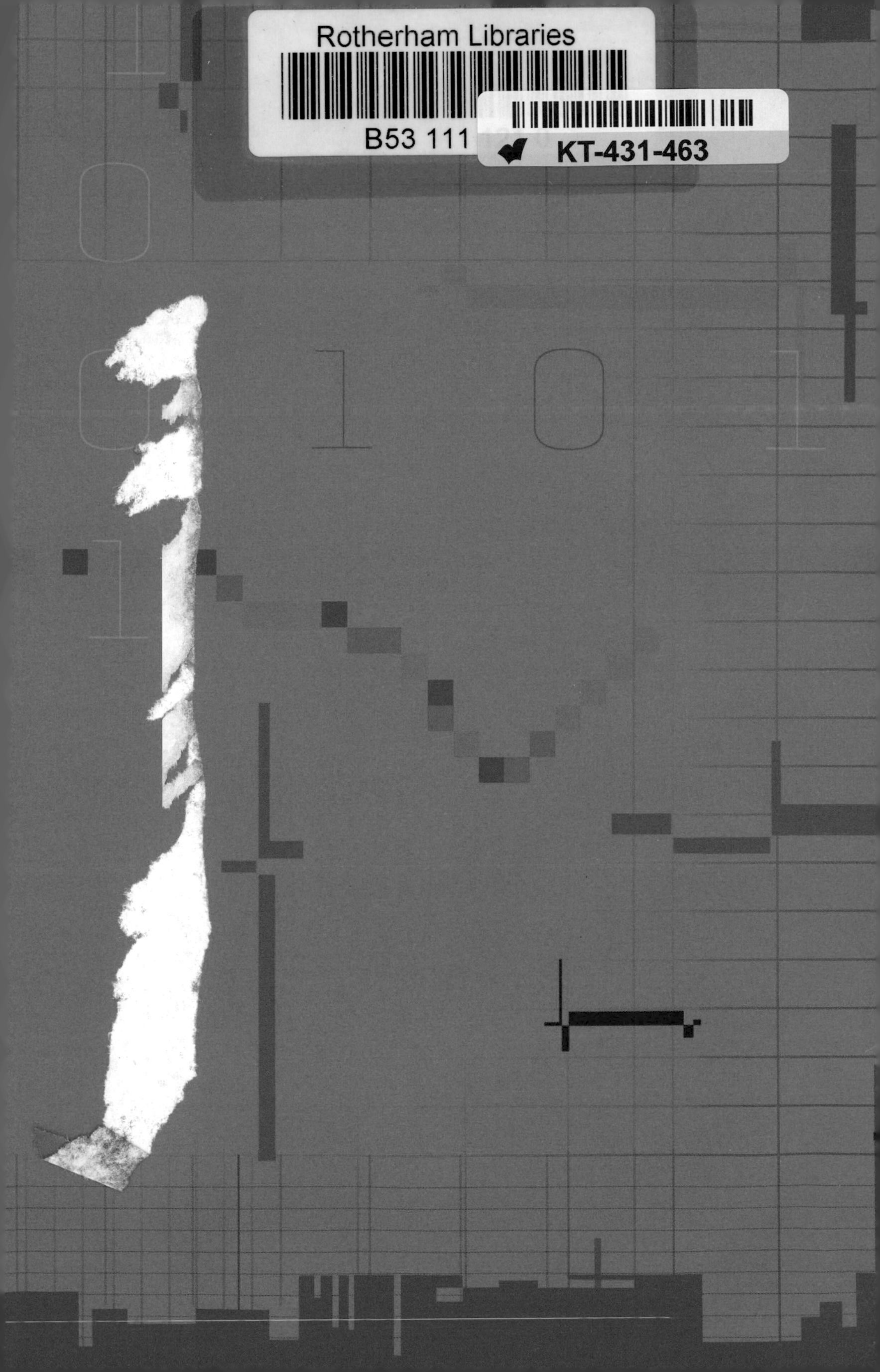
Rotherham Libraries
B53 111
KT-431-463

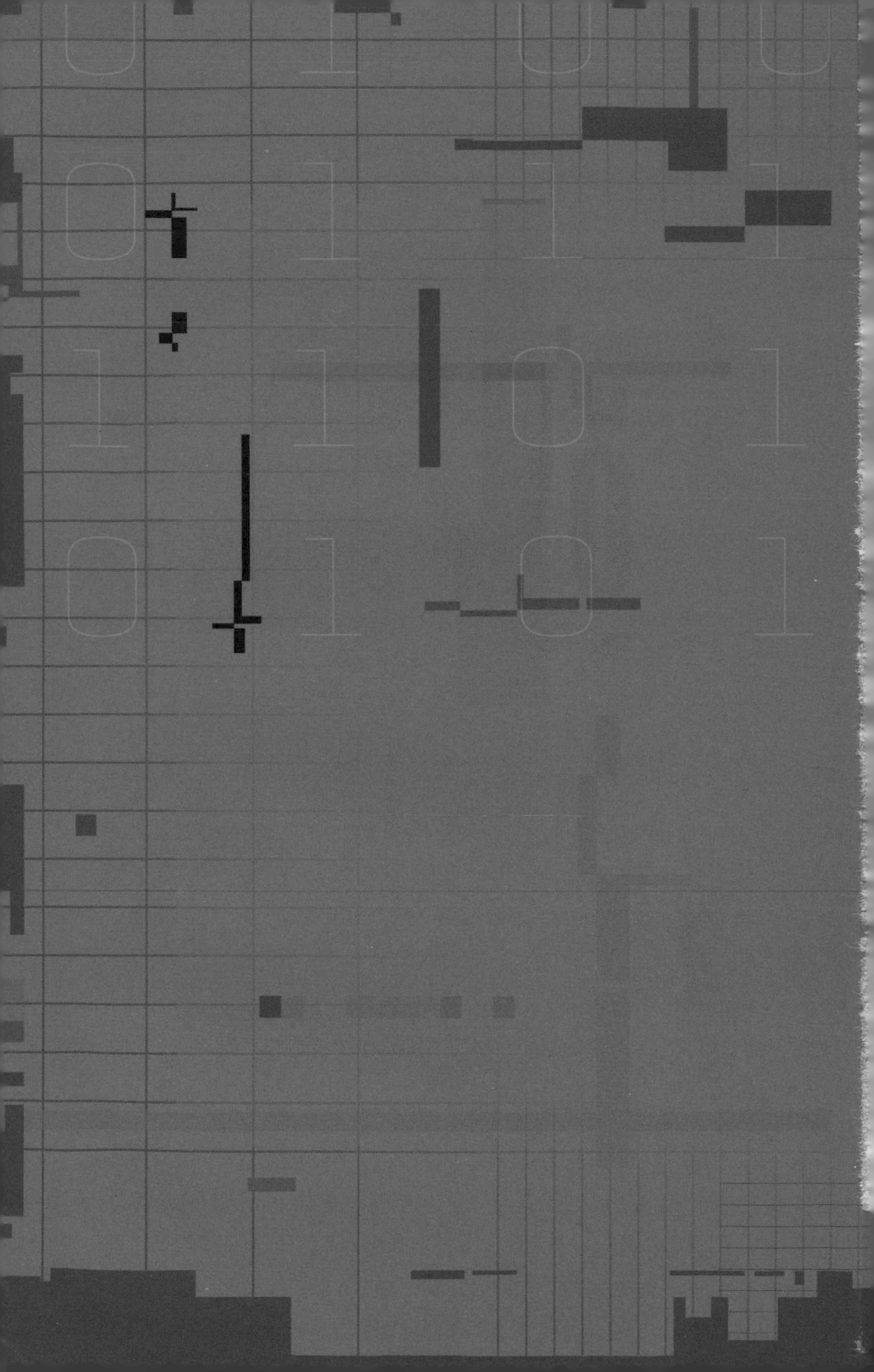

MICHAEL OWEN

REBOOT

Reach Sport

MICHAEL OWEN

REBOOT

With Mark Eglinton

There are so many people who assisted me along the way from being a kid with a dream, to a man leading the line for his country at three World Cups.

From coaches to teammates, not to mention family and friends. I needed them all at various stages of my journey. My amazing wife Louise has been a rock throughout my career and life couldn't be better being the father of four amazing children.

But there are two people who were there from the start and have lived every high and every low I've ever encountered.

Their unwavering belief in me, their selfless dedication towards all their children and their insistence on bringing us all up with the right values instilled in us, created the most perfect environment in which to thrive.

Forget the Ballon d'Or, numerous medals and Golden Boots, my greatest sense of achievement is that I made my parents proud.

Thanks Mum and Dad,
I dedicate this book to you.

Reach Sport

www.reachsport.com

Written with Mark Eglinton.

Published in Great Britain and Ireland in 2019 by
Reach Sport, a Reach PLC business,
5 St Paul's Square, Liverpool, L3 9SJ.

www.reachsport.com
@Reach_Sport

Reach Sport is a part of Reach PLC.
One Canada Square, Canary Wharf, London, E15 5AP.

3

Hardback ISBN: 978-1-911613-33-6
eBook ISBN: 978-1-911613-34-3
Trade paperback ISBN: 978-1-911613-42-8

Photographic acknowledgements:
Tony Woolliscroft (front/back cover images).
Michael Owen personal collection, Reach PLC, PA Images.

Design and typesetting by Reach Sport.

Printed and bound by CPI Group (UK) Ltd,
Croydon, CR0 4YY.

CONTENTS

Forewords		09
Introduction		17
1	Certainty	23
2	Trust	34
3	The Hierarchy	47
4	Culture Shock	68
5	Through The Mayhem	78
6	Fame	89
7	The Trigger	102
8	The Pinnacle	120
9	Momentum	143
10	Scars	157
11	The Decision	172
12	A New Dynamic	193
13	Losing Control	211
14	Mixed Signals	231
15	Respect	253
16	Heroes	285
17	The Badge	300
18	The Fall	325
19	Stick	336
20	Asking For Help	354
Acknowledgements		368

FOREWØRDS

THE MICHAEL WE KNOW

No matter which route Michael took in life, I always knew he would reach the top. When he was a child, his co-ordination was exceptional but it was his mentality that always set him apart. He was a forceful character, relentless in his pursuit of getting his own way. Winning meant everything to him.

Michael loved every sport but football always took priority. I took him to the local leisure centre as a six-year-old and was immediately struck by how clinical his finishing was. I remember turning to his mum and saying: 'Wow, if he develops any real pace we've got a player on our hands!'

Throughout his time in junior football, he was unstoppable. Goals came thick and fast and it was fantastic hearing praise from far and wide. Those were the days; we had so much pleasure as a family watching him play.

Having had a career in the game myself, I knew the importance of mental strength and self-belief. These key ingredients prevented me from playing at a higher level. Michael naturally had these attributes; my role was to simply develop them further.

Making it as a professional footballer was never spoken about. It was a given. The only question was: what level would he attain?

Throughout his career, the remarkable thing about Michael was that his confidence never wavered. Despite serious injury, loss of form or the occasional goal drought, not once did he lose his desire or self-belief. I've never met anybody with a mind as strong as his.

As parents, we shared the highs and lows of a career that took him right to the very top.

But, as with his brothers and sisters, the thing I'm especially proud of is the way he has turned out as a father himself and an all-round decent person.

Terry Owen Senior,
Michael's dad

'He's the best sixteen-year-old I've ever seen, and he'll play for the first team at seventeen' – that was what Steve Heighway told me about a kid who was still at school and who he was bringing into our youth team to try and win us the FA Youth Cup. It was Michael Owen and in his first game, he scored a hat-trick against Manchester United at Anfield to take us into the semi-finals!

What stood out was his pace. He wasn't quick, it was more turbocharge pace that would take your breath away, and his aggression in the tackle left a team of streetwise, tough Scousers open-mouthed.

He did play for the first team at seventeen (and scored obviously) and with me being eighteen months older, we almost started in the team together and ended up rooming together for the next seven years.

It's fair to say for the majority of those years he was as a superstar – Golden Boot winner twice, BBC Sports Personality of the Year winner, PFA Young Player of the Year, having an FA Cup final named after him in 2001, the Treble season, *THAT* goal in the World Cup and the Ballon d'Or. It seems to me, at times, that all this almost gets forgotten when Michael's career gets talked about. He was one of the greatest strikers this country has ever produced and but for injuries would be England's greatest ever goalscorer.

There's no doubt, in speaking to Michael, he's been desperate to do this book and get a lot off his chest for a while – that is mainly down to his decision to leave Liverpool and, years later, join Manchester United.

I tried to stop him doing both!

He'll fill you in later on how it all came about, but I must say I think some of the stick from Liverpool fans is bang out of order considering what he did for the club and the reaction other players get who did nothing for Liverpool.

It hurts Michael and his family, but hopefully this book will let people know the real story and why he came to these decisions.

My only hope in reading it is he doesn't go into too much detail about the Liverpool FC Christmas parties!

Jamie Carragher

MICHAEL_OWEN

The first I heard about Michael was when I spoke to some England coaches who had coached him at Under-18 and Under-20/21 level. They were so excited to tell me about this young kid at Liverpool who was so quick and made such intelligent runs and could finish too.

So, as you could imagine, I was looking forward to seeing this lad break into the Liverpool first team.

I wasn't let down when I did eventually see him in that famous red shirt. It was a match against Wimbledon away on a very poor pitch and he was outstanding for one so young – making clever runs off the ball, not always being seen by his teammates. But eventually one ball was delivered for him that pitted him one on one with the keeper. He calmly tucked the ball past the oncoming keeper into the net. A new, young star was born – pure class. It excited me to see Michael, with his pace and intelligence.

As England manager at the time, I felt that Michael could give us new options with his blistering speed. I knew he would complement the likes of Alan Shearer and Teddy Sheringham. Keeping an eye on his games for the rest of that '97/98 season, he just got better and better, scoring all kinds of goals. My motto was always: if you're good enough, no matter what age, you're in. So, by the time it came to pick a squad, he was a must to go to the World Cup. And what an impact he made in France …

He came on against Romania, scored, and was full of youthful confidence. That was what was so impressive about Michael: at a tender age he was fearless and knew he could cause any defence in the world problems. And, my word, didn't he show it that night against Argentina. When he dropped deep into the centre circle, received a pass from David Beckham and turned on it instantly, he didn't know that his life as a footballer was about to change forever.

With his pace, running at the two defenders in front of him, within seconds he was goal side of them. From my view from the bench I didn't see Ayala so deep behind the rest of his defence. But I could see enough to know that he was coming to Michael square on, not showing him one side or the other. It was at that moment I knew Michael was either going to pass him with that pace we all knew he possessed – or Ayala was going to chop him down and get sent off!

Young Michael flew past him and was at an angle to the goal on his favoured right foot. Paul Scholes got close to maybe taking the shot himself but Michael was having none of it. Instead, he reversed his shot across the keeper into the opposite top corner of the Argentines' net! What a wonder goal – and a strike that announced Michael Owen to the world.

It never went to his head. That's another thing that was so impressive about him. He kept his feet on the ground throughout his career and was a credit to all the clubs he played for and, of course, his family. He's such a great example for all youngsters but particularly those wanting to be footballers.

I now really enjoy working with Michael as a pundit with BT Sport and, again, he is excelling at that.

Glenn Hoddle

Cyrille Regis once told me that athletic ability only gets you so far in football – then the head takes over. I thought that if you were able to get into the family home and see where the 'head' was formed, you would have a better chance of gauging a player.

MICHAEL_OWEN

I met Michael at his childhood home in North Wales when he was yet to make his debut for Liverpool. His incredibly supportive family were crammed into the front room, along with a boisterous dog who kept leaping all over me.

Michael was reserved, polite and mature beyond his years. His mum was a former athlete and his dad an ex-professional footballer: textbook DNA!

My background was sports marketing and I knew that, in image terms, Michael's first sponsor was important. We chose Tissot watches and launched the deal at the Café De Paris in London's West End with Michael, just seventeen, well groomed in his best suit and polished shoes.

After that, Michael let his football do the talking.

So many wonderful memories. A goal on his Liverpool debut, BBC Sports Personality of the Year, the World Cup goal against Argentina, the FA Cup win over Arsenal and the Ballon d'Or in 2001.

Whilst working on David Beckham's 2003 transfer to Real Madrid, I spent considerable time with their President, Florentino Pérez, and felt that I knew what he looked for in both a player and a person.

I had a detailed one-off DVD created, encompassing Michael's key attributes on and off the pitch and played it to the president in his Madrid boardroom surrounded by club executives.

At the end, he went to a nearby desk and picked up a calculator and a few weeks later Michael was presented with the number 11 shirt in the Bernabeu.

Unlike his friend David Platt, who really enjoyed his four successful years in Italy, Michael found it hard to embrace the change in lifestyle and although he scored quite a few goals in his season in Spain, it became clear that a swift return to England would be his preferred option.

The later years of his career were affected by injuries that inevitably took their toll.

Fortunately, Michael, with the support of his family, has always been blessed with great mental strength and his determination will ensure success in the future in whatever direction his career takes him.

Great names in football like Steve Heighway, Gérard Houllier, Glenn Hoddle, Kevin Keegan and Sir Alex Ferguson were really proud of Michael. So am I.

Tony Stephens,
former agent

It was easy to follow Michael's career from a very early age as Manchester United had him at our training school when he was about thirteen years old and we were really optimistic about securing him on a schoolboy form. Then the silly young boy signed for Liverpool!

We were gutted as at that stage we reckoned he was going to make it. It's not an easy thing to predict a young lad's future at such an early stage of his career. We had the same feeling with Ryan Giggs, Paul Scholes and Nicky Butt. From that moment on, we watched and suffered every time he played against our youth team.

I always think that there are crucial moments in a player's career – their first team debut, first goal or getting married, because they are all stepping stones. For me, in tracking Michael's career, one crucial moment was in 1997 when he played for the England youth team in Malaysia.

In the team were two of our players, John Curtis and Ronnie Wallwork. They were away for a month in gruelling conditions, so we made the decision to give our two lads a month's rest in order for them to recover physically – but not for Michael, he went straight into Liverpool's first team! I spoke to Gérard Houllier years later and he agreed with me that Michael lost out on time to develop technically and physically. I can't with complete certainty say that this was the main reason for Michael's hamstring problems.

When I heard that Newcastle were prepared to let him go, I acted in a flash and got him over to my house to talk about joining Manchester United. I know this may go down as a bit of blowing United's trumpet, but I and my staff believed he improved as a player at United and he was an influence on young strikers like Wayne Rooney and Danny Welbeck.

His timing when he made these penetrating runs and his composure in scoring goals was a reminder of the great Jimmy Greaves, whose side-foot finishes were pure genius. I can't think of the number of times I cursed Liverpool for snatching him from under our noses!

Another factor in Michael's career was the way he led his life; no arrogance, no partying, a good family life, respect for his parents, his manager and teammates – all in all, a completely rounded young man.

The game was lucky to have him.

Sir Alex Ferguson

INTRØDUCTION

WIRED DIFFERENTLY

From a very young age, I've always known that I have a hell of a lot of self-belief. Not only that, I know that I've always possessed this innate knack of finding the positive in absolutely every situation and completely ignoring what somebody else might consider to be a negative.

I don't remember trying to perfect this particular skill; it was always just the way my mind worked. I applied it across the board.

If I was doing a warm-up at Anfield ten minutes before a game and someone passed me the ball, which then bounced off my shin, I wouldn't bother at all. Instead, I'd think that's my bad touch for the day out of the way – now I'm going to be on fire.

Equally, if I missed three chances in a game, instead of even considering that I'd had a bad game, my first thought would be that nobody else would have even got into the position to have those three chances.

On that basis, in my mind, I never had a bad game.

Some would say that this attitude is at best laughable, or at worst completely delusional. But, honestly, thinking that way gave me huge confidence from one week to the next. I'd never go missing in games because my belief had been bruised by on-field events. I was never recovering mentally. It worked for me.

Similarly, in my post-playing career, the ability to banish negative opinions and criticism has been an important attribute. When I wrote my first book, many years ago, with retrospect, I wasn't in the position to be able to look back on events of my life with the kind of perspective and maturity that I now have at the age of thirty nine.

Also, whether you do so subconsciously or not, when you write a book while you're still playing, there's a tendency to play things a bit safe for fear of either offending people, or jeopardising future relationships.

But, in the years since the first book and especially since my retirement from the game in 2013, the world – and how people engage in discussing it – has changed beyond all recognition.

Back in those early days, the power of social media was so much less. If someone wanted to criticize somebody, the available mediums for doing so were limited. Nowadays, everyone has an opinion – and, not just that, everyone has, via social media, freedom to express it.

Over the years I've inevitably run into a fair amount of criticism about various aspects of my career. Few players haven't. In my case, people complained that I wasn't loyal enough to this or that club, was 'always injured', boring – amongst other gripes.

The nature of media nowadays is such that, in the absence of any response, myths and rumours start festering into fact.

By and large, I ignore the mythology I hear and the criticism I get. As much as I know it's there, I filter it out. There's little value in trying to respond on social media where there (a) isn't sufficient scope for context and (b) there's a small percentage of people who, regardless of what they're told, will continue to believe what they want to believe. To attempt to influence that would be an exercise in futility. I've got better things to do than sit on my phone battling Twitter trolls.

A throwaway line from Alex Inglethorpe, Academy Director at Liverpool, summed up everything for me. He told me that I had the best shit-filter of anyone he'd ever met.

In my current role in Michael Owen Management – where I'm mentoring young players and representing them in relationships with academies – Alex and I have inevitably talked a lot about the various attributes of young talent.

Immediately we can both identify the kids who can technically play – that part is obvious to anyone inside the game. What's also important is to be able to notice the ones who can both play and have the kind of positive mind-set needed to go further.

During our conversations, inevitably I related some of my experiences and attitudes from my playing days – specifically this tendency I had to turn negatives into positives. Alex identified it straightaway as being a key component of my psyche.

When he first said it, I laughed it off without considering what he meant. But when I thought about it a bit more, what he said made perfect sense. Alex had read me exactly right.

As much as he isn't a big part of my story and is only someone

I've come to know relatively recently, in the context of my life, what Alex Inglethorpe said was indeed very significant. I'd just never thought about it in such simple terms.

When the idea of writing a post-career book came up out of the blue, I wasn't sure what to think. Did I really want to go deep into my feelings? Was I prepared to explain myself in terms of how my mind worked? Those were just two of the many questions I asked myself.

As I deliberated about it all, the fact that the last book only covered up until 2006 was one obvious reason to consider the idea.

Beyond that, I'd come to realise that my opinions over the years had changed with age. I've also got more of them. I'm now a family man with four children; I'm far more mature and world-wise than I was fifteen years ago.

I am so proud of my career and like to think that I conducted myself with nothing but integrity throughout it – regardless of whether I was representing Liverpool, Real Madrid, Newcastle United, Manchester United, Stoke City or England. Also, unless I missed something, I consider my football career to have been a very successful one. At no point did I drag the game through the mud.

Consequently, I came to the conclusion that the fans deserved to know the ins and outs of the various aspects of my life that perhaps weren't clear or made public at the time – and in some cases have been skewed somewhat over time by the internet rumour mill. People, especially football fans, can make snap judgements. In my case, people have made a few while perhaps knowing maybe twenty percent of the facts.

I started considering the events that were most important along the way and how I could present my life – the good, the bad and the indifferent – in a manner that wouldn't be trying to change anyone's mind, but could at least help people understand me better. To many, all I've ever been is a voice – a not very interesting one at that, some would say – or a face on the television screen.

To get there, I knew I had to also lay bare the unique way I think in order to make it all relatable. This shit-filtering is at the core of it all and I hope everyone enjoys getting a brief glimpse into my head.

And if people don't, I'll obviously shit-filter the reviews anyway!

Michael Owen, 2019

REBØOT_1

CERTAINTY

When I was a kid I often used to sit on the couch in my parents' sitting room in Hawarden, eating an apple. My mother, Janette, would be on my left in a chair. My dad, Terry, would be on the couch beside me. In the corner, against the wall, sat the bin. It might have been twenty feet away.

As I finished the apple each time, we all knew what was coming next. I'd eye the bin across the room and then lob the apple core in its direction. I was never just trying to just hit the target. Considerable precision was needed.

If it went directly in, everything was fine. If it hit the white wall behind and left a mark, I'd get an absolute bollocking from my house-proud mother and be told to wipe it up.

My dad would just sit and watch all this. Knowing what was at stake each time, I'd still take this long distance shot on whenever possible. Inevitably, some would miss, but most would go straight in. I was constantly pushing the boundaries.

As time went by, I started to realise that, while my dad wasn't exactly endorsing me risking my mother's ire by making a mess on the wall, he definitely admired the fact that this cocky kid of his had the arsehole to even attempt this feat of accuracy under pressure. While my mother glared, he'd sit there with this look on his face that said *go on then* …

On reflection, I think my dad admired me because I had a confidence that he just didn't have. Beyond that, although I was too young to realise it at the time, in the most understated way possible he was giving me license to trust this innate self-confidence I possessed under pressure – and this was a trait that I'd carry into everything in life, including football.

The unfortunate issue was, when I was young, there just wasn't the range of kids' football opportunities as there are nowadays – where state of the art academies take on kids at five or six years of age. Really, you couldn't play any kind of structured, official football until you were about ten years old.

None of that discouraged my dad. By the time I was six or seven, he never stopped pestering the local youth football team, Mold Alexandra, to let me play for them.

'We can't; we just can't,' the coach would say, 'he's way too young.'

'Just put him on the bench!' my dad would tell him.

Eventually, after much discussion, my dad persuaded the coach to let me join the club, even though I was three or four years younger and half the size of everyone else.

Regardless of my physical shortcomings, they'd use me as a sub most weeks and I'd come on and score more often than not.

The only other football that was available was something called 'mini-club'. It was a loose formula. You could go to

Deeside Leisure Centre, pay a quid or so to get in, and then play football for an hour. There were no age groups per se; it was just a bunch of twelve, fifteen and eight-year-olds mixed in together.

My dad tells me that, when he used to take me there when I was six, he'd watch from the side while I'd just goal-hang, ten yards out. Seemingly, even when I was just this tiny dot of a kid, whenever the ball came to me, I'd never lace it. Instead, he said, I'd coolly stroke the ball into the corners. I'd come away having scored three or four in that manner every time. I was six, and I was prolific.

As early as my mini-club days, my dad says that he knew I had everything: balance, composure – all the attributes needed to go all the way in the game.

While I do have vague memories of mini-club, I don't ever recall feeling like the prodigy my dad thought I was. That's one of the amazing things about my dad: he believed in me long before I ever believed in myself. From an early age he was preparing me for a destiny that he knew was coming.

For example, every Sunday, me and my two elder brothers Terry and Andy, would go down to the local park with my dad – who must have been about thirty-five at the time. Before we could play a two-against-two game, my dad always wanted me to practise heading the ball.

From what I have seen and heard from fellow players, my dad, being a forward also, was always a good header of the ball. And I think, from very early on, he wanted to instil that quality in me. Although I was still so young, I think part of him wanted to make a man of me – as perverse as that might sound given my tender years

Having had a fifteen year-long professional career at Everton,

Bradford City, Chester and Port Vale among many others, and then gone on to play non-league football thereafter, he could still run and play. He'd tear down the wing, pretending, commentating – 'And here's Terry Owen, running down the wing … and he crosses it …' And I'd have to head every ball. And these were often wet, heavy balls.

Even I could deduce that me showing the bottle to head the ball in was much more exciting to him than if I bicycle-kicked it into the top corner. And he wasn't interested in flick headers either; he hated that. To him, that was just me allowing the ball to hit my head. That was a passive act in his eyes.

Instead, he wanted me to rise, with bravery and purpose, and power the ball back in the direction from whence it came. Whenever I did that, he bloody loved it. And I thought that if I did two or three of those on the spin, he might stop crossing it and we could play football. Meanwhile, I felt as if I had a bad case of concussion after I'd headed a few.

As I've got older, I've occasionally given a bit of thought as to what exactly my dad's motivations were back then. By any standards, his approach and dedication to developing my talent was extreme. As some might speculate, I don't think it was because he felt that he underachieved in his own football career. He had no need to relive his life through me.

Among other clubs, he'd played at Everton, in one of the club's best eras – with Kendall, Harvey, Joe Royle, Alan Ball and so on. Granted, my dad only played a couple of games for the first team, but this was an era of the game where there was only one sub permitted.

Regardless, he earned money by playing football, and you've got to doff your cap to anyone who's able to do that.

But with me he had this belief that wasn't just the kind of

hopefulness that any parent might have when their kid shows a decent level of aptitude towards something. He planned my life, our lives, with the certainty that I'd be a professional footballer, at the core of everything. As sure as the sun rose each morning, it was *going* to happen.

Every Tuesday, like clockwork, he'd go to the butcher and buy a massive lump of steak for my dinner – just *my* dinner. Meanwhile, my brothers and sisters would be having beans on toast or whatever they normally had.

The reason for this was understood between us: I'd need beefing up because I was going to be a professional footballer. The physical act of buying the steak and me eating it was significant enough. But the mental strength I took from what he was prepared to do on my behalf was very much more so.

Similarly, when he encouraged me to try my hand at boxing years later, because, as he said, it would toughen me up for when I played football, it wasn't the physical act of boxing that benefitted me down the line. It was the thought and planning that my dad was willing to invest in me that really counted.

Interestingly, at no point did my dad ever actually tell me that I was good at football, or that he thought I could become a top player. The only time he ever let anything slip was when I heard him talking to his mates while he was playing snooker one day and I was watching.

'How is Mike's football doing?' one of them asked. 'Got a chance of making it?'

From my position in the corner of the room, clutching a bag of crisps, I could see that my dad just looked at him and said, simply but very profoundly: 'Ain't no doubt. He'll play for England one day.'

He'd let his guard down momentarily, and his mates took

note. It transpired that a few of them clubbed together shortly afterwards and placed a bet – a bet that they would have to be patient with, but that they'd later collect nevertheless.

My dad didn't know I'd heard him but that was the only time I ever witnessed him voice his view.

What I always had that my dad never had, was between the ears – and I'm not referring to intelligence in a traditional sense as much as I'm talking about mind-set.

My dad just isn't the most outwardly confident. When he walks into a room he's never loud. He needs time to warm up – maybe even needs a couple of pints under his belt. Looking back now, when you come to the realisation that you're exceptional at something; that feeling in turn makes your whole life better and confidence comes with that.

I first became aware of this feeling, albeit on only a subtle level, when I was just a young lad. When I went from playing at Mold Alexandra, coming on as a sub every week, to the Under-11 Flintshire team, formerly known as Deeside Primary Schools, I became as self-aware as a young kid has the capacity to be.

It was a county team in everything but name. Ian Rush held the goalscoring record there and the late Gary Speed had the all-time appearance record – and my dad decided to send me for a trial at the end of that same year I'd been coming off the bench at Mold Alexandra.

I was still just a seven-year-old. On paper it was unthinkable that someone so much younger and smaller would be able to hold his own with ten and eleven-year-olds. Yet, I got picked for Flintshire Under-11s straightaway.

By the time I reached the end of my last year at the appropriate age for the age group, I had scored ninety-two goals in that season across thirty odd games. Ian Rush's record, which had stood for however many years previously, was seventy-two. To say that I was a million miles ahead of everyone else would be an understatement.

In parallel to county football, I'd been running amok at every stage of school football, too – first at Rector Drew Primary School in Hawarden and latterly at Hawarden High School.

I played every week and scored goals every week because I got so many chances to score. Instead of getting one chance and maybe missing it, I probably got ten chances and scored five of them.

I can't understate how important this all was for my confidence. If I just had one chance each game, I'm sure I would have played safe and thought, *Ok, just hit the target* ...

Incidentally, that lazy expression, *hitting the target,* we hear all the time nowadays in modern football commentary. You won't hear me say it though. For me, it's absolutely poisonous – and I'm sure most top strikers would agree. My mum could probably come on the pitch and hit the target. As a striker, you've got to be more precise.

Once you reach the top level of club and international football, goalkeepers are no mugs. Often there are only inches to spare when you're trying to finish. Playing safe is for nobody. You've got to go for corners and tight angles. As a striker, if you want to be elite, you've *got* to take risks.

Consequently, in addition to bolstering my confidence, this glut of opportunities gave me scope to experiment a great deal with *how* I finished. As a striker, I could hone my craft. And I took great pleasure in doing it throughout my childhood.

I explored all sorts of approaches. I tried going around, I'd dink, I'd scoop, I'd slot it – I tried everything. Of course, I scored with all of these methods at one time or another. But I also figured out that each one came with its own set of risks. If I tried to scoop the keeper, I might have scored one in ten. If I tried to slot it I'd maybe convert six out of ten. Round the keeper … four. And so on.

With practice I quickly realised that, of all the methods, the dink finish was right up my street – and for a couple of reasons. I obviously already had pace combined with a good touch. Better still, I found that I had the ability to touch the ball further than the keeper thought I wanted to. They'd then think they could get it and so they'd dive. But because I was so fast, I could inject a bit of pace at the last second, and then dink. I loved that finish. It felt so comfortable for me.

At the other extreme, I eventually came to the realisation that I didn't particularly like having to go around the goalkeeper. I did it four or five times and soon realised that – instinctively – I just didn't like how it felt.

With the benefit of hindsight, my being better than everyone else didn't make me complacent – quite the opposite. It made me wary of resting on my laurels. I had to *keep* getting better.

Nowadays, I'm not sure this happens like it did in my day. Instead, if a kid shows ability, he or she is often pushed up the levels.

Eventually they reach a standard where they're starved of opportunities and/or no longer stand out. When they no longer shine, discouragement often follows. And then they become cautious.

None of this happened to me.

■■ ■■■■■ ■

My dad's dedication to my footballing ventures was even more admirable when you consider the financial dire straits we were in as a family when I was a young lad. Yes, we lived in our own house in Hawarden, but there were a lot of us and we were mortgaged up to the hilt. The money that my parents made was just never enough to cover everything so the bailiffs were at our door every week.

Even I could recognise the perilous situation we were in. It was hard to ignore.

There were five of us kids upstairs at night having to listen to my mum and dad screaming at each other about finances. They loved each other deeply, but the pressure of money was just too great. My mother and I were sharing underpants at times because she couldn't always afford to buy her own. Sometimes I'd catch her raiding my drawer!

And there wasn't an obvious solution to these problems either. My mother was always the real grafter of the two. She'd never stop working, worrying – while my dad always took a bit of an 'it'll be alright on the night' approach to things like money.

On weekends I'd follow him around while he played golf or snooker with his mates, almost always for money. I'd sit there and watch him lose a tenner and, even at that young age I'd be thinking, *Oh, no. We might not be eating much this week now.*

As insignificant as a tenner might sound, it was a lot of money back then in the context of the Owen family. But my dad never once lost any sleep whatsoever over losing. He just shrugged it off and I know that's a trait I have definitely inherited from him.

Even nowadays, if somebody told me I was going to lose my house tomorrow, I wouldn't lose any sleep worrying about it.

Instead, I'd get up the next day and think, *Ok, how can I resolve this?* My dad was exactly the same when I was a kid.

After he retired from football in 1985, he and my mother took over a clothes shop in Liverpool that had belonged to her parents.

In a way, my granddad had been ahead of his time in that he loaned money against the value of clothes that were purchased in the shop. If something cost twenty quid, he would charge five pounds per month over five months.

My parents' job was to go out and collect this money from the various people who had outstanding loans.

As time passed, the clothes part of the business went into decline because of the availability of cheaper imported clothes I'm told. But the money loaning part of it continued to be worthwhile for a few more years. Sadly, even those proceeds weren't enough to service the family debt and so my mother took on a full-time job at Iceland's headquarters in Deeside.

She'd work there from eight until five then she'd drive to Liverpool and collect money in the evenings until midnight. Consequently, I really didn't see much of my mum when I was young, certainly not on weekdays. She'd have done anything for us. She's always been absolutely selfless.

Meanwhile my dad's focus was split. When the money collecting business eventually wound down, he could very easily have gone down to the job centre to look for something else. He just didn't want to do most of the jobs that were on offer. But eventually he found another position selling insurance for the Co-op.

On one hand he absolutely hated it. Knocking on people's doors trying to coldly sell them something was in direct conflict with his reserved nature. He'd tell stories of having to sit at monthly sales meetings where he'd feel humiliated because he always seemed to be the worst performer.

On the other, he liked the job because it allowed him the flexibility to come and watch me play football. If I had a game at ten in the morning, he could manipulate his schedule so that he could be there. He knew my timetable better than I did.

During the winter months when we were doing cross country running at school, I'd be jogging along and then, all of a sudden, I'd see my dad's car parked up on the side of the road. He'd be sitting there not wanting to be seen by anyone – just to see what position I was in. If I was in sixth place when his car pulled up, I'd absolutely bust a gut to improve.

No matter what I was doing – football, cross country or whatever – he wanted me to do well. My dad lived for my progress and, because he demonstrated to me that he did, it only made me want to prove myself to him more. I've got nothing but admiration for how he nurtured me.

REBØOT_2

TRUST

When I moved on from Deeside at the age of eleven, I joined the Liverpool Centre Of Excellence (Academy). This could best be described as a loose arrangement to train every week. There was no written contract or particular obligation at that time. It was just the place where the best players in the area aspired to be.

As such, this was where my path crossed with Steven Gerrard for the first time. From memory, he'd already been at Liverpool for a year or so prior to my joining.

Even in those days it was blatantly obvious to everyone, myself included, that Steven was absolutely exceptional. Both he and I were miles ahead of anyone else and this soon turned into a magical, almost telepathic understanding whereby he knew what I was good at and vice versa. It was almost embarrassing at times. Whenever he got the ball: pinpoint pass … goal. If I scored four goals, Stevie would have four assists. This would continue for years.

As much as Steven and I clicked on the pitch and were good mates, we weren't, and never have been since, particularly social off it. This relationship is very different to the one I'd develop over the years with Jamie Carragher, for example.

With Carra, I got to know his family and I'd go over to his house and meet his friends. The friendship was deep. With Steven, it was never quite like that. Because he was from the other end of Liverpool and I, in effect, would jump ahead of him by a couple of years in a developmental sense, we never saw each other as much as I would have liked to off the pitch.

I will never have anything but great things to say about Steven Gerrard though. We've obviously been in the trenches together many, many times. Our friendship runs very deep. We still text each other every couple of months nowadays.

Anyway, as much as my dad had probably identified that I had a future as a footballer by the time I was seven, there remained a difficult balance to manage. While my mother was working all hours to bring money in, my dad's reliance on this belief in my bright future – in combination with just a token effort on his behalf to bring in his share – often caused considerable conflict at home.

I suppose I could see both sides of the argument. I recognised the very different qualities that my parents had. But there was still an obvious problem in terms of how an unerring belief in my future, and the investment of time and money it would need, could sit with the more pressing concern of how to keep a roof over the Owen family's heads. It was such a tough position, and by the time I was twelve or thirteen, it wasn't just my dad who knew that I represented the only conceivable way out for the family. I knew it too.

Faced with a life or death situation of this kind, some

youngsters might have succumbed to the pressure. For me, it didn't work that way. The possibility of providing an escape for my parents and my brothers and sisters only made me more focused and more single-minded in terms of what had to be done. I didn't view any of it as a burden – I was motivated by the chance.

Nevertheless, by the time I was eligible to be picked up by a club on a schoolboy signing, the family was faced with a moral dilemma. By this point, even though I was training with Liverpool, every club in the land was scouting me with a view to securing my signature for schoolboy forms.

As much as I was comfortable with the arrangement I had to train at Liverpool, my dad wanted me to remain open to the attentions of other interested parties. He wanted me to look around, he said.

I remember one occasion where he came to me one day with a proposal. 'I've agreed that you'll go up to train and play a game at Sheffield Wednesday,' he told me, 'but don't worry, there's no obligation beyond that.'

It should be said that I didn't want to do this. Liverpool was the only club I wanted to train with. Grudgingly, I agreed. So the whole family got in the car, drove up to Sheffield and I played in a game. At the end of it, as we were getting back into the car, my dad was handed an envelope containing money for his mileage expenses. It was probably twenty quid.

On the two-hour drive home, we drove past our usual Hawarden turn-off. As we did, we all looked at each other as if to say: 'Where are we going?'

Meanwhile, my dad stared ahead and kept driving – all the way to Rhyl – where there was a little theme park with a few rides.

During my childhood, we never had days out like that – we just didn't have the money.

Yet, with this small amount of expense cash, my dad decided to treat us by letting us all have a couple of hours of fun. It was a brief escape from the realities of life for all of us – and just one example of how totally selfless my parents were. Time and again, they'd go above and beyond.

Looking back now, by encouraging me to look at other clubs, my dad was doing the right thing by all of us. By doing so, not only was he giving me added experience and game time, it also served to generate fervour among clubs looking to position themselves to acquire me. And there were plenty of them queuing up. I could see it.

Whenever I played, my dad would always stand behind the goal. No exceptions – that's where he would be, usually alone, while my mother did the talking with the other fifty or so parents at the side of the pitch. This dynamic became very comfortable for me – to the extent that, if he wasn't there for a game, I almost felt lost. I needed my buddy there.

Although he was there, Dad never gave much away in his facial expression. Even so, if I touched the ball and did well, I couldn't help but have a sly glance over.

Nod of approval.

Equally, if I gave the ball away – a stern look or shake of the head would be waiting. On reflection, I think I was addicted to this type of synergy. I just couldn't get enough of trying to impress him and receiving affirmation, as understated as his was.

Whenever I saw somebody stood next to my dad, I *knew* it was important. Not just anyone would stand next to my dad; it could only be a scout – and a lot of the time there were five or six people standing around him. On these occasions, I didn't hide. I thought, *I've got to be the best player on this pitch.*

Seeing scouts on the touchline was something I got accustomed to. That year, 1993, Arsenal courted me first. They sent a club official to meet us and put my mum, my dad and me on a first class train to London. We were taken to Highbury, met by George Graham, introduced to Ian Wright – and then given a tour of the dressing room and executive boxes before Arsenal lost 3-0 to Coventry when Mick Quinn scored a hat-trick.

Not long afterwards, Chelsea did the same. I was taken to Stamford Bridge, introduced to Glenn Hoddle and the Chelsea players.

Then it was Manchester United – who had sent Brian Kidd several times over the preceding years to watch me. We went to Old Trafford and Alex Ferguson took me into his office, stared into my face from a distance of about one inch and said: 'Do you *want* to be a Manchester United player?'

It was all so intense – and I didn't know what to say. All I know is that this kind of attention just didn't happen to every young player. Without meaning to sound arrogant, I doubt there was a young footballer in the world in such high demand at the time.

And then Manchester City came along, and with them that moral dilemma I referred to. Because my dad is so nice, maybe too nice, you could say that City caught him off guard by offering him fifty grand in cash for my schoolboy signature.

While this was, frankly, a bribe, it also represented a life-changing opportunity for a man whose family eternally teetered on the brink of being evicted from their home. As much as he knew how much I wanted to sign for Liverpool, my dad came to me and said, 'I've got no option.' But there was one option.

My dad phoned up Steve Heighway, the academy boss at Liverpool, and pleaded our case.

'Listen, Michael desperately wants to sign for Liverpool when he's old enough but we're in a financial mess right now. We need you to match what we've been offered by Manchester City.'

'Leave this with me,' Steve said.

Even this was something of a departure for my dad. He never liked asking anybody for favours. Even nowadays, he wouldn't dream of asking any of his former clubs for free match tickets.

When I was young and wanted to go to games, I'd say. 'But Dad, you played for Everton; you played for Chester. Why can't you just phone them up for a couple of tickets?'

He just wouldn't do it.

Yet, this was a different situation and he knew it. We all realised that this was a huge crossroads for all of us. Fortunately, Steve Heighway was wise to all the signals. He clearly understood our predicament, and at the time he also recognised my huge potential. There was an obvious opportunity to fulfil both purposes.

He took our proposal to the Liverpool board and came back to us a week or so later with an arrangement whereby my dad would be employed as a Liverpool scout – and would be paid the equivalent of the money we required. In return, I agreed to sign schoolboy forms for Liverpool Football Club – which would cover the two years up until I was eligible to turn professional.

It should be said that this offer was a major statement of investment on Liverpool's behalf. The agreement only required that I signed with them as a schoolboy, nothing beyond that. I would have, in theory, been free to walk away thereafter – not that that thought ever occurred to me.

To employ my dad was the only workable solution – to have a deal structured in any other way wouldn't have been legal. I was delighted – I'd be going to Liverpool. And, equally significantly, this money was absolutely vital in terms of buying our family time. We never looked back financially from that day forward.

■■ ■■■ ■

As a fourteen-year-old who'd guaranteed two years of his future to Liverpool, in addition to being available to represent the club's youth team, Steve Heighway was also keen that I attend Lilleshall – at that time the Football Association's 'university' for the country's most promising young players.

The aim was to find the best one or two players from all the various academies around the country, and then nurture them, in a controlled, structured environment, into the best.

This was when, at the age of fourteen, I got my first sponsorship deal with Umbro after we were approached by Simon Marsh who at that time was an executive responsible for managing assets like football clubs and footballers – one being Alan Shearer.

Simon was a person with whom I felt a certain affinity right from the start. As much as my parents had been beyond supportive, subconsciously I think I needed someone in the wider football world to guide me – somebody who wasn't an immediate family member. Simon Marsh became that individual, and he's never left my imaginary circle of trust since.

Obviously, the concept of a fourteen-year-old kid being sponsored by one of the leading kit manufacturers in the world wasn't exactly normal. But nothing about my young life was. At every stage it seemed like I did things – and had things happen to me – that were unprecedented back in 1993. As surreal as it might seem to the outsider, this was just my life. It felt normal.

While there was no actual cash offered for this first sponsorship deal with Umbro, there was a significant benefit in terms of kit. From memory, I believe there was an initial advance of five thousand pounds made available for Umbro gear: boots, tracksuits, jumpers the lot.

I was the only player at Lilleshall to have a sponsorship deal so this kit came in quite handy. I'd sell it to the other lads for cash and I even traded it to one of the lads in the group in exchange for some homework – specifically, as I recall, an English essay for which one lad in the group got a B grade for me. It was a good investment! As you might expect, I became quite popular within the group.

Above and beyond a few brighter sparks than me on the homework front, there were some very good footballers in our group. Wes Brown was absolutely exceptional. Then there was Michael Ball and John Harley who could really play too. I was considered to be a standout among that year group also.

Under the guidance of head coach Keith Blunt, my two years at Lilleshall were the perfect preparation for when I'd later sign for Liverpool as a pro at the age of seventeen. At Lilleshall, I became more of a man in both a footballing sense, and a day-to-day sense. The life skills that were instilled in me during those two years in residence have stayed with me ever since.

Being residential near Telford in Shropshire, my attendance at Lilleshall meant that I left Hawarden High School and went to another school, Idsall High School, which was local to the centre. Throughout our time at the centre, it was impressed on us (and our parents) that, while we were in the very top category of promising footballers at that time, a future at the top level of the game was in no way guaranteed.

Education, therefore, was considered to be a vital component in our overall development process. As much as I didn't personally enjoy academics, I was able enough to pass all of my GCSEs – albeit with grades that might have been better had I not been so dedicated to football.

In any case, I was motivated to get good academic qualifications in my own right. It wasn't a 'just in case' situation – I did it just because passing exams and getting qualifications felt like the right thing to do. That's something I impress on youngsters now. Don't do something just in case – just do it.

Under Keith Blunt's watchful eye, my football ability developed faster than ever. As much as I was already fast and able to score goals in all kinds of ways, Lilleshall was where I added other important elements to my game that would be pivotal for my future.

Added to being taught yet more subtleties of the art of finishing, it was here that I learned other, deeper nuances of the game – how to keep possession, turn with the ball, use what limited physicality I had to thwart defenders and to link play. By the age of sixteen, I had added the attributes of an even more rounded footballer to my searing pace.

In their capacity as my parent club, for want of a better

description, Liverpool recognised the scope of my development all too well. One day, Keith Blunt came into my dormitory room with some news.

'Liverpool have been on the phone,' he said, 'they want you to go back and play in a Youth Cup game against Sheffield United at Anfield.'

Given that this was under-18 football and I was still not quite sixteen, it was absolutely unheard of for someone of my age to be called up for such a game. Seemingly though, one of the strikers had got injured and I was their next choice. I was given special dispensation by Lilleshall to go back to play in a team that included Jamie Carragher and David Thompson.

I returned to Liverpool and played in the fourth round game and scored twice on the main pitch at Anfield in a 3-2 win. At this point I'm thinking, *oh my God. Not only have I played at Anfield, I've scored there ...*

My head was spinning. I was still just a kid, and I had a shirt with a number nine on the back.

Lo and behold, two weeks later we're into the quarter-final of the Youth Cup. The call comes again – 'Is Michael available to play against Manchester United?'

Again, I went back to play. And again, I delivered. We beat them 3-2 while I scored a hat-trick – all of them at the Kop end. Looking back, that was the moment where my life changed most. The Youth Cup is a big deal – and everyone who mattered at Liverpool at that time: Roy Evans, Ronnie Moran and the entire first team, were becoming aware that I wasn't just another promising youngster. There's no doubt that my developing reputation was reaching far beyond Liverpool.

I scored five more goals across a two-legged semi-final against Crystal Palace, and then, coincidentally, I *did* receive the call to represent the England Under-16 team at the European youth championship in Austria.

This trip coincided with the first leg of the FA Youth Cup final away at West Ham – a team that included Frank Lampard and Rio Ferdinand. In my absence, Liverpool won 2-0 in front of 15,000 at Upton Park.

For the second leg at Anfield in front of a crowd in excess of 20,000, and a week after the first team's infamous 'white suits' final at Wembley, I returned to score an important header to level the score on the night. Thereafter, Stuart Quinn scored the winner and we were crowned 1996 FA Youth Cup champions – the first Liverpool side to do so.

At the age of sixteen, I already had quite an impressive résumé stretching behind me. I'd won a Youth Cup and scored many goals in the process. Not just that, in parallel I'd also set records for the England Schoolboys by having scored twelve goals in eight games in the various fixtures we played. The previous record was a joint one held by Nick Barmby and Kevin Gallen.

From memory, eight or nine of us from the sixteen in my year at Lilleshall made it to the England Schoolboys set up. These were serious games, played against established football nations – including a home nations tournament contested annually called the Victory Shield.

My achievements with the schoolboys still rank among some of my proudest moments.

In general for me, being so young, this period where I was resident at Lilleshall, playing with England Schoolboys, while also representing the Liverpool youth team, was all such an incredible rollercoaster ride. I also still consider that Youth Cup win to be one of my best footballing achievements.

To have shared it with someone like Jamie Carragher, who'd

become one of my best friends in the game, only made it even more significant.

As years have gone by, the public perception of Jamie has been that he's very intimidating, uncompromising and doesn't mince words. He has done nothing to disprove that.

The truth is, when he was younger, he was far worse! He was so confrontational as a teenager that it was almost impossible to have a conversation with him. He was very loud, and you certainly couldn't win an argument with him. In the end it was much easier to let him just have his way. Consequently, I was always a bit submissive around him in the early days. You had to be – otherwise he'd just overpower you with his opinions!

Carra and I became matey by chance really, just because we got into the squad together. It then made sense that we started rooming together. We always had loads of laughs together. We talked about football a lot. From that perspective he's an interesting character in that where I had releases in the sense that I played golf and liked racing; he was all about football, day in and day out. I'm sure people thought that, having roomed together so often, we'd be talking about cars and girls or whatever, but we rarely did.

Looking back now, Carra and I were good for each other. He'd had a tough upbringing; I'd had a relatively protected one. Initially he was very streetwise; I was much less so. Because our friendship quickly extended outside football, I remember going with him to his local pub one afternoon after training early in my Liverpool days.

The moment we walked in the door, it was like entering a different world. Carra knew everyone, and everybody knew him. As we stood at the bar, he'd nudge me, point to a corner at a group of people and tell me what crime they had committed or were probably orchestrating – 'Those lads there will likely be plotting to rob the next ship that comes into dock. These lads here are on the run from the police …'

It was an eye-opening scene. I'd never encountered this side of life and I suppose that spending time with Carra toughened me up to life's rugged realities. Similarly, spending time with me probably served to smooth away some of Carra's rougher edges over the years. I'd say we were definitely good for each other.

Although his parents probably had more money than mine when we were growing up, thinking about it nowadays, in some ways he probably had to be a bit nasty and tough to get to where he got in life.

Despite his tough edge, however, Carra has always had an absolute heart of gold – even when he was a teenager. Even today I know that, if I were ever in serious trouble, Carra would be the first person to stick up for me. He's always been a true friend.

REBØOT_3

THE HIERARCHY

After I finished my two-year stint at Lilleshall, I came straight back home and signed for Liverpool on a YTS at the age of sixteen years and eight months. As an aspiring footballer, this represents your first main target in that you're getting paid for the first time to play the game.

For this privilege I would be eligible to receive forty pounds and fifty pence per week for either the two year length of the contract, or until I signed a full professional contract.

At this point, Liverpool were promising me the world – and that world consisted of a YTS contract plus four years of a professional deal beyond that.

For any club, this represented an unprecedented degree of commitment to place in a young player. The reality was that, if I were to sign a professional contract on my seventeenth birthday (the earliest date I was legally allowed to do so) I'd only be on the YTS contract for four months.

It was during these four months that I did all the jobs you

hear about young football apprentices being subjected to: cleaning senior players' boots, scrubbing down the toilets and the showers and so on. My specific job was to keep the boot room clean and tidy every day. It could have been a lot worse.

As long as they were, those early days at Liverpool were good days. I felt like I had a definite purpose each morning – and that purpose was the culmination of everything I'd done since mini-league at the local leisure centre.

For the first time I thought, *I'm a footballer.*

My dad would drop me off at the station near our house each morning. Then I'd get a train to Bidston near one of the Mersey tunnels, followed by another train under the tunnel to Liverpool Lime Street. From there I'd get the number twelve bus to Melwood, Liverpool's training ground.

I did this routine every day, there and back, for four months until I turned professional, and then for another two months thereafter until I passed my driving test.

Interestingly, when I went to collect my first car, a racing green coloured Rover Coupé, I was told: 'Don't worry, this has been taken care of by Umbro'. It wasn't just shorts and boots after all!

During this period after leaving Lilleshall is when my relationship with my now wife Louise cemented into something beyond an unresolved childhood crush.

We had actually known each other since we were two years old, given that she lived a few doors down from us growing up. But to be honest, it wasn't until I met her in my local pub, the Crown and Liver Inn in Ewloe, when I was out one night with my brothers, that the romance developed in earnest.

Throughout our lives we'd been at infant school, nursery, primary school and high school together. I'm sure, at various times, there had been flirtatious catcalls across the playground, notes of romantic interest passed to each other via friends and the odd peck on the cheek here and there when we were very young.

As we grew older, the relationship developed into much more of a boyfriend and girlfriend type – albeit that we both had other boyfriends and girlfriends along the way. But it wasn't until our eyes met across the Crown and Liver that we both knew our futures belonged together.

The problem was, I'd been seeing another girl while I was living at Lilleshall. So, when it became clear to me that Louise and I were about to become a couple, I drove straight down to Lilleshall to do the decent thing by telling the other girl that, sadly, it wasn't going to work out between us. I wanted to do the right thing by her.

In many ways, it should have been obvious to me all along that Louise Bonsall was the girl for me. She and I had been a constant in each other's lives. And now that we've been together for more than twenty years, I know more than ever that that was for good reason. Without wanting to sound cringeworthy, it was destiny. And it has been, with the odd glitch, a case of happily ever after for us.

■ ■ ■

I signed a professional contract on my seventeenth birthday: December 14th, 1996. From memory, my dad negotiated a deal that involved a twenty-grand signing on fee that was paid straightaway (and went directly to my parents).

Beyond that, for the first year I would receive a wage of four hundred pounds a week, followed by five hundred the next year and so on, for the duration of the four-year deal.

Sitting here now, I think I should probably have a word with my dad about this first professional contract! It wasn't the best. As nice as the signing-on fee was, the weekly pay wasn't going to bowl anyone over. With all due respect to my dad, perhaps it could have been negotiated a bit better. I reckon Liverpool were wise to that fact too at the time although Roy Evans, of course, waited until I'd physically signed. Then he came to me with a word of advice.

'You need an agent!' he told me.

In my mind, naïvely I thought my dad and I could handle the business side of things. I felt that – given how he and I had overcome every barrier that had been put in our way thus far – I didn't see the need to upset the apple cart.

Furthermore, in this era, 'agent' was something of a dirty word anyway. That's still the case to some extent and I've always considered that view to be a little unfair. Just like any industry, it only takes a few unscrupulous ones to tarnish the reputation of all the others who are doing a good job every day.

'Boss, I don't think I really need one,' I countered. 'My dad used to be a professional footballer. I think we're fine.'

He looked at me again, more pointedly this time.

'You *need* an agent ...'

Roy wasn't just making a casual suggestion. He was *telling* me. Immediately, panicking a little, I thought, *this is the kind of stress I do not need.* I was realising that the life of a professional footballer didn't just involve pulling on the boots and scoring goals. There was a whole new, complicated commercial world to navigate beyond the pitch.

That evening, I went home and told my dad what Roy had said. The next morning, I went back in to talk to the boss.

'I've spoken to my dad,' I explained. 'We have no idea who any agents are so would the club be able to help steer us in the right direction?'

At that time, Liverpool put the names of three agents in front of me. They were: Leon Angel – who continues to be an agent now. Jon Holmes – whose understudy at the time was a lad called Struan Marshall. Struan became the main man and would look after fellow Liverpool players like Steven Gerrard, Emile Heskey and Carra. I can't recall who the third option was.

Having been told in no uncertain terms that this was a route I had to go down, I didn't come away from any of these meetings with any sense of comfort.

As much as I liked Jon Holmes – and he was the one I would have picked out of the three at the time – if anything, I was left feeling more scared about the complexities than reassured by the guidance I'd be getting, and would be paying handsomely for.

I decided to call Simon Marsh – one of my few trusted confidants outside of the family.

'Simon, I've been told I need an agent,' I explained. 'I've met this and that person and discussed this and that with them. What should I do?'

'Let me have a word with Alan Shearer's agent, Tony Stephens,' he said.

At that time, Tony's client list comprised of David Platt, Alan Shearer, David Beckham and Dwight Yorke. Those, I was told, were his four clients – and he didn't have any particular desire to expand. Regardless, we arranged a meeting and he came round to our house to meet me, my mum and dad and my brothers.

As much as he went through the process of pitching to us, he really didn't know much about me beyond the few grainy videos I could show him of me playing for Liverpool reserves. Given that this was 1997, there was little other option. He was really going on hearsay.

Anyway, we liked Tony so much and were so impressed by his attributes that, when he left that day, we all pretty much high-fived each other as he walked out the door. We all thought we could have a great relationship with this man who was clearly the agent to be with and I personally thought, *finally, I've found the right person.*

I called him the next day and told him that I'd love to become one of his clients.

Tony had other ideas.

'I can't really take anyone on at the minute,' he explained, 'but between me and you, David Platt is retiring at the end of the season and you could replace him as my fourth client.'

I remember being a little deflated thinking, *uh, okay – but the end of the season is quite a while away …*

To cut a long story short, we agreed that he'd take me on right then, and wean himself away from David Platt at the end of that 1997 season. From that day forward, Tony Stephens would represent me throughout my whole career.

My relationships with Tony and Simon Marsh would set a precedent for the rest of my time in the game in the sense that I liked establishing lasting relationships and didn't particularly relish the idea of letting new people come in to my life. Once I trusted somebody, they were with me and became a friend for life.

On reflection, this approach was probably a by-product of how I was living at that time. It was all so frenetic – it felt like people from all walks of life perpetually circled me. Some, I'm sure, were good intentioned. Others probably wanted to squeeze whatever juice they could from a hot commodity while they could.

As naïve as I was, I soon learned to become, on one hand, highly suspicious of newcomers, and on the other, loyal to those I could trust. I have never regretted that approach. I'm still insular to this day.

When I first arrived at Melwood, Steve Heighway was in charge of everything at the academy and Sammy Lee was also a member of the backroom team.

By the time I started actually playing for the reserves, Sammy was managing the team. From memory I played ten or twelve games for Liverpool reserves during the early part of 1997. Higher up the ladder, Roy Evans was the manager, and Ronnie Moran was the first team coach.

Playing in the Liverpool reserves was a huge jump in standard, and this is where football kills itself nowadays. We had a first team squad of eighteen players at that time at Liverpool. If you weren't in that squad for any reason you didn't just not play, you played in the reserves – no matter who you were.

For example, if Stig Inge Bjørnebye playing at left back meant that Steve Harkness wouldn't – then Steve Harkness would play in the reserves. If Robbie Fowler was playing in the first team and Stan Collymore wasn't – Stan would be in the reserves.

Basically, anybody could be in the reserves: John Barnes, Jan Molby, Nigel Clough or Paul Stewart. Nobody was exempt.

At any one time there might be six or seven players in the reserves who just weren't in the first team that week, mixed with the various kids who were knocking on the door. In those days it was Jamie Carragher, David Thompson and I who usually filled these three spaces.

Straightaway, you were playing first team football in everything but name – albeit that it was dressed up as a reserve game. Just because there were two thousand in the crowd as opposed to forty two thousand, didn't mean that it wasn't proper, hard men's football. Trust me, you learned quickly. It was the best stepping-stone you could ever have because the move into the first team proper was so seamless.

None of this happens nowadays. Reserve teams don't even really exist. It's all Under-23 teams and so on. With player power being as it is, if you were to say to player X: 'Player Y is playing this week. Will you play in the reserves?' it's just not going to happen – players just won't do it. That's not a reflection on the actual players either, I should probably say. It's more that the broader culture has changed within football. To my traditionalist eyes, the game has to be lesser for that.

Anyway, after one game on the bench in April of 1997, away at Roker Park, I made my first team debut for Liverpool off the bench against Wimbledon at Selhurst Park on May 6th, 1997.

At the time, when people asked me questions like: 'Were you excited?' or 'were you really proud?' I just said yes because it was easy to.

But the reality was that I approached my Liverpool debut just like every other game I'd ever played. As much as it was a vital game for the team in the context that we were still vaguely in the hunt for the league title along with Newcastle and Arsenal, I had just one focus: I wanted to score.

And I did score.

Although we lost the game, my debut goal was one of those finishes that I'd executed a thousand times prior.

Stig Inge Bjørnebye threaded a nice ball in from the left hand side. I ran into the channel and around the ball before side-footing it with absolute precision into the bottom left hand corner. It might as well have been Deeside Leisure Centre.

Five days later, with a Champions League place to play for, I made my first full start away at Hillsborough.

We drew the game, I was affected by horrendous cramp that could have only been as a result of nervous energy, and we missed out on that Champions League place on goal difference to Kevin Keegan's Newcastle United.

Cramp aside, it was a strange day. I'd been picked up front alongside Stan Collymore – without doubt one of our biggest stars. So keen was I to impress that day, I probably ran double the distance I normally would have in forty-five minutes. I was headless. No wonder my calves and groin were seizing up at the break. As we sat discussing tactics, Roy Evans spoke.

'I'm going to make a change up front,' he said.

In that split second I thought, *that's a bit harsh. I thought I played well in the first half.*

After all the excitement of getting a start, I was bitterly disappointed.

Then he looked at Stan Collymore.

'Stan, you're coming off ...'

That moment gave me a real boost at the time. I wasn't suddenly thinking that I was ahead of Stan in the pecking order. It just gave me confidence to think that the gaffer thought enough of me to leave me on for the full ninety minutes.

On account of a combination of factors, from May 1997 onwards, I was more or less a fixture in that Liverpool team under Roy Evans.

As it happened, Stan Collymore left the club for Aston Villa during the summer and Karl-Heinz Riedle was brought in from Borussia Dortmund to be what seemed his like-for-like replacement. On paper, it looked to me as if he and Robbie Fowler would be our first choice strikers for the 1997/98 league season.

How wrong my speculation turned out to be ...

■ ■ ■

As a Liverpool player, the main time when you're most in tune with the Kop is when you run out onto the pitch. When I first started watching Liverpool when I was fourteen or fifteen, I used to assume that the songs the Kop sang when the team ran out were in some sort of hierarchical order.

Robbie Fowler would get his song first and then it would go down the list from there. Whether there actually was an order or not, I'll never know, but when I got into the team, did well and started hearing my name being sang first, I felt a huge amount of pride to think that the fans appreciated me. The little things mattered to me – to feel that for a couple of seasons I was at the forefront of the Kop's affections. It gave me so much more positivity and self-belief.

So, for those few minutes prior to kick off, you just drink it all in. You can see and hear everything. The Kop flows through you. But once the game kicks off you become totally focused as peripheral vision retreats like fog. Your eyes go lower and tighter. All you're left with are the minutiae of the game you're playing.

Still, when you're in battle, in a game of football, there are always moments where your backs are against the wall and you need something. In an individual sport like tennis for example when someone's under the cosh, you hear of players changing something in order to alter the course of a match. Maybe they'll go to the net more or serve to a different side. In a team game you draw on little things to change the flow of a game: a tackle, a decision for or against you or, if you're a Liverpool player, shooting into the Kop. These things can give you momentum and over time you learn to use them.

I often hear people say, 'Is there a pressure shooting into the Kop because everyone expects?' If you think like that, you'll never be a Liverpool player. You've got to draw on the positives. In many, many half time team talks where maybe we were one nil down, I heard: 'Don't worry, we're kicking into the Kop second half ...'

It's still the same pitch, the same ball, still the same teams. In theory it's nothing. The Kop has never scored a goal. But in practice, as much as it's an external factor that shouldn't matter, if it works in your mind and you can draw strength from that, it plants a legitimately viable seed that can bear incredible fruit. And we've seen it time and time again that kicking into the Kop can trigger an incredible comeback.

When I first got into the first team at Liverpool, I soon became aware of a definite pecking order among the players. What's more, I knew full well that I was at the bottom of the pile.

As much as I scored goals in those very early days, I still knew I hadn't achieved much in terms of the hierarchy while I still had the likes of Collymore and Fowler sitting on the bus.

From the beginning, Robbie Fowler and I got along as well as anyone in our position could. With strikers, it's always a bit territorial. You're always looking over your shoulder thinking, *who's this young lad coming through trying to take my place?*

Although he never said, I'm sure Robbie would have felt that way about me. All things considered, though, we were absolutely fine. He had the kind of personality that was hard not to like.

I always admired the way Robbie played too. He and I, as much as we were both instinctive goalscorers, didn't have too much in common stylistically. I was quick; he wasn't especially. I was right-footed; he had one of the sweetest left foots I've ever seen. I liked to finesse my finishes; he wasn't averse to powering them in.

We were different in almost every way – yet we were both very effective in terms of putting the ball in the net in whatever way we could.

Interestingly, after I'd won two Golden Boots, *even then* I never considered that I might be even close to the same level as someone like Robbie. While I was arguably a more important player in the context of the club than he was by that time – it didn't matter. In my mind I was still beneath him and aspiring to reach his level. That was just how it worked.

As far as what the rules actually were, there wasn't much

guidance offered. It was left to the player to gauge what the lie of the land was and my God, if you did something wrong, you'd hear about it.

For example, there were certain cars that I simply wouldn't have turned up in. I would have been petrified of anyone looking at me and saying: 'Oi, you. I've seen that bloody Porsche you're driving,' or anything else like that. Equally, there were certain places in the car park where you just didn't park.

There were other strange quirks of the hierarchy too. Around this time, mobile phones had just started becoming readily available. All the senior guys would put their mobile phones in the cup holder of their tray table on the bus. As a seventeen and eighteen-year-old who'd just got my first phone, I would never have dreamed of doing that. Mine stayed in my pocket.

As time passed and after I'd maybe banged in a few more goals, if people were happy and having a few bottles of beer on the bus, maybe then and only then would I consider popping the phone out of my pocket and positioning it in my cup holder. Yes, I was in the first team and scoring goals, but I was always respectful of my standing. Everything was based on respect and hierarchy. I still had senior players above me and I never wanted to overstep that mark. I don't think concepts of this kind exist in the modern game.

When it came to gambling (and I had always liked a bet since I was a kid) there was a similar pecking order. I remember the first time I climbed aboard the team coach on one of the first away trips at the end of that 1996/97 season. Because I was young, and keen, I arrived early and sat down.

'That's my seat. Get out!' Stan Collymore said when he arrived. 'Who do you think you are?'

'Sorry, Stan,' I said 'Are there any spare seats?'

'I don't know, really,' he said – as if he couldn't care less.

I sat somewhere else and I got kicked out of that seat too. Eventually I found myself just stood there in the aisle waiting for everyone to get on so that I could see which seat was left. Naturally, wherever I ended up was far away from the clan in the back.

In those early days in the first team, that clan usually consisted of the likes of Robbie Fowler, Steve McManaman, Paul Ince and John Barnes. Then you'd have other lads like Steve Harkness, Dom Matteo, Rob Jones and Razor Ruddock who were often back there too. There were strong personalities wherever you looked.

As great a team spirit as it all was, I was nowhere near the core of all the fun and games. On away trips, after we'd played and won, we'd stop at the first chip shop on the way home. Ronnie Moran would jump off and say something like: 'Twenty five fish and chips please.'

As we went down the road, the fags would come out, the booze would come out. There'd be crates of lager appearing from nowhere. Soon, the cards would come out. And then the newspapers would appear, closely followed by the porn magazines. I'd never seen anything like it. In a sense I was born into that lifestyle.

As time passed, I was desperate to get into that bloody card school! I wasn't bothered about smoking and I wasn't much of a drinker or a reader of porn magazines. But I did like to gamble.

Gambling had been an integral part of my life since my early teens. I just always loved it. I regularly spent all my YTS money in betting shops, backing horses and dogs. I couldn't play anything: golf, snooker or whatever, without there being money at stake. Some people might consider that to be quite a sad attitude but it was always that way for me. Obviously the pride of winning was important, but the buzz was even greater if there was money at stake.

Obviously, as time passed, people left and you could hope to move one more rung up the ladder. But it was a gradual process – allied to the fact that I was only paid in the hundreds per week initially whereas the top guys were earning perhaps thirty to fifty grand.

Even if I'd wanted to, I didn't have the means to meddle in the card school – where you might lose a grand or two on a bad day – in those early days anyway.

■ ■ ■ ■

My days of relatively low earning didn't last long, however. As that 1997/98 season began, and with it a starting berth in the first team on account of Robbie Fowler's ankle injury, I embarked on the first of two landmark seasons at Liverpool.

As confident as I was, scoring a penalty in the first league game of the season to get us a draw against Wimbledon at Selhurst Park just lit a fire under me.

Goals away at Blackburn and Crystal Palace, and several more at home games against Tottenham, Coventry and Leeds followed – in addition to a hat-trick against Grimsby in the Coca-Cola Cup and another goal in the next round away at Newcastle. Earlier in the season, I had scored the first in a 2-2 draw at Celtic in the first round, first leg of the UEFA Cup to get off the mark in Europe.

Liverpool renegotiated my contract to reflect not just my value in terms of goals, but also my rapidly escalating profile as probably the most valuable teenager playing the game. I signed a new five-year contract and my six grand a week salary made me the highest paid teenager in Premier League history at that time.

All this good news was tempered slightly by the fact that I was sent off for losing my rag and butting a defender in a game against what was then Yugoslavia, for Howard Wilkinson's England Under-18 team at Rotherham. Not my proudest moment, let's just say that. I'd like to say it was just youthful exuberance, but really it was this aggressive streak that I've always had, but generally been adept at channelling.

By Christmas of that year, I'd also been called up to train with the full England squad.

With a World Cup just around the corner in June 1998, there was much optimism under manager Glenn Hoddle's management. At his disposal was undeniably a great if slightly ageing group of players. As made-up as I was to be part of Glenn's squad at all, the idea of my being in France in June, other than for a holiday, nevertheless seemed remote to me.

The turn of the year changed everything, however.

Robbie Fowler would eventually be ruled out for the remainder of the 1997/98 season. But before he was, I initiated what could only be described as a goalscoring frenzy.

In January and February I scored at home against Newcastle and Southampton (two) and away at Villa and Sheffield Wednesday (three). While our title challenge would later falter, I'd never felt better in terms of my own form. Goals, it seemed, were never far away. Neither, as it turned out, was a full England call-up.

I remember being out playing golf at Curzon Park with my dad on a day off in late January. From memory it was the day after we'd drawn 0-0 against Blackburn at Anfield. After a few holes my phone went – even though you weren't really allowed mobile phones on golf courses at that time.

On the screen it said *Doug Livermore* – who was our assistant manager at Liverpool at that time. Puzzled, I thought, *what's this all about?* He's never called me before.

I told my dad to wait while I slunk sheepishly into the trees.

'Hello?'

'I've got some good news for you,' Doug said.

I honestly had no clue what he was going to say.

'You've been picked in the England squad,' he told me, 'it'll be announced tomorrow.'

Looking back now, I have no idea why I'd been so oblivious to this possibility. Maybe I was just naïve at the time, but really, given my profile and goals, I shouldn't have been as surprised as I was. Regardless, I tried to play it cool.

'Ok, that's great,' I said, 'thanks for letting me know.'

Then Dad and I erupted.

'Dad!!! I'm in the England squad tomorrow!'

We both punched the air like madmen.

The only upsetting thing was that we were playing for a tenner, and I was four up at the time. My dad ended up beating me one up in the end because my golf game went to pieces. I was phoning everyone for the rest of the round between shots!

Walking into the England team hotel ahead of my full England debut against Chile at Wembley on February 11th was a surreal experience too. There I was, still a young kid, mixing it with a squad of household names – many of whom had been heroes of mine. Some of them still were.

Also of considerable comfort to me was the fact that there were at least a few familiar faces around me, with Paul Ince and Steve McManaman often part of the England set-up at these initial squad get-togethers.

Beyond that, Alan Shearer and Tony Adams were very much the two senior figures in the dressing room at the time.

In many ways they were similar characters: tough, perhaps a little overbearing and unapproachable to a youngster on his debut – but nevertheless inspiring guys that you just knew you'd want alongside you on a pitch.

Both were old-school lads that commanded total respect at all times. As a striker, I couldn't help but see Alan Shearer as everything I should be aspiring to.

The game itself is another one of those events where people always say: 'How did you feel?' And my answer, as was the case with almost every milestone event in my career, was: 'Nothing very much.'

This isn't in any way meant to denigrate the act of representing my country at senior level for the first time – not at all. It goes without saying that it's an honour we all aspire to. I'm as passionate about England as the next man.

But for me, walking out onto Wembley's pitch for the first time, in the pouring rain as I recall, my first thought wasn't *yes, here I am in the England squad.* It was much more a case of *I've got to score here – preferably more than once …*

This total inability to rest on my laurels would become a hallmark of my career. The way I saw it, after something good had happened, it was over. If I scored, I was only thinking about the next goal. If I scored a hat-trick, I'd think *that's fine. Next time I'll score four …*

Playing for England was exactly the same. The record books

will tell you that I had a more than respectable debut in a 2-0 defeat. I had a few good runs, created a few chances and was awarded man of the match for my troubles.

As soon as the whistle blew, I revelled in this limelight for perhaps five seconds as Wembley's lights dimmed.

Then I thought, *what's next?*

And then, *I've got to stay in this England team forever now...*

And then, *I've got to win the World Cup.*

It's important to add that, at the time, I didn't see these lofty ambitions as pressure. As far as I was concerned, if you're good at something, as I was, and your destiny is in your hands, as mine was, it's not pressure.

Nowadays, if you put me on the first tee of the Old Course with a golf club, and just three people watching, I wouldn't know whether the ball would go high, low, left or right. That would be pressure to me, and that's because I'm relatively crap at golf.

But football, for me, because I genuinely felt like I had no equals, never felt like pressure. If there had been ten million people watching me, I wouldn't have wilted – quite the reverse. My only reaction would be to do even better. Just like when I saw scouts standing with my dad, all those years previously.

My inclusion in England's plans, unfortunately, would come at the expense of another hero of mine from closer to home – my Liverpool teammate Robbie Fowler. As I mentioned, his season was over on the back of a serious knee injury sustained in an innocuous challenge in the Merseyside derby in late February.

Liverpool's title challenge faltered shortly afterwards on the run-in. Despite more goals for me in a significant loss away at Villa – where my former teammate Stan Collymore came back to bite us with a goal in either half – and other goals at home to Bolton and away at Coventry and Manchester United, it was defeats to Chelsea and Derby at important moments that probably sank us.

My getting sent off for the second time in six months for diving in two-footed on Manchester United's Ronny Johnsen didn't help us much either.

I'd gone into that game as a pumped-up kid who on one hand recognised the rivalry with United while on the other was possibly a little jealous of them. With hindsight, my performance that day was like some kind of out of body experience. I was so keen to win, so zoned-in. I was running everywhere, kicking every ball, kicking everyone! I was out of control.

Despite my knowing all too well that this aggressive streak of mine was often a positive, the tackle that day that saw Johnsen taken away later in an ambulance, was many steps too far. It was a moment of absolute red-mist madness that I'm not proud of to this day.

After I was dispatched, I remember standing in the shower on my own, crying. As the tears fell I was learning an important lesson. As much as you can have fire in your belly, you've also got to have ice in your brain.

The end of Liverpool's 1997/98 league season left a slightly sour taste in everyone's mouth. We were in contention, but faded away into a distant third place behind eventual winners Arsenal who just edged out Manchester United by a point to give forward-thinking Arsenal manager Arsene Wenger his first league title.

For me, though, the 1997/98 season was an unmitigated success – a breakout year of epic proportions that included eighteen league goals and twenty three in all competitions. As if to confirm it, I was awarded the Premier League Golden Boot and the PFA Young Player Of The Year Award.

As you'd expect by now, I rested on these two impressive laurels for all of a few seconds. With a World Cup looming, there was much more to do.

REBØOT_4

CULTURE SHOCK

Between my England debut against Chile in February of 1998 and the World Cup in France in June, a thirty-man squad was announced at a bonding session convened by Glenn Hoddle in La Manga.

My first impressions of Glenn Hoddle as a manager were nothing but positive. Glenn was an intriguing character. I got on with him fine, and have done even more so in recent years having worked with him as a pundit at BT Sport. But at the time you'd have never called him a players' mate.

Where a Keegan or a Harry Redknapp-type would give players confidence by getting close to them and being part of the laughs and jokes, Glenn was more reserved. He used his number two, John Gorman, to do his bidding for him. John would be the one to ferret among the lads to gauge the mood of the camp. Glenn was a great man manager, but he always seemed to want to do things from a distance. Horses for courses, I suppose.

Prior to the squad announcement, having been the Premier League's top scorer in the 1997/98 season, I was quietly confident that I would be going to the World Cup by the time March came around. I'd played two more friendlies for England in the interim, one in Berne against Switzerland and a second against Portugal at Wembley.

I scored in neither. I'd have to wait until another pre-World Cup game in Casablanca against Morocco – where I came off the bench to replace an injured Ian Wright – for my debut England goal. It was all the more memorable given that I could have easily been replaced myself a few minutes prior, following a nasty boot to the head.

As confident as I was, as a striker, goals are what you're after, especially when you're trying to persuade a manager to take you to a World Cup. With hindsight, I suspect the goal in Casablanca was what sealed an already reasonably convincing case for my inclusion in Glenn's mind. I'd shown I could play and handle big occasions. Now I'd showed him I could score.

And it wasn't just Glenn who I'd made a believer of, either. When the newspapers started speculating about who they thought would go, as they liked to do, I seemed to fall into the category of being a probable as opposed to a possible.

In La Manga, all kinds of drama ensued.

At some point on that trip, we were all assigned a five-minute appointment to see the gaffer in his hotel room. As I recall, I was about two thirds of the way down the list. While me and all the later guys were sitting around the pool speculating about who'd be in and who wouldn't, someone came out and said: 'Lads, Gazza isn't in the squad.'

To me, this was unfathomable news. Initially I thought, *God, he'd have been the first name on my teamsheet alongside Alan Shearer.* And I doubt I was alone. Nobody could believe it.

Then another rumour spread that all meetings had been pushed back by half an hour because Gazza had flipped – thrown chairs around and generally smashed the room up. David Seaman had then been detailed, we were told, to find him and calm him down. There was a collective sense of shock around the England camp that afternoon.

Gazza was one of the household names I mentioned who were around the England squad in the spring of 1998. When I was younger, it was impossible not to admire everything about Paul Gascoigne.

To me, in his days at Newcastle, Tottenham and Rangers, he had everything: charisma, confidence and, obviously, a footballing brain and skill the likes of which is rarely seen.

I also admired the fact that he had – being an obviously home-loving lad – the bottle to leave England for Lazio at all. Even though it hadn't been a total success, at least he'd done it. For me, Gazza was one of my absolute heroes. Italia 90 was the beginning of that adulation.

I first met him in person when I first joined up for an England squad session at Bisham Abbey in October of the previous year. We'd just beaten Chelsea 4-2 at Anfield in a four o'clock game and Steve McManaman, Paul Ince and I had to then make our way to the team hotel, Burnham Beeches, to join up with rest of the lads. It was a Sunday – it was past two in the morning when we eventually arrived.

Steve McManaman showed me around.

'Here's where we have breakfast in the morning,' he said.

'There's where we have our team meetings,' he added.

He opened the door to a room with a giant screen on the wall and there was Gazza, sitting playing video games on the big screen.

'Alright?' he said, barely looking up.

As I walked over to shake his hand, I took careful note of the empty wine bottles on the table in front of him – and the empty sleeping pill packets.

I thought, *oh my God. This is bad.*

From that moment on, Gazza and I formed as comfortable an affinity as anyone could with him. I would never say that we were friends who talked every day. But there was definitely a healthy degree of mutual admiration that continues to this day. I always and still do want the very best for him

Anyway, when my appointment time came that day, I walked into the room and looked around for signs of Gazza's reputed damage. There was none. Everything looked perfectly orderly and Glenn himself was calm as if nothing had happened.

'First of all,' he started, 'you're coming. You're in the squad.'

Phew.

'And I don't want you to think you're just coming for a ride. You'll have a big part to play in this tournament,' he then said.

He explained, as I thought he might, that Shearer and Sheringham would start the first game against Tunisia in Marseille. They were tried and trusted, he told me. And I agreed. But then he was very keen to stress that I'd be coming on and that there was real scope to break that partnership up.

I walked out of that room delighted with what I'd just heard. As much as I knew that I was third choice, he had really made me feel that it was in my hands to change that.

When you consider the wealth of other strikers that were around the English game in 1998: Robbie Fowler, Ian Wright,

Chris Sutton, Les Ferdinand, Stan Collymore, Andy Cole and Dion Dublin – all of them top, top players, it was no mean feat that I was considered third choice in such company. Going into that World Cup in France, I couldn't have felt more confident about my status or that of the squad as a whole.

As far as the Gazza situation goes, after the initial shock of his omission had passed, I personally understood why Glenn had made the decision he had.

Paul Scholes was doing an amazing job for Manchester United. Glenn obviously saw him as the type of player who could be the orchestrator in a three-man central midfield that would include Batty and Ince sitting. It all made sense.

I think it was clear to everyone that, as much as Gazza probably still had the ability to affect a game despite being just past his best, if you were going to actually play Scholes instead of Gazza, the latter's disruptive influence off the pitch might be too much of a risk.

The other thing with Gazza was that you had no choice but to take both sides of his personality. The laughs you'd have, of course, would be amazing. But if you were to pick the team and have him sitting on the bench, there's every chance he'd have a face on and do his fair share of whining. Nobody needed that, and I'm certain that Glenn knew it. On reflection, as much as Gazza was one of my all time heroes, I think Glenn made a shrewd decision.

As it turned out, when June came around, the World Cup in France was a huge eye-opener. As much as the public forms an opinion based only on what they hear in the papers, if it had been me managing an England squad twenty years ago, I'm not certain I would have done it in the manner that Glenn Hoddle did.

Firstly, Glenn was adamant that our squad environment at La Baule in Brittany should be a camp in the purest of senses. Within that camp we weren't allowed newspapers and we weren't allowed the radio on. We weren't allowed to interact with any of our family or friends – even after games. These were big calls Glenn made at that time.

However, in hindsight, given what would happen in later major tournaments, few would argue that Glenn's thinking in '98 was spot-on. But at the time, instead of us living in a travelling circus like later years when WAG culture came to the fore, it felt more like a hard labour camp.

Food and nutrition was a significant part of Glenn's regime. Up until that point in England, we had been very much backwards in comparison to how the continentals approached the subject of nutrition and dietary supplements and so on.

By and large, we were all still on the pie and pint regime – where you'd return from the summer break two stone overweight and use the pre-season to get fit. It was all old-school stuff.

From 1996, Arsene Wenger at Arsenal had sparked at least the beginnings of a new dietary culture in the English game. Other clubs, including Liverpool, were still miles behind Wenger by the time the 1998 World Cup came around.

But Glenn had worked abroad. By 1998, he not only knew how to prepare from a nutritional perspective, but he also knew how to achieve the best recovery after games. Really it was a new frontier, and Glenn was miles ahead of the curve.

Consequently, while we didn't exactly rebel against any of Glenn's ideas, it was nevertheless a bit jarring – only because it was all so new to us.

Food would be boiled chicken, boiled rice or boiled pasta and broccoli for every meal. No sauce, no nothing. And the motto above the door of the camp canteen was 'Chew To Win'. Basically what this meant was that he didn't want any of us eating loads of food. Instead he wanted us all to chew every mouthful three or four times more than we normally would – the theory, we were told, being that (a) we'd extract more nutrients and (b) the food would be more easily broken down and digested. Let's just say that meal times were something of a culture shock.

The broader daily regimen was no more palatable.

Each day we'd wake up, have breakfast, and then train from ten until half eleven. You'd have lunch at one o'clock and then, between then and seven o'clock at night you'd do absolutely nothing whatsoever, other than staring at the wall in your room.

By the time dinner rolled around you'd be genuinely excited to go downstairs – not because of the bland culinary delights that awaited, but more because you could actually talk to someone. Then you'd go back to your room and stare at the walls until you went to sleep again. And repeat. It was all so sterile and boring.

More than anything, all of this opened everybody's eyes to the level of focus that Glenn wanted from us. And as much as we missed our family, friends and kids, we also knew that we were no different to people who went away to work on oilrigs, down coalmines or in the army.

Don't get me wrong, none of us exactly cried poverty – but my personal view, with hindsight, is that if you want the best from a group of people you should do whatever you can to keep them happy. If someone's bored or depressed or is missing their family, are they really going to give their best in a game?

I guess the jury is still out on that.

Anyway, we flew to Marseille for the game against Tunisia and I vividly remember flicking on the TV in the hotel to be greeted with CNN pictures showing England fans fighting everywhere. At times we could hear it outside the window of the hotel.

Before we'd even played a game, there was talk of England getting chucked out of the tournament. Lying in bed, as battle royal raged outside, I can remember thinking, *what the hell is going on here? This could ruin it for us.*

As Glenn had intimated, I sat on the bench for the vast majority of the first game at Le Stade Vélodrome against Tunisia. Shearer scored in the first half and then Scholesy added a bit of gloss to the performance with a last minute curler to kill off a spirited Tunisia side.

For me, coming on in the scenario that I did was one of those horrible no-win situations. As good as it was to be comfortable in the game, because I wanted to start the next game, I really needed us to be drawing 0-0 so that I could come on and score the winner. As it stood, I was sent on there in the boiling heat, just to keep the ball and kill the game.

In the next game against Romania in Toulouse, it was frustrating for entirely different reasons.

After what seemed like an eternity, I came on to replace Teddy Sheringham after seventy two minutes. We were 0-1 down at the time, desperately in need of something. As fabulous a player as Teddy Sheringham was, I felt that, in those circumstances where outright pace could be the key, I had a much better chance of scoring than he did.

As time passed, I became more and more deflated waiting to come on – especially given that we needed a goal. As a few of us warmed up behind the goal, I kept glancing over trying to catch Glenn's eye. All I can remember thinking before Glenn eventually gave me the signal to go on was, *I can't believe how long this is taking. I'm not going to have time to score here.*

Not long after getting on, I made an immediate impact. I wriggled past a couple of players, shot from outside the box and hit the post. Immediately, I was brimming with confidence.

Two minutes later, bang – I scored to equalise. Then they went straight up the other end and scored to beat us. But importantly from my perspective, I'd come on, scored and changed the course of the game. As a result of my impact, I'd start the next two games.

Looking back, the outcome of the final group game was somewhat informed by Glenn's preparation back at our base in Brittany. Having just lost, tensions were understandably high as match day approached. During one of our morning training sessions, two days ahead of the game, we were all practising free-kicks and corners.

At this stage it's important to mention that, if the gaffer had a weakness at all, as brilliant a tactician as he was, it was that he thought everyone should be as good as he was. And he was bloody good. The reality was that, even though he was working with a group of top international players, not many of them had anything close to the touch that he had.

He'd devised this complex free-kick routine whereby Becks was going to run up and hit it while Scholes was to put his foot right in front of the ball. The gaffer's idea was that, when it hit Scholes' foot, the ball would acquire massive amounts of topspin that would send it up then bring it rapidly down.

We started practising this.

After a few goes, Becks couldn't do it. Then Scholesy tries it – couldn't do it either.

Meanwhile the gaffer started to lose his head a little because he could do it and nobody else could.

'Ok, you clearly can't do it,' he said, 'just do what you normally do.'

We started practising corners and what the various hand signals meant. The lads who weren't playing were meant to be listening while they stood behind the goal.

But Glenn eyed a few of them talking to each other. He shouted over to a couple of them: 'You, what does one hand mean?' No clue. 'You, what does two hands mean?' Didn't have a clue. He was furious, and made them all stay behind.

As it happened, I played quite well against Colombia in a game we had to win to progress to the next phase. We won 1-0.

Ironically, David Beckham's free-kick from the edge of the box was the difference on a nervy night in Lens. Instead of the complex two-man routine that Glenn had dreamed up, Becks did what he normally did and just whipped the thing into the top corner. The second round beckoned.

REBØOT_5

THROUGH THE MAYHEM

Everybody always talks about the game at Saint-Étienne against Argentina on June 30th. Whether I like it or not, the events of that night have become part of football folklore. Those 120-plus minutes had all the elements of a final and more: edge, great goals, controversy and a penalty shoot-out to top it all off. But it was just the second round.

For me, I'd be lying if I didn't admit that, among a few life-changing moments across my football career, that goal in Saint-Étienne was the most significant for all kinds of reasons.

Along with the huge buzz I experienced in the moment (and I can still feel it now if I try hard enough) came an awful sense of anti-climax.

As much as – being the guy tasked to score goals, the game *within* the game, I'd done my job – we nevertheless went out of the tournament and got on a plane home. Did the goal soften the blow? Maybe just a little.

Even now, I need to look at a TV replay to remember exactly what happened that night. As time passes, you forget the moments, the angles – but never the rush of adrenaline you felt when you saw the ball, spinning in slow motion, silhouetted against the top corner. I can remember the faces behind the top corner, frozen in time, waiting, mouths open with excitement, for the ball to arrive.

Before the game, I had no idea who any of the Argentinian players were. At a push, I could probably have named you Batistuta, but that's about it.

At that point in my career, I knew little about many other players. Defenders' attributes – whether they were left-footed or right-footed – didn't even enter my mind. Even if they had, these attributes wouldn't have concerned me at all. Because I was so confident about what I could do, I just thought: *I'll run past you ...*

As much as I hadn't researched Argentina, it was clear to me that – after our first goal where I ran at their defence and won a penalty – they didn't know much about me either. But thereafter, I noticed panic in their eyes anytime I received the ball.

Few would argue that Roberto Ayala is one of the best defenders we've seen in world football in recent years. Yet, on the build up to our second goal that night in Saint-Étienne, a world-class defender found himself in a position that just beggars belief. This was only because of what I'd done to the defence a few minutes earlier. I'd scared them.

Funnily enough, as the goal sequence developed when Becks' pass reached me just inside the opposition half, my first thought was to keep the ball and potentially link play. Then, when I looked up and saw what was in front of me, my eyes lit up. Everything changed.

Unsettled by what had transpired a few minutes previously, the Argentinian defenders must have thought that they couldn't just squeeze up on me again. Instead, backs to goal, they just gave me a run on them. Play broke down into something you might see in a school playground: no structure, assignments lost. In truth, they had no chance. I would have run past them all even if I'd been slow!

I was thinking, *they're sitting ducks …*

Initially, the shape of José Chamot came into the corner of my eye. In a split second I thought, *he's too close to me.* He was cheating, edging, gambling – hoping he could nick it, or use his strength to put me off. He had underestimated my pace too.

I felt he was in the wrong position and, if I took a good touch, I could just run away from him. I made an instinctive decision. I used the outside of my foot and took that touch. I wriggled free of him and it was then, when I lifted my head again, that I thought one thing: *oh my God … goal.*

Bizarrely, at no point in any of this did I feel any pressure whatsoever. Regardless of the enormity of the stage, because I'd rehearsed every conceivable way of scoring goals throughout my young life, what could have been a nerve-wracking, do or die moment was reduced to just familiar routine.

I went into automatic mode.

As I got closer, I was always thinking a little ahead. As I was sprinting towards Ayala, of course it would have been piss-easy to just run past him. The risk was that, by going past him, I might take the ball too near the corner flag.

Conversely, if I took it too close to him, I'd be risking him nicking the ball or bringing me down.

Angles and distance of touch became my sole focal points. I had to take it as close to him as I dared, but not so far away that I'd be making the finish too hard. In a situation like this, you're weighing all this up subconsciously, but you're not aware that you are. It just happens.

Everyone always asks me about Scholesy – because, if you watch the replay, he comes into view on my right-hand side. Honestly, it was never a question in my mind to pass to him – not because I'm selfish, but more because I was in already in a rhythm, a pattern, that ruled it out. Had I wanted to pass to him, I would have already instinctively started moving to my left to give him more room.

As it stood, Scholesy never even shouted for the ball. I think we both knew that it would have been a really difficult finish for him anyway – running straight onto a ball that was coming across him. Once I'd moved it to my right, it was the easiest thing in the world to clip it back the other way. It was on my right foot; it was a great angle.

When it came to it, the clipped finish was something I'd practised so many times. I need to stress again how important my childhood experimentation was for moments like this. If you had a camera at ball level, you wouldn't have seen a lot of net. It would have all been goalkeeper.

In that situation, I could have perhaps rolled it through his legs. But even that would have been risky. If I'd gone low or mid-height, there wouldn't have been that much goal either. Had I been further right, a near-post finish would have entered the equation because the natural shape of that shot moves right to left. I could have started it outside and brought it back in. But by clipping the ball high and back across the keeper, I was giving myself the biggest target.

As soon as I touched it I thought, *that's in …*

As much as scoring a goal in any situation gives me a huge rush of adrenaline, the aftermath of that goal in Saint-Étienne was memorable for other reasons.

As I scored and peeled away towards the touchline to celebrate, my teammates submerged me for what seemed like forever. In reality, it was only a few seconds.

Amid all this chaos, I lifted my head, looked up at the crowd to punch the air one more time in celebration and the first eyes that met mine were my own mother's.

In a crowd of 30,000-plus I had absolutely no idea where my family was. I knew they were in there somewhere – but never did I suspect that they'd be the first people I'd see in the midst of the mayhem. It was so bizarre. What were the chances?

Obviously, when we later went to the penalty shoot-out, I knew exactly where to look for them.

As an Englishman, it was impossible not to be aware of our history in penalties over the years. I'd been a fan sitting in front of the TV. I'd seen Gareth Southgate in a pizza advert walking into a post. I'd seen Chris Waddle blaze it over the bar. I'd seen Stuart Pearce miss. I could name everyone who'd missed for England.

We'd *all* seen what the press did to people when they did things wrong – the objects that would be placed on their heads in photos in the next morning's paper. This was an era where the press seemed to be particularly vindictive and nasty. People were disproportionately castigated and had to live with mistakes they'd made for the rest of their lives – to the extent that one bad move could eclipse an otherwise brilliant career.

Rightly or wrongly, prior to that penalty kick competition, my only thought was, *just don't let it be me.*

Was that a selfish thought? I don't know. Did everyone else feel the same? You'd need to ask them. Should I have been more positive as I was walking towards the ball? Probably! But I only felt what I felt because I didn't want to be on the wrong side of history.

What didn't help me much was that I had no idea where I was going to put the ball, right up until I struck it. I didn't like penalties and I didn't have that good a record with them for Liverpool. Really, the only aspect I ever liked about penalty kicks was that they were helpful for my goalscoring tally.

With retrospect, I maybe didn't like them because I never practised them enough. Firstly, it wasn't that enjoyable and secondly, no goalkeepers want to come out after training for half an hour while you lash balls past them.

If you practised them together as a group of lads, ego became a factor. If you missed one you looked a bit of a dickhead so you just didn't do it. I got round it all by thinking, *I'm a good finisher. Let's just hope that when it comes to it I score.*

With hindsight, not practising penalties is a mistake that I'd rectify if I could have my career over again. When asked in the papers, I just gave the same reason everybody did: you couldn't practise them. Of course, I said this to justify my own actions.

But sitting here now, I know that, while you can never perfectly imitate a high-pressure situation like a World Cup penalty shoot-out, by practising you can at least come to trust the required process more. After all, just because Tiger Woods can't recreate the pressure of standing on the last green of a major tournament where he needs to hole a four-footer to win, that doesn't mean he can't practise the process of holing four-foot putts. Surely the whole point of practising is not only to perfect a technique, but also to create a mind-set and a muscle memory that will stand firm under the most severe pressure?

The same logic should also apply to penalty kicks. While there would still be some variables obviously (what the keeper does, for example), at least you could remove some of them by being better at the act of taking a penalty. We're always wiser after the event!

Anyway, I had no clue where I was going as I stood in the centre circle awaiting my turn. Alan Shearer had just taken one and had scored. I was fourth in line.

Nervous, I said to him: 'Al, which corner should I go for?'

I just wanted some moral support.

He just looked at me with that quizzical, withering expression that sometimes crosses his face.

'Do what you normally fucking do,' he said. 'Stick it in the back of the net.'

That was Al's style – and it wasn't exactly what I wanted to hear.

For whatever reason, my standard finish was always low down to the keeper's left-hand side – my right. I don't even know why I favoured this because, on paper, it's harder to put the ball in that corner as a right-footed player.

Standing there in the centre-circle, I looked over at my mum and dad. I pointed left and right as if to say 'which way?'

What the hell was I thinking?

On reflection, I don't think I was thinking at all. I was afraid and was half-joking with them in an attempt to alleviate my own nerves.

My mother, the worrier, couldn't cope with it. She covered

her face – I assume to make the situation go away. Dad, ever the implacable one, just stared ahead.

As I walked to the ball, I was no less conflicted. Going through my head was the fact that, for all our previous penalties, the keeper had guessed correctly. In a brief moment of paranoia I start thinking, *maybe he's spotted something in the run-ups?*

Armed with this suspicion, I only made my decision as I stood by the ball. I decided that I was going to open my body up in the run-up as far as I possibly could as if to exaggerate that I was going right. Then, at the last second, I decided I'd drag it left into the other corner.

It sounds simple, but you've still got to do it.

Fortunately, in that situation, you get very little time to consider whether it's missing or not. Just as well, really. The ball flew into the top corner, hitting the post as it went in. The keeper dived the wrong way but you could have put five keepers in there and they wouldn't have saved it.

Did I really mean to put it that high? Absolutely not – I was aiming for something of mid-height, into a particular area – just to throw the keeper off the scent. I got away with one.

And when it went in, there was no joy – only extreme relief. As embarrassing as it is to admit, it's a very selfish state of mind that you go into at that moment … *thank God it wasn't me …*

Maybe it was my age and immaturity at the time or maybe I would have felt the same way if I'd been thirty five – I'll never know. I just felt like a miss would have ruined my life. And I certainly didn't want to be the one to walk back into the dressing room having cost us.

Unfortunately for David Batty and Paul Ince, it was them who experienced the heartache. And we exited the 1998

World Cup with a feeling that, yes we'd lost, but that we'd held our own against one of the best teams in the tournament – even with ten men.

Having mentioned that we played some of that game with ten men, it would be remiss of me to *not* comment on David Beckham's sending off that night.

I'll start by saying that David and I always got on well on a personal level. But after that World Cup in France, few would argue that his and my paths were different. I became the darling of English football for a period of time whereas he became the villain. The press loved playing us off each other as opposites. As we all know, we were in the midst of an era where the press were just merciless. David certainly bore the brunt of that.

The general feeling in the dressing room immediately after the match was that there was nothing to say about him getting sent off. We were all disappointed about going home under the circumstances.

But when you boil it down, what could any of us have said to him that would have changed anything? The damage was done.

However, some time later, I got wind from Tony Stephens' assistant that Victoria was in some way disappointed in me. She felt, I was told, that while all the limelight was on me after the World Cup, I should have publicly and voluntarily come out and backed David. Had someone specifically raised it, and I can't recall anyone doing it, I may have considered saying something along lines of: 'Come on, everyone – leave off him.'

The truth is, as an eighteen-year-old kid, I didn't feel that I had the standing in the game to have done that off my own back. In my first two seasons at Liverpool, I'd become accustomed to that idea of hierarchy I described. At every stage, I believed, a player should know where his place is. As you progress up the ladder, that place changes. Although it was unsaid, I felt the same about the England dressing room.

As much as I'd scored a wonder goal in many people's eyes, albeit in a game that we ultimately lost, I certainly didn't think it was my place to play in the card school in 1998.

Similarly, I was hardly going to waltz into the dressing room after the game, shake Tony Adams by the hand and say: 'Congratulations on a great career, pal.' I wouldn't have dreamed of doing that. Equally, I didn't consider myself senior enough to pat David Beckham – twenty times more famous than I was at the time – on the back and say: 'Keep your chin up, mate,' either.

Whether I thought his actions lost us the game or not didn't matter. For me, at that time, it was about hierarchy and standing. I was just a junior member of that squad. I was really just a kid.

But …

Sitting here now, with the benefit of hindsight and perspective, I feel differently.

First of all, let me pre-empt what follows by saying that what David did probably wasn't a red card offence in the first place. While it was clearly pre-meditated, it was immature and petulant more than it was violent. But for me, that almost makes it worse. Had he stood up and just punched someone in the face, somehow the disappointment would have been easier to take.

But because his flick-out was so childish, it also seemed so much more unnecessary. People will say it was just a mistake, but my feeling is that, if you want to win World Cups, you can't afford to make mistakes. This is a tough world we're living in. You've got to be bob-on with everything you do because the margins are tiny.

Would we have beaten Argentina with eleven men? We'll never know – but we were playing well enough with ten at the time. Would we have gone on to beat Holland and then Brazil and so on? We'll never know that either.

All I can say is that, as I sit here now writing this book, knowing how lucky a player is to appear in one World Cup, never mind more than one, I'd be lying if I didn't say that what David did that day hadn't let every single one of that England team down.

Did he deserve the abuse he got from the press afterwards? Certainly not. What human being needs to see his or her effigy being burned? But David let us down, and I still hold some resentment about it today.

REBØOT_6

FAME

The adulation really was heaped on me after that World Cup in 1998. It was unprecedented and, obviously, I'd never experienced anything like it. Even before we got back to England – and we flew back on Concorde from Paris to Luton – events got a little out of hand. As we began our approach, one of the crew came to my seat and asked me to go up to the cockpit.

Walking up the aisle I thought, *what's this all about?*

As it turned out, what they wanted me to do was hold the England flag out of the cockpit window when we landed at Luton. Who else can say they've done that?

If you could find footage today of that plane touching down, you'd see two arms appearing out of the window holding the flag. Those were my arms. That alone was a nice moment. And again, it felt entirely normal.

When we all disembarked at Luton, we got our bags together and sorted them into the right cars and then said our goodbyes.

But as soon as I turned into my mum and dad's estate in Hawarden, I got a first sense of what the next few weeks might look like. Camped out, pretty much, were members of the press, cameramen from various news stations and pretty much everyone that lived on the estate. Our neighbours clapped me out of the car into the house.

As much as we all like to be recognised and to be famous to some degree, I actually think that the family tendency is to be quite shy. My dad and my brother, Terry, are certainly that way. Confronted by so much interest in me in the weeks after France was quite a culture shock to everyone.

And, inevitably, it became invasive at times.

My dad and I would be out playing golf and then, the next thing we'd hear would be rustling in the bushes – there were photographers everywhere, snapping away from concealed positions behind the green.

Wherever we drove for a while, two or three cars full of paparazzi would follow us. At that point, any enjoyment there might have been in being appreciated just melted away. It became a stressful game of cat and mouse with no winner – an emotionally stressful slog.

On a purely practical level, the volume of mail that arrived for my attention was every bit as overwhelming as being followed. At one point we were getting four large mail sacks delivered to the club every day containing all kinds of correspondence: letters, things to sign, photo requests, charity enquiries and, inevitably, some commercial opportunities mixed in.

Initially, it being new to me, I was enthusiastic about reading and replying to them all.

But when I got home from training every night, had something to eat and then emptied my car boot to start wading through what was only a fraction of one sack of mail with my mother's help, I soon started thinking, *where do I even start?*

I was just scratching the surface – and then more sacks would arrive the following day.

Obviously, as the days and weeks passed, the volume tapered off. But even still, faced with a huge backlog, I was forced to call Tony Stephens and ask his advice.

He suggested I employed a designated assistant to look through all the correspondence, sort it into piles according to each one's nature and then process it from there.

In addition, and this didn't feel great at the time, we had a standard photograph of me made with a printed signature on the front. Instead of me having to physically sign thousands of items, we had thousands of these cards printed and sent them out. I'd like to have personalised everything, but it just wasn't possible.

In parallel, Tony had been proactive on my behalf during the summer of 1998. His job as my agent, in addition to the football side of things, was threefold.

One, develop a public persona/image for me as his client. Then, secondly, as an extension of that, use that image to secure the best possible commercial opportunities for me on my behalf.

Finally, and he was good at this too, he was responsible for managing my interview time carefully. As much as I was in high demand, Tony didn't let just anyone talk to me. He protected me, and I appreciated it. And those outlets that he did allow time with me, he ensured paid handsomely for that time. Basically, Tony controlled the headlines.

All in all, Tony did a great job creating the Michael Owen brand – not harmed at all by the fact that he already had experience of mopping up great commercial deals for David Beckham. His contacts were all in place.

In his eyes I was arguably every bit as marketable as David was. Post '98, the press had seemed to enjoy playing David and I off each other as good cop/bad cop types. In a way it helped me because the negative focus was on him and not me. From a commercial perspective, that should have made me attractive.

And so I proved to be.

Within a few weeks of the end of that World Cup, I was one of the public faces of as many blue-chip companies as you could think of: Jaguar, Walker's Crisps, Umbro, Pepsi, Persil, Tissot, Lucozade – and a whole host of others too numerous to list. I was a walking advertisement.

Jaguar's endorsement was particularly appealing to an eighteen-year-old who liked his cars. They gave me two new cars every year for many years thereafter. Amusingly, years previously when it was clear that I was going to make it as a professional footballer, my dad and I had a semi-serious conversation on the golf course one day.

'How can I repay you for all you've done for me?' I asked.

'Oh, just buy me a Mercedes one day,' he replied.

Well, I never did buy him a Mercedes. But I have given him a few free Jaguars over the years on the back of my endorsement. He had two of them at one point – which led us to give him the nickname Terry Two-Jags.

He loved being called that – not least because it poked a bit of fun at himself. There he was, fending off bailiffs, then, lo and behold, he's got not just one car but he's got two Jaguars. We still joke about it now!

Anyway, to secure these relationships, Tony created an image of me that to this day I feel a little conflicted about. Given that the thrust of this image was that I was a whiter than white, angelic family man, I'm grateful that he perpetuated it back then because on one of those counts he was correct: I am, and have always been a family man.

On paper I should be saying, 'Nice one, Tony!' because he made me a fortune. On the other hand, I should have a word with him for lumbering me with an image that's hard to shake off. I never felt that the angelic, whiter than white part was accurate.

Don't get me wrong, I get why he pushed it. Had I been more rugged and edgy, maybe I wouldn't have secured those commercial deals. But I sometimes feel that this image has disadvantaged me in the years since – not least because it gave the impression that I was a little dull. The truth is, I'm not like that at all.

I am, and have always been a practical joker and a wind-up merchant, and a gambler – to the extent that Rio Ferdinand has said to me more than once over the years: 'I have no idea how you have got away with this image of yours for so bloody long.'

The problem is, once you have an image in the public's eyes, it's very hard to change it.

Regardless of what my image said about me in 1998, the truth is, as much as the adulation was a novelty for a few days or a few weeks, the idea of being a celebrity was not something I was ever particularly comfortable with. I'm still not.

While I understood the need and the obligation to be visible in the context of my commercial deals, I was never comfortable putting myself out there in the world. I did it – but only because I had to.

Fortunately, Louise was of similar mind. Despite the fact

that she had known me when I was a relative nobody with very little money, Louise had no option but to be thrust into the same crazy world that was overtaking me.

On one hand it was a nice, easy passage into what became a very comfortable lifestyle.

On the other, it meant that she would invariably have to contend with the same irritations that I would. It took some adjustment, I can tell you. I'm sure she'd agree. Unlike other footballer's wives you could probably name, Louise always preferred to be in the background.

From the beginning, we both grew to dislike that everybody we met only wanted to talk about the World Cup. As much as I understood how my performance had impacted people, I personally had started looking to the future as soon as we'd trudged off the pitch in Saint-Étienne. I was focused on what was next, where the next game was, where the next goals were going to come. But, yet, people still wanted to talk about France.

We also developed a distinct aversion to getting cornered in restaurants whenever we went out for a meal together or with my family. Sitting at a table, with my fork halfway to my mouth, I'd spot someone first clock me from afar – then start to head in my direction as if they knew me personally. As soon as you've been on TV and done a few interviews, you're everyone's friend.

At that point you just feel trapped. Given that you're not exactly going to get up and leave every time someone recognises you, all you can do is sit and be polite. It did get tedious though – I can't deny it.

Nowadays, I'm much the same I might add. If you see someone walking down the street in Chester with their forehead so bowed that it's almost touching their shoes, you can guarantee that it's me. I don't enjoy being recognised and never have. Fame, I suppose, isn't for everyone.

■■ ■■■■■ ■

I have no doubt that Gérard Houllier came on board at the beginning of the 1998/99 league season as a direct reaction to the success that Arsene Wenger was bringing to North London. After all, his Arsenal teams that we were playing seemed to be running faster, further and more often. They also seemed never to be getting injured. It's no surprise that they won the league title.

Meanwhile, we were still drinking pints, not conscious of our diets and weren't exactly being too scientific about our training. That is in no way meant as a knock on past managers – that's just how it was in the '90s. It just so happened that Arsene Wenger was a few of years ahead of his time when he brought success to Arsenal in '98.

As good a manager as Roy Evans was in an old-school sense, Gérard Houllier was simply the bridge into a new era at Liverpool. Regardless, on reflection, the appointment of Gérard as a joint manager initially was quite an unusual arrangement. There was, I believe, a specific reason: Roy had done nothing to deserve the sack. If anything he'd been the fabric of the club and had done well to get us into third place.

I just think that the club was in a corner. The opportunity to sign Gérard Houllier was too good to miss – so they decided to retain them both. What's obvious to everyone in a situation like that is that, when something later goes wrong, there's only one person that's going to leave. That's exactly what transpired later that season.

Initially, however, Roy and Gérard's very different attributes worked in our favour.

Roy, obviously, was a football man with an excellent football brain. He understood the game inside out and his preferred domain was the training ground.

Gérard, having never kicked a ball at all at any sort of level, could have managed any group of men in any discipline. He was so intuitive in an organisational sense. But that wasn't all he could do.

As much as he hadn't played the game, he nevertheless knew enough and had sufficient confidence in what he had learned to put on training sessions and talk tactics at a more than respectable level. At no point did I think, *this guy doesn't know what he's doing ...*

Incidentally, the playing credentials of a football manager are an interesting concept for players. Rightly or wrongly, if a manager walks into a dressing having won a European Cup as a player, he commands instant respect.

When Zinedine Zidane walked into a dressing room for the first time, I doubt anyone questioned him. Even if he couldn't coach to save his life, he'd be off to a head start.

None of this is to say that a manager who has no or limited playing credentials gets zero respect, it just means that they usually have to work extra hard to earn it by having other very obvious qualities.

Despite being a former schoolteacher, Gérard Houllier also had the kind of qualities that players could recognise. Despite his calm, media-friendly front, Gérard was a surprisingly tough taskmaster, particularly during those early days. He knew very well the nature of the out-dated culture he was walking into and it was clear from the start that he wasn't in any way concerned about what people thought of his disciplined methods.

With him came his implacable assistant Patrice Bergues – a guy he'd worked with since back in his days at Lens in the 1980s I believe. They'd been coaching partners ever since, all the way to the French national team.

If Gérard was tough and uncompromising at the beginning, Patrice was even more so. He thought nothing of telling supposed superstars to do endless laps of the track and he orchestrated fitness sessions without the faintest flicker of a smile. I'm sure Patrice was human, but he never gave you much indication of it.

Predictably, as with any new regime, there was resistance at first. It's natural that everyone should get entrenched in their established ways and, equally, that they should resist new ones. I've seen that happen with almost every manager transition throughout my career.

Some of the lads grumbled about Patrice's tough sessions, others whined about the new diets or the pettier rules like not being allowed to chat while we stretched at warm-ups. But as time passes and the old ways are forgotten, everybody usually just gets on with it – particularly if the fruits of all this labour are borne out in actual results.

And they were.

When I think back, my primary thought at the beginning of the 1998/99 season was, *let's show everyone that I'm more than that goal in Saint-Étienne.*

I was so conscious of how my life had been publicly transformed and I suppose was desperate to show how little that change had affected me. In no way did I want to be seen as a one-hit wonder who burned out as fast as he had ignited.

Beyond that, I wanted to cement my position as a *Liverpool* fan favourite. Robbie Fowler had done it by scoring goals. It seemed as if the fans worshipped him no matter what he did. Although my fame had come on the back of an England performance, I saw no reason why I couldn't do the same.

As such, I could hardly have started that season better than I did. Despite scoring only once in pre-season, in the Carlsberg Trophy final against Leeds United, I began the league campaign with serious intent.

With Robbie still side-lined with a cruciate ligament injury, Karl-Heinz Riedle and I started up front for our opening game away at The Dell against Southampton. In a 2-1 win, he and I scored in either half.

Following a 0-0 draw with defending champions Arsenal at Anfield, we travelled to Newcastle and I scored a first half hat-trick. Less than a month later I'd eclipse even that when I scored four in a 5-1 pasting of Nottingham Forest at Anfield.

St. James' Park was one of those days where everything went right. Their manager Ruud Gullit had arrived promising fast-flowing, incisive 'sexy' football. Unfortunately for him, it was us who provided it. That was the afternoon that I famously rubbed my hands together with delight after my third goal. People were inquisitive as to why I'd done it. There was a funny back story …

For every away game, as players we were given an allowance of two tickets each. Inevitably, people like Carra, who always seemed to have loads of mates wanting tickets, would ask other lads if they had any spares.

The norm would be, when we were at an away game in the

hotel (Carra and I always shared), we'd get a knock on our hotel room door three or four hours before kick-off and this would be people he'd texted the room number to, who'd been looking for any spare tickets.

On this particular occasion, one such chap called Tom – seemingly one of Carra's dad's friends – appeared in our room. Given that I'd not long come back from the World Cup, let's just say that Tom was more than a bit nervous and excited to meet me.

As we were talking, Tom just stood there and couldn't help rubbing his hands together. Carra I were having a right laugh about it.

'I tell you what,' I said, just as he was leaving, 'if I score today, I'll rub my hands together just for you.'

During the game, when I scored my first goal, I forgot all about it. Then I scored my second. Nothing happened. During the celebration, Carra came over to me.

'I thought you were going to rub your hands together for Tom?' he said.

'Oh my God,' I answered, 'I totally forgot!'

Obviously, I scored the third – and this time I remembered to rub my hands together.

The funny thing was, when he saw me doing it, Paul Ince instinctively started rubbing his hands together also. The problem was – he had no idea what I was doing. Incey wasn't in on the joke! Tom, on the other hand, was a local hero after that!

I'd like to say that I knew how good that day at St. James' Park would be from the first kick of the ball but nothing could be further from the truth.

That was the day that Stuart Pearce tried to intimidate me. I knew Stuart and had never had anything resembling a crossed word with him. Yet, as we lined up at kick-off with my foot on the ball ready to move it backwards, he edged forward and said his piece for the day.

'You better fucking watch yourself today, boy,' he snarled.

I thought: *So that's why you're nicknamed 'Psycho'.*

I actually said ... nothing whatsoever.

As young as I was, I'd already learned that there was nothing whatsoever to be gained by mouthing off at the opposition. In fact, I only ever talked back at one player in my entire playing career. Given some of the abuse I got from defenders over the years, that's no mean feat.

I do recall Everton's centre-half Alan Stubbs saying some derogatory stuff about us in the build-up to a Merseyside derby at Goodison in April 2003. I don't even think it was anything out of the ordinary – just the usual sort of pre-game 'pop' players sometimes take. But for some reason, whatever he said really riled me.

So, when I scored in the game after half an hour I remember grabbing the ball out of the net and running past him shouting something like: 'You won't be spouting any more shite now, will you?' in his ear. Not exactly angelic or whiter than white, eh?

At that moment, it felt satisfying. But I never did it again. Fortunately, we won the game and there was no lasting grudge held on either side. I've met Alan many times since and everyone knows he's a lovely guy.

As much as Gérard Houllier's appointment had brought the beginnings of a new culture to Liverpool, it didn't necessarily translate to instant success on the field.

Seemingly uncomfortable with the shared coaching dynamic,

Roy Evans left the club in a flood of tears in November after successive home defeats against Derby and Spurs.

I, for one, was very sorry to see Roy go. As a young player, I believe that your first manager leaves an imprint on you that no others can. Because you knew nothing else prior, their influence and advice stays with you long after they've gone. Roy Evans gave me my first start for Liverpool. For that reason alone, I'll be eternally grateful to him.

REBØOT_7

THE TRIGGER

I showed up to the BBC Sports Personality Of The Year awards in December of that same year with a nice black eye thanks to a Chris Perry elbow earlier that day at Selhurst Park. Just being nominated was a proud moment. To even be considered among such household names while I sat beside Glenn Hoddle felt so gratifying. To win was surreal. Meanwhile, unknown to everybody, Glenn's days as England boss were already numbered.

As I've mentioned, Glenn had a unique approach to many aspects of coaching. Tactically speaking, there's no doubt in my mind that Glenn was the best England manager I ever played under. With him, you always felt that there was a belief that we could have won a big tournament. It's just a shame that, when we had arguably the best players in the world in 2002-2006, we didn't also have a coach like Glenn Hoddle overseeing us.

It's hard to ignore the fact that with Glenn's shrewd coaching acumen also came an odd kind of eccentricity that wasn't everyone's cup of tea. I always knew that he had the capability to say and think some fairly off-the-wall things. You could tell he was a deep thinker – a seeker of knowledge and enlightenment. To find these things, it was clear that he'd go further than most.

And then there was Eileen Drewery – who Glenn brought in as an unofficial member of the wider support network. The press latched on to her and never let go. To that end, you'd never see her floating around the squad. But whenever you joined up with the group, the option to see her of an evening was offered by the manager.

I should say at this point that I am not what you'd call a spiritual person. If anything, I'm the absolute opposite: I'm a cold, hard realist.

Given the understanding that Eileen Drewery's work was centred on her belief in spirits and angels and so on, when the manager asked if I wanted to see her, she was always going to be up against it. I was sceptical before I even sat down.

Nothing changed when she started discussing which particular spiritual enemy may or may not have been perched on my shoulder at any given moment.

As much as I have complete respect for anyone who believes in such things – including Glenn himself, it just wasn't for me. I sat there feeling a little uncomfortable – and I only agreed to do it because the manager had asked me to.

Glenn was leading edge, but not everyone bought into every aspect of his systems – including the press. I can recall that much of what Glenn was doing was absolutely ridiculed.

It wouldn't be fair of me to suggest that it was Eileen Drewery's direct influence that led Glenn to say what he said. I wasn't even sure at the time what he actually *had* said.

Obviously though, it was spelled out in black and white by the press who, predictably, had an absolute field day with it all.

As always seems to be the case, there was never any comeback on people in the press who took great pleasure in writing nasty things about Glenn's ideas throughout his England tenure – many of which are standard practice nowadays.

For example, if you're not offering a service at a football club today for players to discuss mental health, you're an absolute dinosaur. At the time, however, the press got lots of free laughs out of Glenn's approach to subjects like psychology. But the truth is, he was ten or fifteen years ahead of his time.

For us players, the end of Glenn Hoddle triggered something of a cold war between the press and us. Relations had been cooling for a while as it was. The problem on our end was that it felt like every article we agreed to sit down and do turned into a hatchet job. It felt like you just couldn't say anything without it being misinterpreted. Soon, we didn't trust them and they didn't trust us. We started dreading doing any sort of press.

It got so bad with England that your biggest fear became not who you were playing on the pitch on a given day, but who was going to have face the press beforehand. When it was your turn, going into the pressroom felt like going into the lion's den. It wasn't that I was scared per se on the occasions I was called upon – just so on edge about the possibility of saying something that would get twisted, spun and recycled. If it wasn't your turn on the rota, you'd let out the biggest sigh of relief imaginable.

As we withdrew, the press inevitably started complaining about not getting access. They wanted it both ways. But it was clear to everyone that they needed us more than vice versa. We all understood that hard questions had to be asked at times. Nobody had an issue with that. It was the spun headlines that resulted when every paper seemed to want do outdo the other that soured things. I think the press really shot themselves in the foot with England for a few years. Thankfully, nowadays, there seems to be a bit more mutual respect.

Regardless of how cutting-edge he was, in February of 1999, Glenn's time with England was up. He left without a word to any of us – he was just gone in a shit-storm of press furore. We were left feeling empty and disappointed.

Some people suggested at the time that Glenn had already lost the dressing room prior to his infamous remarks. I personally didn't feel that was the case – even though the three initial qualifying games for Euro 2000 in the autumn of 1998 had hardly been convincing.

There's no doubt that Glenn had had personality clashes at times with David Beckham. As England's emblematic player of that era, he perhaps wasn't the best enemy to pick.

The press, again, blew that out of all proportion and gave it a good spin. And they did the same with comments Glenn publicly made about me not being a natural goalscorer.

At the time, when I first read what the headline said, even I was a bit puzzled. Then Glenn phoned me. 'The press have misquoted me here,' he said. What he'd seemingly said was that I wasn't *just* a goalscorer (which implied that I was a goal-hanger).

After he explained it to me, I actually took what he said as a compliment. He was merely stating, as he reiterated, that I was capable of doing a lot more than hanging around the box waiting for the ball to arrive. I agreed with him. Saint-Étienne should have been evidence enough of his point.

I really appreciated the call from Glenn. Firstly, it put my mind at rest, as I would have hated to think he didn't regard me as a natural finisher. Secondly, during future dealings with the press, I now had a stock answer to reply with that would kill the subject straightaway

In a nutshell, I really rated Glenn as a tactician. At least he played 3-5-2 when he could – as I always felt that system played to our strengths. On a human level I trusted and respected him too. He was, in my opinion, a proper England manager – not least because he was actually English …

Another Englishman – Kevin Keegan – would eventually step in to the breach to replace Glenn in late February, 1999. The few weeks prior to Keegan's appointment were as bizarre as it gets, however.

I'd be surprised if anyone remembers Howard Wilkinson's two brief spells as England caretaker boss in 1999 and 2000 with much in the way of affection in years to come. No offence to him personally – he was a good football man who was first brought in at less than no notice after Glenn was unceremoniously bundled out of the door.

But honestly, for us players, being under his management at any time felt as if we'd all been loaded into a time machine and transported back to the 1970s.

The training sessions alone were bewildering – and he only presided over two games. In the first, for our very first session prior to a friendly against France, when we were used to being ferried around by air-conditioned coach, he literally walked us down the road to what looked like a piece of waste ground.

'Let's work on a few set-pieces,' he said.

We all stared at each other – and then at him. It was all so amateur.

I thought, *is this guy for real?*

It wasn't that we were entitled arseholes used to luxury at all times – that wasn't it at all. It was more that he didn't seem to know, or care, what level of training and facilities a top group of international players required.

His first friendly, as I mentioned, was in February of 1999 against France at Wembley. I started and was pulled off after sixty-odd minutes in a disappointing 2-0 defeat.

And, with that, he was gone. Howard Wilkinson's first caretaker stint was over as quickly as it had begun. It wasn't what you'd call inspiring either. Nobody knew what he was thinking. I sometimes wonder if he even knew.

In contrast, Kevin Keegan offered something very different – in theory at least. As much as he was the people's choice (and he definitely was), we as players also recognised the kind of relentless energy Keegan could bring to the job.

Whatever the outcome, you knew you'd get everything with Kevin: passion, energy and great quotes in the press – he'd lay it all out there with seemingly no fear.

Who, after all, could forget his passionate Sky Sports rant while trying to haul Newcastle over the line to win the 1995/96 league title? What team wouldn't want a manager who went out on his shield like Keegan always did?

Having said all of the above, he and I didn't always see eye to eye. I'll explain why shortly.

First, to rewind slightly, by the time Keegan came in, if I was the Titanic, there was an iceberg on the radar that I hadn't noticed.

It would be no exaggeration at all to say that the 1998/99 season at Liverpool changed the trajectory of my career. In an innocuous 0-0 draw at Elland Road on April 12th, I badly ruptured one of my hamstring muscles. It was bad at the time, but I had no idea that this injury would scar my entire life.

As much as people would see me, years later, doing my knee in a World Cup, your knee is your knee. It can be fixed, and in my case you can come back as good as you were before.

Hamstring injuries, on the other hand, are much more complicated. They have a much more creeping, insidious effect on the human body – certainly mine – in a way that you just don't realise at the time.

To put it plainly, there are three hamstring muscles in each leg, all of which provide a slightly different function within the act of running. I totally snapped one of them in two.

When this happens, the force causes the damaged hamstring to recoil and, in my case, one end ended up down behind the back of my knee, while the other found its way to a place up near my arse cheek.

Nowadays, this situation would be a relatively straightforward surgical fix. The rogue ends could be retrieved and repaired.

I know this because, years later, I did the almost identical injury playing for Manchester United in the 2010 Carling Cup final against Aston Villa. I'd just scored to make it 1-1 and then I did my left hamstring – I had surgery straight afterwards. It was still a bad injury. I was out for four or five months. But as I sit here today, I still have all the muscles in my left hamstring intact.

Back in 1999, however, things were so different. Surgery just wasn't an option – the muscle ends were just left where they were to re-attach to whatever tissue happened to be around.

So, from nineteen years of age onwards, I was running, essentially, on three hamstrings on my left leg and only two on my right. Big deal, people might say, what difference does it make?

Well, while it wouldn't necessary feel different to run, I was nevertheless operating with a third less power in my right leg for the rest of my career. One way or the other, the body has to find a way to adjust to this imbalance. And by doing that the pressure is focused onto another muscle group, which then overworks to compensate and tears, and so on and so forth.

As someone who was so reliant on running very fast, this would become a constant issue over time.

None of this I knew at the time in April 1999. But with retrospect I recognise that, from that day forward, it was a slow, agonising decline. When considering this first hamstring tear, I have often thought, *things could have been so different* ...

Having done my hamstring at Elland Road, I stayed overnight at the hotel because, coincidentally, one of the best hamstring specialists in the UK at the time was based in Leeds. As the team coach left that next morning, an appointment was booked for me. It was his scan that revealed what was already clear: the rupture to the muscle. From there I was sent away to rest.

I don't think it helped that we had just one doctor and one physio at that time at Liverpool. I'm not certain, but both of them might have even been part-time. Nowadays, of course, this would be unheard of. Most big clubs have two or three doctors and five or six physios.

Anyway, with little fanfare, I just went off on holiday to Barbados in early May, 1999 and quite literally sat around doing nothing. I'd been given no instruction to speak of really other than being told: 'Rest because it has to heal.'

Nothing was too scientific in 1999, it seemed.

Before I returned for pre-season, because he was on holiday at the time, I went down to Cornwall to spend the week with Mark Leather, the club physio. He and I did some very basic initial rehab on my leg that involved gentle stretching and deep massage – to prepare me for the next stage of my recovery. The injury was healing well but I was still a few weeks away from exposing my muscle to full load.

In my head, I was just keen to maintain my momentum. While Houllier's first season – a seventh place finish – had all the hallmarks of him feeling his way into the English game, I personally had continued to score goals and ultimately shared the Golden Boot with both Dwight Yorke and Jimmy Floyd Hasselbaink on the back of eighteen league goals and twenty three in total. Had I not got injured at Elland Road, I would have certainly won it outright again.

The start of the 1999/2000 season, the first with Gérard Houllier in sole charge, was when he started putting his unique identity stamp on the team from a transfer perspective.

All kinds of players arrived at the beginning of that campaign; the dressing room had an unfamiliar look when I first walked in. Sami Hyypiä turned up and along with him, as if to become half of a ready-made centre-half partnership, Stéphane Henchoz – who had signed from recently relegated Blackburn Rovers. Erik Meijer also appeared, as did striker Titi Camara.

I remember talking to Gérard a lot about players he could

potentially sign and when the subject of sitting midfielders came up I clearly remember saying: 'What about Didi Hamann?' The boss said nothing more and then, in the blink of any eye, we'd signed him! Looking back, being part of the process perhaps made me feel quite close to Didi, even before I'd met him.

As I did, Didi loved racing, golf and a few pints where appropriate. He did it all with a positive attitude that made him so infectious to be around every day. Better still, he could play a bit too.

I've often thought about his attributes when it came to that sitting midfield role. I think the casual observer sees it as an easy position – one for the less gifted players among us maybe. But the truth is that it requires more discipline than many others on the pitch. And Didi always had that discipline.

He wasn't the quickest or most athletic but he didn't need to be. He kind of shuffled around that midfield area and always resisted the temptation to join in the attacks. He didn't get excited and get caught out of position. He had the willpower to not get drawn in and did his job incredibly well. If you ask Liverpool fans I think the majority would say that he was a really good signing for the club at the time. Even after I left Anfield, Didi Hamann continued to be one of my best friends in and out of the game.

As fresh as this Liverpool dressing room was, I was a mere spectator when the season finally began in early August with a 2-1 win at Sheffield Wednesday.

In the background, Gérard and club physio, Mark Leather, had been in dispute throughout pre-season. The conversation had seemingly gone something like this:

'Michael needs to be joining in with training,' Gérard said.

'He can't', Mark countered, 'he's not ready.'

On paper, Mark was right. Everybody knew that a hamstring injury was a four or five month affair. At this point, I'd only been off for a little more than a couple of months. Not just that, because I'd done only very light rehab in Cornwall, I was generally very weak.

A major fall-out seemingly ensued. As a result of this impasse with Houllier regarding my recovery, Leather left the club by mutual consent shortly afterwards.

The last thing I want to do is accuse Liverpool of neglect. But in this day and age, people would be horrified by what happened. Modern medical treatment would be to get rid of any scar tissue straightaway, before slowly getting your flexibility back and doing a bit of strengthening. I hadn't done nearly enough to warrant being back in full training.

As much as this could have happened at any club, nowadays I rue the fact that this injury happened during this era. A few years later, and it would have been surgically repaired. I'd have been like new and as fast as I ever was – all the way through my career.

Instead, this hamstring injury was the first of a whole series of others up until my retirement in 2013. Because I was so reliant on busting a gut to be as fast as I possibly could be, this tiny one per-cent of weakness continually showed itself in different forms over time: thighs, groins, more hamstrings, knee …

Again though, at the time, in the absence of a crystal ball, I was just focused on returning to play for Liverpool as soon as I could. And when I did make my return – in a 2-0 win against Arsenal on August 28th, 1999 – I wasn't just undercooked, I was positively raw.

While I didn't feel as if I was a lesser player as such (my youth ensured, I assume, that I was still able to generate enough power to be fast) I must admit to being constantly aware of my fragile hamstrings for much of that season.

Regardless, I could still score. After a confidence-building double at Leicester in mid-September, I'd have to wait until November until my next league strike away to Sunderland at the Stadium of Light. We ultimately finished fourth, booking ourselves a UEFA Cup place.

In the context of the previous two marquee years, I was there, but only just. I ended that season with just twelve league goals and thirteen in all competitions.

By my standards, solely because of injury, the 1999/2000 season had been a disappointing year.

On the England front, I remember feeling devoid of confidence in the immediate build-up to the 2000 European Championships in Belgium and Holland.

As much as I'd lit up the World Cup in '98 and won two Golden Boots in the period thereafter, I still came to the squad for the Euros under Keegan mindful of the hierarchy that was in place. Some might argue that perhaps I'd moved a step or two up the ladder because of those accolades, but personally I still didn't think I'd done enough to join the card school, for example.

In the qualifiers, we'd been far from convincing. Then Glenn went halfway through the campaign in early 1999, which didn't help much either. Kevin Keegan's first game in charge was a win against Poland at Wembley.

Subsequent games against Sweden and Luxembourg culminated in a do or die rematch with Poland in Warsaw with second place in the group at stake. We drew 0-0. A complex series of mathematical permutations thereafter brought us to a home and away play-off against Scotland in November of 1999. Over the two legs, we prevailed, but we were far from persuasive. It's fair to say that we staggered into the final stages and no more.

From a playing perspective, I thought I'd earned my stripes. Although I'd had a disrupted season from an injury perspective, I still thought I should be in the starting line-up particularly after I scored in a friendly against Brazil at Wembley at the end of May.

The problem was, on the immediate run-in to the tournament proper in June of 2000, I got the impression that Kevin Keegan wanted to make me into the kind of player that I just wasn't designed to be.

From a striking perspective, Alan Shearer was Keegan's kingpin still – which was fine. But I felt that, given everything I'd achieved, I was every bit his equal.

For reasons I never understood, Keegan wanted me to be less of a threat in behind. Instead, he wanted me to come short, hold the ball up and bring other people into play. As much as I'd practised these skills over the years at various times, I didn't think this type of role played to my strengths. From a purely physical perspective, I wasn't built for it.

Although I could always come off and show, I was never the kind of striker who would pin a defender. I relied on being better at angles and turning. Unlike a Shearer-type who'd be forever feeling, grabbing and pinning opponents to gain ground, if a defender got too close to me I'd turn them – then they wouldn't get too close next time. I could do all of this, but really it wasn't my game.

Consequently, Keegan's requirements just confused the hell out of me. In addition to asking me to do things that didn't come naturally, I didn't enjoy his training sessions either because of that.

With hindsight, I felt like I was being picked on all the time – not just by him, but also by his coach, Derek Fazackerley. Had it just been me, that would have been fine – I would just have assumed that there was a clash of personalities. These things happen all the time in football. It wasn't just me though. Steven Gerrard felt exactly the same about Keegan and Fazackerley.

I'm sure even Steven himself would have admitted at the time that he was a surprise inclusion in Keegan's Euro 2000 plans. As much as Steven had barely kicked a ball for England, they certainly knew he was a great player. He had been due to start a game in the tournament – I can't recall which one – but got injured in the days immediately prior to the game.

Steven was really upset. I went to his room to console him and he said more or less the same thing as I felt. 'I can't even sprint without feeling I'm going to pull something – my groin, my hamstring, my thigh,' he told me, visibly upset.

Given that Steven used to be smaller than me growing up, it was pretty clear that he'd gone through a very rapid growth spurt – with the result being that his muscles just couldn't keep up. If he *thought* about jogging, he'd pull a muscle.

There was no sympathy offered whatsoever – no arm around the shoulder and no 'don't worry – you'll be fit in a couple of weeks. We'll get to the quarters ...'

At the time, all of this led me to believe that Keegan – this man that everyone said was such a great manager and so good at motivating players – was doing exactly the opposite. I felt awful about the Keegan situation on the pitch.

Off it, the atmosphere was much lighter than it had been under Glenn Hoddle.

Instead of being devoid of all stimulation, at our base in Spa, Belgium, Keegan had arranged for loads of entertainment: pool tables, pinball machines and so on. Also, there was a cinema room in the basement that we used for watching games and even horse racing. It was a place where we could all meet and enjoy each other's company. Euro 2000 was the polar opposite of France '98.

This tournament was when the press first latched on to our gambling habits in a big way. Journalists would see us turning up to games in the bus and there'd be a group of three or four in the back row playing cards. They didn't like that.

I was never totally sure what their beef was. Some suggested that they felt we were publicly flaunting the money we made and that somehow, large losses might affect our performance on the pitch.

Possibly they thought we should have been focusing more on football than playing poker. Whatever their reasons, we were given a really hard time about it in the papers.

The other tradition, which we continued at Euro 2000, was that we'd run a book. Then, for every game, we'd all get together and watch with a bit of our cash at stake. In '98, Shearer and Sheringham had been the bookies; in 2000 it was Shearer and me. Guys would come down in the morning with their fifty quid or whatever in hand and say, 'I'll have twenty quid on Thierry Henry to score,' or whatever they fancied.

I was in awe of all this in '98. I loved the fact that we could create our own bookies – they were taking two or three grand every game. And then, when I became one of the bookies myself in 2000, I loved it even more.

I remember one game in particular involving a Scandinavian side where all the lads clubbed together in an attempt to take us down. A win for this team would cost us bookies a right few grand.

We locked ourselves in our own room while the game played out while the lads were all together in another room. When the wrong result did come in for us bookies, we had twenty-odd guys banging on the door and laughing – demanding a pay-out. It was all a great laugh.

When the press got wind of this book, they were horrified about that too. They had no idea about the boredom of being away from home in a camp. They had no clue about how much it bonded us when we all sat in a room to watch a game knowing there was a few quid riding on it. All they saw were the negatives.

The reality was, the book (and all the other gambling) was just a bit of fun to add variety to the time away from family and friends. Losses at anything were forgotten as soon as they happened. Me, having been a gambler since my teens, never bothered my arse about losing a few quid anyway.

And what the press failed to grasp was that, in relative terms, the sums we were losing were less than if the average guy in the street lost twenty quid out of his two hundred and fifty quid per week pay packet.

My own brother is case in point. Nowadays, when he has a bet, he'll have fifty quid on a horse without even blinking. He only earns around three hundred quid a week!

None of this is meant to rub the extent of our wages in anyone's face. It's just a fact of life that, whatever losses were incurred, nobody's performance at Euro 2000 suffered as a result. As is often the case, these things were only magnified by the fact that we'd eventually come home early. Had we gone further, I doubt the gambling would even have been mentioned.

Anyway, right up until the first game against Portugal in Eindhoven, I don't think Keegan had a clue as to whether he should start me. As it turned out, he did. But when we came in at half time, tied at two each, he made a beeline for me.

'What were you doing out there?' he began, 'I told you to come deeper and link.'

In an attacking sense, last time I checked, that first half had been fine. We had been 2-0 up after twenty minutes. Yet, he had a right go at me in front of the rest of the lads. Then he subbed me in the break and put Emile Heskey on in my place. As I was sitting there getting changed into my tracksuit, I was thinking, *what is going on here?*

It felt like this massive fall from grace. And then, to add insult to injury, Nuno Gomes completed Portugal's comeback with a winning goal midway through the second half.

The most bizarre moment was still to come. Keegan came rushing up to me after the game.

'Don't worry,' he began, 'you're going to start the next game.'

He then explained that he just wanted me to do *this* more and *that* more – hold the ball up more. I was getting so many mixed messages, and I wasn't buying any of them. After all, I knew very well that if Emile Heskey had gone on and scored, I would have been relegated to the bench. Nothing of what Keegan said added up.

During the following week in training, he continued to single me out by taking me to the side. Then he'd ping balls into me and have me control them and hold play up. I felt these were things I would have been doing when I was much younger and inexperienced. These were not the qualities that had won me two Golden Boots.

In the next game against Germany in Charleroi, he pulled me off after about an hour and stuck on Steven Gerrard in my place in a dour affair that we won 1-0. Again, I was bewildered by Keegan's approach. My head was in turmoil. I was mentally out of tune.

Against Romania, also in Charleroi, I scored on the stroke of half time to put us 2-1 up. When the ball hit the net, I looked over at the bench. Keegan's and my eyes met. Every single part of me wanted to cup my ear as if to say: 'Stick that up your arse.' I didn't do it. Later, I kicked myself because I hadn't.

Despite having scored against Romania, true to form, Keegan subbed me after sixty-odd minutes. It felt like for that whole tournament I was forever looking at the bench to see if a sub was warming up to replace me. And there always was.

Anyway, it all became immaterial in the end. Phil Neville conceded that penalty, Romania scored and we were off home early. Euro 2000 was all so unsatisfactory.

It was just a sad era for me with England.

REBØOT_8

THE PINNACLE

A few people in the game, Sir Alex Ferguson included, have gone on record as saying that they felt I was overplayed in my first few years at Liverpool. The inference being that, because I'd played so many games when I was young, that's why I got injured. Sir Alex even went on to say that – had I been a Manchester United player at that time – he wouldn't have used me like Liverpool did.

However, if you examine the facts a bit more closely, during those seasons in question, Sir Alex had young players who played almost as many games as I did.

But, and here's the difference: his young players were not made available for every single international game, whereas there I'd be, off representing England Under-20s at tournaments like the World Cup in Malaysia and so on. Because of this, he feels that he protected his players better.

What do I feel?

Well, given that I was there throughout, I think it's impossible to say that, had I played less, I would therefore have got injured less. It's just not that simple.

My injuries were always muscle-related. Even my freak broken foot and my major knee injury, which I'll discuss later, were muscle-related. The reason for this is quite simply genetic. I am injury prone from a muscle perspective. It's just the way I was made.

My dad was a professional athlete for fifteen years and pulled muscles. And my brothers are exactly the same. Because we were all so fast, we were also serial muscle-pullers. It's in the family.

My brother Terry is forty nine. Even now he could turn up at circuit training with a bunch of twenty-year-olds and whip their arses at sprinting. We are just naturally very rapid – all of us. But he's pulled muscles all his life.

Saying all that, there's no question in my mind that, regardless of how old I was – eighteen, twenty or twenty five – it wouldn't have mattered.

Equally, whether I'd played five games or five hundred, this susceptibility to pulling muscles would have been exactly the same. And throughout my career, with a couple of anomalies mixed in, that's what I did: I pulled muscles.

Looking back now, perhaps Sir Alex had a fair point in the respect that Liverpool might have been more strategic with me between 1997 and 2000.

But the truth is, we just didn't have the luxury of being able to play Teddy Sheringham one week, Andy Cole the next, then Ole Gunnar Solskjær the week after that, then Dwight Yorke. We had Michael Owen and Robbie Fowler, essentially – and both of us got injured at some point.

What were we supposed to do?

I know what Sir Alex meant, but I don't think it's anything like as cut and dried as he put it.

Always seeing the positive in everything, the way I see it is that, if I had been protected when I was eighteen or nineteen, maybe I wouldn't have won two Golden Boots.

Extending that thinking further, had I been at Manchester United, I might have only played five games in a season and might not have even gone to the 1998 World Cup at all. I conceivably wouldn't have been in the position to score anywhere close to the number of goals I needed to grab Glenn Hoddle's attention and force my way into his squad.

Given that theoretical scenario, I'm sure people like Sir Alex Ferguson would say, 'Yeah, but you would have been brilliant at the next World Cup.'

My view is that I don't care whether I was very good at eighteen years of age or thirty. It just happened that I was ready to be the best I could possibly be at a young age. I'd never want to change anything.

When you look at the early part my career – the goals, the Golden Boots and, ultimately, the Ballon d'Or, how can you say that was the wrong way of doing things? There's no wrong way of winning a Ballon d'Or. I'd reached the peak of my career. It just happened to be between the ages of eighteen and twenty two.

You can, of course nit-pick and say, 'Yeah but you might have been better for longer …' But the way I saw it, I might never have been there at all. My shit filter always made me think, *accept what you have, forget what you might have.*

■■ ■■■■ ■

I returned to pre-season in the 2000/2001 league season, physically reasonably fit, but still mentally scarred by the happenings of Euro 2000 under Kevin Keegan.

Meanwhile, Houllier had signed a new five-year contract and, again, he had freshened the squad by bringing in guys like Gary McAllister, Nick Barmby and Markus Babbel. The squad was growing, toughening – and it needed to given the volume of games on the horizon.

In addition to thirty eight league fixtures, we'd be in three cup competitions in 2000/2001. When we kicked off on August 19th with a 1-0 home win against Bradford City, nobody would have guessed that we'd go on to win all three of them.

Again, I got off to an absolute flier with a brace in a 3-3 draw away at Southampton. A week later, in a home game against Aston Villa on September 6th, I went one better with a hat-trick that might have been a little reactionary.

Three days prior, we'd been back with England in an international friendly against France in Paris. It was a bad case of déjà vu for me, only slightly worse. Instead of starting me then later hooking me as he'd done throughout Euro 2000, in Paris, Keegan didn't even bother going that far. He started with Andy Cole up front and put me on the bench. I was unimpressed.

Then, when he eventually did bring me on for Paul Scholes after eighty minutes and I scored, I stared at him in the dugout for a few seconds longer than I had in Charleroi. I'm sure I got my point across!

Whether I did or not, Keegan was gone a month later after that infamously dull 1-0 defeat to Germany – the final game at the old Wembley stadium where my mate Didi Hamann's skidding free-kick got England's qualifying group for the World Cup in 2002 off to a depressing start. I wasn't in the squad that night, Keegan's final game in charge. Suffice to say given our history together with England, I wasn't exactly sorry to see him go.

Four days later, again at very short notice, Howard Wilkinson stepped in once more for an away World Cup qualifying tie in Helsinki against Finland.

Credit to him for doing so, but his antics in Finland were no less bizarre. As if his training methods weren't bad enough, some of his comments when picking the team would have been comedy gold had they not been so surprising from an undeniably experienced coach.

'I could toss a coin …' he said – when talking to David Seaman and Nigel Martyn about who he was going to go with that night, was one.

'I don't think you know your best position …' was another Wilkinson gem directed at Emile Heskey – before playing him out of position anyway.

All in all, Finland was a strange mess – not least because he left me on the bench all night in a deadlocked game that was screaming out for fresh legs. I sat there stewing. But alas, no call came from the dugout. The game finished 0-0 – and off Howard Wilkinson went again to be replaced by Sven-Göran Eriksson in January of 2001. It was always bizarre stuff with Howard.

By December of 2000, Liverpool's season was taking serious shape. We were fifth in the league – five points adrift of leaders

Manchester United. Having beaten Fulham courtesy of three extra time goals (one of them mine) we'd booked ourselves a place in the two-legged semi-final of the Worthington Cup, scheduled for mid-January against Crystal Palace.

Europe was equally successful. An away goal in Bucharest settled a dour two-legged affair with Romanian outfit Rapid Bucharest in the first round. In the second round, at the end of October, we beat Czech side Slovan Liberec 1-0 at Anfield. I was absent that night, for all the wrong reasons. Ten days prior, we were playing Derby at Pride Park. It was a game that we'd eventually win 4-0 with a hat-trick from Emile Heskey.

During the build-up to his first goal, I made a near-post run and somehow tripped over. I lay there on the ground for a second before rising to my knees. Meanwhile, behind me, Derby defender Chris Riggott was sprinting up from behind me. As I got up, unable to stop, he tried to hurdle me. He didn't quite make it. His knee slammed into the back of my head instead.

It went dark – and from this point I'm only relating what I've been told since because I have no recollection whatsoever.

Apparently, after being stretchered off, I then began arguing with the doctor and the physio, claiming that I was fit and able to go back out. Meanwhile, the doctor was putting thirteen stitches in a nasty gash in the back of my head.

As it transpired, the cut was the least of my worries. The impact had rattled my brain enough for me to lose all grasp of reality. Having wanted to go back out, I seemingly then decided otherwise and then collapsed again in the dressing room, after which an ambulance was called to take me to hospital.

The next thing I actually *do* remember is waking up in hospital in a state of complete panic. Somewhere, deep in my subconscious mind, I was aware of voices. It felt like a dream, but I instinctively knew that it wasn't.

'I think we might have lost him,' the voices said, 'he might be dead.' There's nothing like hearing that you might be dying to spur you into action, let me tell you.

'I'm awake! I'm awake!' I shouted across the room to where I thought the voices had come from. Someone came over to my bedside and they checked me over to make sure there was no lasting damage, bleeds and so on.

It's hard to say how long this whole episode lasted – but I was allowed to go back on the team coach. All I remember about that journey is that I sat there and just cried my eyes out all the way back to Liverpool in front of all the lads.

It wasn't that I was upset – I was later told that the impact of the knee had disturbed the area of my brain that controls emotions. Basically, I had no control for a while; I was bawling, telling all the lads that I could have been dead.

Looking back now, it's all a bit embarrassing. But it was a nasty injury that potentially could have been even worse. Not just that, as it turned out, there was a sad ending to the story. Beside me in the A&E area, behind a curtain, had been a poor guy who'd been admitted following a motorcycle accident. It was he who I'd heard them saying they'd lost. He'd died beside me behind the curtain.

The head knock kept me out for a few weeks. For a few days I was unsteady on my feet and emotionally raw.

I returned and scored in the second round UEFA Cup second leg against Slovan Liberec in the Czech Republic. A fortnight later we advanced to the fourth round after a 4-2 aggregate defeat of Olympiacos. Heading into 2001, the season was nicely poised.

Nowadays, unfortunately, competitions like the Europa League (or UEFA Cup as it was back then) and to a lesser extent the FA Cup, are looked down upon – probably because of how big the Premier League and the Champions League have become.

But at the time, these competitions were extremely hard to win – especially the UEFA Cup. Teams were always full strength; everyone took it so seriously – Gérard Houllier included.

From the beginning of that season we'd all got the impression that winning a European trophy was at the top of his wish list. On reflection, he had the right kind of side to do it. We were, quite simply, suited to knockout football. We could score goals, but we could also defend well.

Sami Hyypiä, for example, was one of the most underrated players I've played with. He was the absolute epicentre of that defence; he proved week in, week out that he was world class. In addition to being unbelievable on the ball in a way that everyone could identify with, it was the little things that Sami did that really made him stand out.

Where other defenders clearing the ball might blindly slash, in turn causing the ball to then come off their shin and go out for a corner – that never happened with Sami. Every single thing he did was as pure as you like. The only thing he couldn't do brilliantly was run – he wasn't very fast at all. That said, because he was so intelligent, he never, ever got caught out.

And then, when you added Stéphane Henchoz into the equation, who was brilliant that year, and Jamie Carragher, who played a lot of that year at full-back, then we undoubtedly had a defence that was hard to break down.

As a team, we had all kinds of options at our disposal in

every position on the field. With Emile Heskey and me as the main strikers, we could afford to sit a bit deeper and then hit sides on the counter-attack if circumstances permitted. We'd play Didi Hamann as a sitting midfielder but we'd never really play wide men, as such. Instead we'd put three in a line in front of Didi and then went from there. We had Jamie Redknapp, Vladimir Smicer, Danny Murphy and Steven Gerrard at our disposal – the list went on. All in all, we were extremely hard to beat that year – and we proved it time and time again against top class European opposition.

People always say to me nowadays: 'In which game was your best ever individual performance?' Many would guess that it would be the game where I scored three goals against Germany in 2001. Or the game when I scored that goal against Argentina in 1998.

But I maintain to this day that my best ever performance was at home to Porto in the UEFA Cup fourth round second leg at Anfield on March 15th, 2001.

Scoring two goals in Rome against Roma in the preceding round had been quite an achievement in itself. But, as important as that night in Rome was, *everything* about that game against Porto was perfection for me – and not just from the perspective of the result.

The record books will confirm that I only scored once – a header at the Kop end. To the spectator, it might have seemed like just another contribution to what was a polished 2-0 victory that took us through to a European semi-final tie with Barcelona.

But sometimes you walk off a pitch knowing deep within yourself that every conceivable aspect of your game was A1: your touch, your hold-up play, your passing, your defending

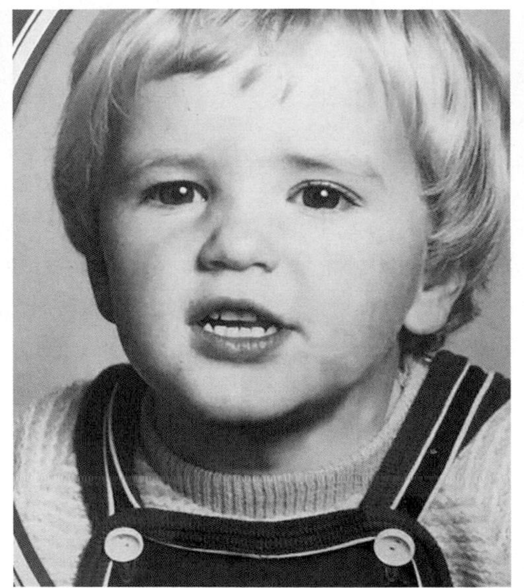

Early days: As a toddler *(left)* and all smiles at Rector Drew Primary School in Hawarden *(right)*

Rising star: Performing the captain's duties before a Mold Alexandra game

Stepping up: From the age of eleven, I trained at Liverpool Football Club's Centre of Excellence

Winners: My goals helped Liverpool to lift the 1995/96 FA Youth Cup *(above)* for the first time in the club's history, overcoming a talented West Ham team that included Frank Lampard and Rio Ferdinand

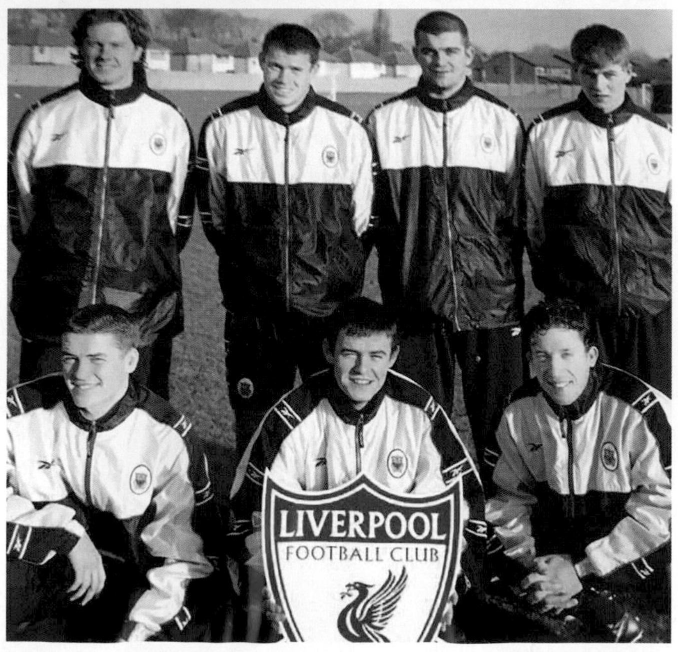

Academy class: *(Top row, from left)* Steve McManaman, Jamie Carragher, Dominic Matteo, Steven Gerrard. *(Front row, from left)*: Me, David Thompson, Robbie Fowler

Strike one: A debut goal as a 17-year-old for Liverpool against Wimbledon at Selhurst Park in May 1997

Public image: Signing an early commercial deal with watchmaker Tissot *(left)* and reading fan mail!

Young Lion: I became the youngest player to represent my country that century when I made my debut for England against Chile in February 1998

Full flow: Netting against Bolton in March 1998 on the way to the Premier League Golden Boot

The joy of scoring: My goals in 1997/98 also helped me to win the PFA Young Player of the Year award *(left)*

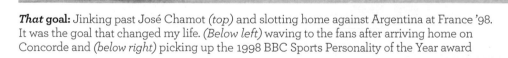

***That* goal:** Jinking past José Chamot *(top)* and slotting home against Argentina at France '98. It was the goal that changed my life. *(Below left)* waving to the fans after arriving home on Concorde and *(below right)* picking up the 1998 BBC Sports Personality of the Year award

New boss: I was unsure about Kevin Keegan as England manager – but all that would change at Newcastle. *(Above)* celebrating a goal in January 1999 with my good mate Jamie Carragher

Kop that: Scoring two goals in a 3-1 win over Manchester United in 2001 felt good

Sweet Rome: I scored twice in a famous UEFA Cup win over Roma in the Stadio Olimpico

It doesn't get better than this: My late equaliser against Arsenal in the 2001 FA Cup final *(left)* was followed up when I beat Tony Adams to the ball *(below)* and slotted the winner past David Seaman. I'm still not sure why I decided to celebrate with a somersault!

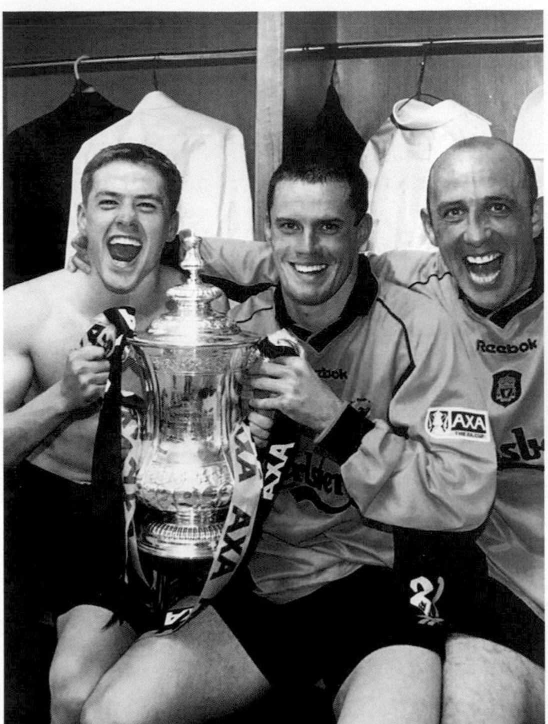

Silver service: *(Top left)* in the dressing room with Jamie Carragher and Gary McAllister after the FA Cup final and *(above)* lifting the Charity Shield and being awarded Man of the Match in the UEFA Super Cup – 2001 was a year I'll never forget

Treble time: Lifting the UEFA Cup after a dramatic final against Alavés in Dortmund

– everything. Of course, there had been and still would be many other great, headline-grabbing moments in my career. But as an entire piece, Porto remains the best game I ever played.

The away leg of the semi-final in Barcelona on April 5th wasn't quite the same. We got absolutely hammered in terms of possession but we hung in there. I literally touched the ball on two occasions at most.

That kind of resilience was a hallmark of that whole season. If need be, we could just defend to keep that all-important clean sheet. And we did – and then went back home and beat them 1-0 with a penalty from Gary McAllister. The season's climax was still to come.

Meanwhile in parallel, Sven-Göran Eriksson had taken over at England. From the get-go, I liked him – everyone liked him.

In many different ways he was a great manager – even though he never did much in the way of coaching or, in fact, talking. Instead, he relied quite heavily on his assistant, Steve McClaren. As much as he knew the game and picked the right squads, tactically he left most of the details to Steve.

There's no denying that this was a difficult period in which to be an England player.

As I mentioned, the press felt like our enemies – to the extent that people didn't even like turning up to play for their country. It was a horrible environment – you just couldn't wait to get to game day. I know more than a few guys who retired early from international football because this whole era was just so miserable.

Nevertheless, as hard a time as it was, with hindsight I think Sven reintroduced a bit of happiness to things. He was smart enough to know that happy players off the pitch probably meant better performances on it. To that end, he was quite relaxed.

At squad get-togethers he let us play golf up until two days before the game. If we wanted to get in a taxi to go to Windsor to do a bit of shopping, he was fine with that, within reason. If he needed to be tough, he could be. He would never have let us walk all over him. I think he got the balance exactly right and I think most of the other guys felt the same.

Fortunately, he had an immediate impact on our performances on the pitch.

While I never felt that he played quite the right formation, you can't deny that he got results – particularly in those early days. His first competitive game in charge was a 2-1 win against Finland at Anfield in March – where David Beckham and I scored a goal each in the first half.

Four days later we went to Albania and won 3-1. I scored there also. The group was set up perfectly for the crunch games that loomed against Greece and Germany later that year.

■■ ■■■■■ ■

Meanwhile back at Liverpool, having picked up our first trophy of the season courtesy of a penalty shoot-out defeat of Birmingham City in the Worthington Cup final at the Millennium Stadium in Cardiff, we were reaching the business end of season 2000/2001.

It would be remiss of me not to mention that it has always irked me that I was left out that day in Cardiff.

Because of the way we played: counter-attacking with two

strikers, one of them a target-man, Emile Heskey had made himself more or less Houllier's first-choice striker. That left the other starting place available to whoever was playing best out of Robbie Fowler and me.

When Emile first turned up at the club, I used to look at him and think, *you're absolutely unplayable …*

On a personal level, I'd met him a few years previously while playing for England in the Under-18 European Championships. I had just hit an Italian player during a game – as was my style when I was younger – and I just remember all the Italians swarming around me at the final whistle while Emile stood by my side and fended them all off. Straightaway I thought, *you'll do for me!*

Despite this willingness in the heat of the battle, Emile was a lovely, gentle giant of a guy. And, as I mentioned, he was a terrific player: big, strong, good touch – he was the perfect type of player for us at that time because he offered something completely different.

Unlike some strikers, Em was very unselfish. Although he could obviously score goals, he was happy to hold the ball up and look for chances to put me in. Not just that, when defending corners he'd win pretty much every header.

While I played with many better strikers with arguably bigger reputations across my career: Shearer, Raúl and Fowler etc. I'd have to say that my favourite partnership was with Emile Heskey – with both Liverpool and England. Throughout those years, he never did anything to compromise my way of playing. He only enhanced it. He was the perfect foil for both Robbie Fowler and me when he arrived from Leicester.

Despite the healthy competition, on many occasions in that season, I got the nod. At Cardiff, it was Robbie that got the shout. I was never totally sure why – although a double he'd scored at home to West Ham a few days prior had probably helped his case.

As much as I always wanted to play – especially in cup finals – I don't begrudge Robbie's selection that day at all – and he repaid the boss's confidence with a brilliant first half goal.

However, as the game dragged on in deadlock after a Birmingham City equaliser, I was sitting there thinking, *surely this situation is made for me?*

I have always considered myself to be a big game player. Throughout my career, the bigger the game, the better I did. There are many examples of when I showed up when it mattered most. And in many of those situations I knew that I'd have an impact long before it even happened.

This game, in my eyes, was another opportunity. *Just bring me on*, I thought, as extra-time wore on, *I'll settle this.*

But no call came – and we went on to win the penalty shoot-out. Afterwards, I don't mind admitting that I was embarrassed to even be part of the celebrations having not actually contributed on the pitch. However, I wouldn't have to wait too long for my next opportunity to impact a big game.

I don't think anyone would look at our list of opponents in the early rounds of the 2000/2001 FA Cup and think that it was the toughest of passages. Shortly after winning in Rome, we came back and comfortably dispatched Manchester City 4-2 at Anfield.

Unbelievably, given their status today as one of the world's wealthiest clubs with a trophy cabinet to back it up, City would ultimately be relegated that season. Manager Joe Royle left the club after they went down and they brought in – guess who? – Kevin Keegan to help them rebuild.

Wins against Tranmere, where I scored, in a 4-2 victory and, Wycombe where I didn't, in a semi-final at Villa Park that we made much tougher than it needed to be, all led us to a final appointment with Arsenal at the Millennium Stadium in Cardiff on May 12th.

Every professional footballer hopes to have a brilliant day in their career – a game where they can look back, later in life, and say *I reached the pinnacle.*

In my case, and over the course of my career, I was lucky enough to have two or three such days – and the final against Arsenal on that roasting hot day was certainly one of them.

On paper, we were massive underdogs. Arsenal had class and experience all over the pitch. Wherever you looked, you saw players that could either score, or stop you scoring: Tony Adams, Patrick Vieira, Robert Pires, Thierry Henry, Ashley Cole – the list went on and on.

As good as we had been that season, and we had been, Arsenal seemed to have just that little bit more in the locker.

Curiously, *my* locker had a part to play in that cup final.

In the weeks leading up to the game, I'd worn my standard Umbro boots. I'd been scoring goals. Before that final in Cardiff, Simon Marsh brought me a pair of a new, special edition boots they'd created for me. In his eyes, the FA Cup final was the ideal opportunity to showcase them, given that millions of TV eyes would have been on one of the game's most recognisable players. To Umbro it was a perfect marketing opportunity – and I, as usual, was happy to accommodate Simon's wishes.

In training during the week before Cardiff, both the assistant manager Phil Thompson and Gérard Houllier noticed me training in the new boots. Gérard called me over.

'What are you doing?' he asked.

'What do you mean, boss? These are my boots for the weekend,' I replied.

'You're not wearing them,' he said.

'I haven't got a choice. Umbro have asked me to,' I told him.

'You *have* to wear the boots you've been playing well in,' he said – clearly getting irritated.

He was adamant. I had just scored two at home against Chelsea. I was in a rich vein of form.

I called Umbro.

'My gaffer doesn't want me to wear the new boots. What can I do?'

To be fair to Umbro, they were very reasonable about it. They actually turned it into a positive and it became a bit of a headline as a result – *The Gaffer made me wear my old boots!*

I put the new boots in the locker and committed to the old and proven ones as I'd been instructed.

For seventy minutes, in one of the hottest and most oppressive days I can remember ever playing football in, Arsenal absolutely battered us at Cardiff. It was a rear-guard action epitomised by our captain Sami Hyypiä.

As he had been many times over the years, Sami was immense that day as Arsenal pressed. He won key balls in the air, put in last-ditch goal-saving tackles and cleared shots off the line. For seventy two minutes, we held firm. And then, as it looked like we'd take the game into extra time, Freddie Ljungberg broke the deadlock.

You would have thought, having survived so long in the heat and then conceded with less than twenty minutes left, that we would have wilted. Well, let me tell you: the opposite was the case that day. Like a boxer that'd been swinging hard for a knockout punch, even after they scored, I could sense that

Arsenal had less left in the tank than we did. They seemed to be punched-out.

In the 83rd minute, the ball dropped to me in the box after Markus Babbel diverted a Gary McAllister free-kick into my path.

As if I'd envisaged it in advance, the moment arrived.

I hooked the ball into the bottom corner and the Millennium Stadium erupted. Five minutes later, things got even better.

I thought: *We'll win this.*

Then I thought: *I'm scoring the winner.*

Like the goal against Argentina, my second goal against Arsenal in the FA Cup final is one I need to re-watch to recall the exact details. The feelings – I'll never forget.

We were under pressure on the edge of our own penalty area, as I recall. In the ensuing scramble, the ball broke to Patrik Berger. As he looked downfield, like a quarterback surveying his wide receivers, I was in the centre-circle.

One look at Patrik's eyes and I set off. His ball was absolutely perfect in that it was inside their right-back Lee Dixon, and outside their centre-half Tony Adams. There was a clear channel in front of me to run in. I ran – and I did so as if lions were in pursuit.

As good a player as Lee Dixon was and as much as he was sitting slightly deeper than I was, I beat him to the ball, held him off and hurtled towards the penalty area.

I should say at this point that, in general, Tony Adams was the kind of traditional centre-half that I always preferred to play against. As strong and wily as he was, I fancied my chances more against him than a really quick defender like, say, Gary Neville – who was quick enough to stick to you and would never stop grabbing and pulling your shirt.

Gary Neville, as much as he was a right back, fell into the category of defenders that we referred to in the trade as 'a rash'. These types – the Keown, Lúcio and Puyol types never gave you any peace. They were always all over you. I hated that.

Then you get the guys who have everything. Marcel Desailly is as good an example as I can think of. He was so big, so strong, so fast – I'd find myself thinking, *how do you even get past him?*

There was one game at Stamford Bridge that I recall specifically. In general, I didn't like playing at Chelsea. I never had a good scoring record there; we never seemed to get good results there.

That day I remember trying to run past and around Desailly, all day to absolutely no avail. I could do nothing. He was too big, too aggressive and was a rash also when he needed to be – he was everything I hated. Whenever I tried to spin around him, he was too quick. It was a nightmare.

Eventually, as I was running behind him as he was shielding the ball out for a goal kick, I suddenly thought I'd kick him. I'd tried everything else. I thought, *why not? If I can't beat him, I might as well hurt him.*

Prepared to take a yellow just to leave one on him, I volleyed him in the back of the leg. Bang!

As I did it, my shin pad hit the back of his boot and I split my shin down the middle. I needed a few stitches afterwards. It was one of those where you just roll your eyes. Desailly was immense.

Meanwhile, returning to Cardiff, Tony had given me nothing that day; any time I took the ball past him he always seemed to find to find a way to block and obstruct in the most subtly brilliant way.

This time, with me bearing down on goal and running flat out, as he scrambled across to intercept, I had the chance I'd waited all day for.

I thought, *I've got you here …*

For a split second, I considered cutting back inside him to manoeuvre the ball onto my favoured right foot. Instinctively, and there was no time for anything else, I realised that (a) to do so was risking bringing Lee Dixon back into the equation. He'd drifted over towards the penalty spot. And (b) I was running too fast to make the change of direction anyway.

I was left with only one option. Given that I was already pretty wide, and being pushed further and further left by Adams, the only way of scoring was to swing one back across David Seaman with my left foot.

Looking back at the replay now, the target was miniscule – there really was only one place the ball could go without David saving it. And because I'd spent my childhood years rehearsing for this kind of moment, that's exactly where I put it. If you took me to the local park now I'd probably have a one in ten chance of repeating it!

Just like Saint-Étienne, as soon as I touched the ball, I thought, *that's in.*

As tight an angle as it was, the connection on the ball was absolutely perfect. As if in slow motion, I watched it head towards the bottom corner. For a horrible moment I actually thought Seaman was saving it – his wingspan appeared huge; I thought he'd done enough. And then it hit the net.

The feelings in that moment are hard to explain even now. It was one thing scoring in an FA Cup final in Wales – where I'd lived my entire life.

It was another thing entirely scoring the winner. Then,

beyond that, the *circumstances* under which I scored that winner: a finish, under pressure, as the clock clicked down, with absolutely zero margin for error, against Arsenal, against David Seaman, with my left foot …

In that moment, it was all too much. So obviously, I did what I felt was the natural thing and performed a weird hybrid kind of somersault as I ran to the corner flag in front of our fans! I'm not sure why I chose that day to attempt it either. As much as I'd done occasional handsprings in the garden when I was a kid, I hadn't exactly been practising them since with an FA Cup final celebration in mind. As embarrassing as that celebration now is, what a day that was. I'll treasure the 2001 FA Cup final forever.

The funny thing is, having watched the replay many times, if you look closely you'll see that David Seaman actually *did* get there.

He was indeed in a position to push the ball round the post. But the ball, unfortunately for him, flew just above his outstretched left hand, on its way into the corner. It was a good break – but I'll take it all day long!

And it wasn't over.

We had no choice but to quickly switch our attentions to the UEFA Cup final in Dortmund, four days later.

Looking back now through older eyes, there's no doubt that the idea of playing Alavés in the final of a European competition felt like something of an anti-climax on a couple of levels. Firstly, we'd just won an FA Cup final against Arsenal in dramatic circumstances, on a Saturday in the baking heat, in front of 80,000 fans in an incredible state of the art football stadium. *Any* game against *any* opposition would have done well to eclipse that.

Secondly, as decent a side as Alavés were that year (let's not forget that they'd turned over Inter Milan 2-0 in the San Siro on the way to the final) they weren't what anyone would ever call a big, or particularly glamorous opponent. It wasn't that we underestimated them – I'm sure we just thought that, in Roma, Barcelona and Porto, we'd already played three sides that were arguably much better.

Consequently, with little time to think about things too much on account of a very quick turnaround, we went into that final in Dortmund against Alavés assuming we'd win it.

For a while, the result appeared to be a formality.

Markus Babbel scored early. I set up Steven Gerrard for a goal twelve minutes later. Then, after they'd pulled one back, I won a penalty after rounding the goalkeeper and getting pulled down just as I was about to tap the ball into an empty net. Gary McAllister stepped up and converted the penalty. It seemed to be all very plain sailing – to the extent that I vividly remember coming in at half time and looking at guys like Carra, Didi and Danny Murphy as if to say: *'Oh my God, how bad are these? How are they even in the final?'* Like a fool, I thought, *we've won this already*.

It almost came back to bite us in the arse when one of the great European comebacks ensued in Dortmund. That second half was just wild: goals, red cards, a Golden Goal and own goal. In the end, we won it.

As fraught as it all might have appeared to television viewers at the time, I honestly don't think *any* of us ever truly believed that we would lose that final. Nevertheless, we still needed a bit of good fortune to get us over the line. And we got it after one hundred and seventeen minutes courtesy of Delfi Geli's 'golden' own goal from a free-kick.

Winning a European trophy was undeniably a great night – particularly for the boss and possibly for some of the foreign lads also. But as an Englishman who'd grown up watching the FA Cup, there's no doubt that Cardiff still had the edge, and not just because I scored twice.

Almost lost amid the excitement of our successful dual cup run was the significance of the next and final league game of the season away at Charlton. To qualify for a Champions League place ahead of Leeds United, we had to win it.

Speaking personally now, I always felt that the things I would look back on when I eventually retired would be the great games, the goals and, more than anything, the trophies. That's just how I am. I prefer tangible things, cups you can hold in your hands as opposed to just the act of taking part in a competition at an elevated level.

Having said that, all of us knew that a win away at Charlton would both cap a wonderful season and take us to the next level, albeit via a qualifying round of European competition the following year. From that perspective, with only a couple of days to prepare, we took the game extremely seriously.

Whether it was fatigue, complacency or whatever it was, the 4-0 win we eventually dug out at The Valley, with a significant financial windfall on the line for the club, was not pretty. For forty-five minutes, they deluged us. They could have easily scored four. Despite our recent successes, Gérard bollocked us in the dressing room at half time.

I should say at this point that, as a player, I never particularly needed motivating by anyone to go out and do my best. I didn't need anyone to come up to me at any point in my life, let alone in a dressing room, and say 'Come on, lads. We need to win this today!'

For me, money wasn't a motivation. Words were never a motivation. My personal pride in myself, my family, the people watching and the badge I was wearing – these were the things that motivated me far more than any speeches managers might have given over the years.

In the second half, we found our rhythm again courtesy of a couple of goals from Robbie Fowler and one from Danny Murphy. Thereafter, we coasted home with a late goal from me adding to the flattering scoreline.

Because the UEFA Cup final was so soon after our Cup win at Cardiff, it wasn't really until after we'd secured a Champions League place at Charlton that we could celebrate in style.

The bus tour of Liverpool – where it was estimated that a million people came out to see us – was incredible. As young as I was at the time, it helped me to acknowledge how much what we do on the pitch means to those fans who pay good money to come and watch us.

As far as wild partying was concerned, the fact that Gérard Houllier had steered the dressing room away from the drinking culture that had preceded him, meant that it was all reasonably subdued. I personally wasn't particularly interested in the idea of drinking to excess anyway.

At that point in my career, as much as I liked a pint here and there, I was still of the opinion that I needed to keep my body as pure as I possibly could to be the best footballer I could be. I even used to berate my dad and brothers on holiday when they drank beer – 'It's unhealthy. You'll get dehydrated,' I'd tell them.

Nowadays my wife laughs when I'm on holiday because I'm the one that's usually queuing up at the bar at midday to get a drink!

Anyway, when all was said and done, 2000/2001 had been a truly memorable season.

On a personal note, I finished the season as our top goalscorer ahead of Emile Heskey with twenty four goals in total – sixteen of those in the Premier League. Best of all, I'd done it all while remaining largely injury-free.

REBØOT_9

MOMENTUM

In August of 2001, we picked up where we'd left off in May with a win against Manchester United in the Charity Shield at the Millennium Stadium in Cardiff. It was great to be back at the scene of such a memorable day so soon afterwards and I marked it by scoring again in a 2-1 win to give us our fourth trophy in that calendar year.

Often forgotten amid our haul of trophies in 2000/2001 is the UEFA Super Cup – which we contested against reigning Champions League winners Bayern Munich in Monaco.

The Super Cup has never had the greatest of reputations among football purists. I've never been sure why not. Although it is contested early in the season, it is still, whichever way you look at it, a contest between the two winners of the preceding season's main European trophies.

Having already picked up four trophies, there was no reason not to bag a fifth and we did just that courtesy of a 3-2 win during which we'd been 3-0 up after John Arne Riise, Emile

Heskey and I had scored. I was also delighted to pick up the Man Of The Match award – a giant slab of metal that now resides, collecting dust, in my cellar at home. It's not something that you'd hang on the wall!

We went there after we'd beaten West Ham at Anfield in the opening league game in which I scored both our goals in a 2-1 victory.

We qualified for the first group stage of the Champions League with a 9-1 aggregate win over Finnish side Haka which included a hat-trick from me in the away leg. The competition proper saw us in a group with Boavista, Dortmund and Dynamo Kyiv. I scored against Boavista at Anfield and thereafter we went unbeaten, topping the group with twelve points at the end of October.

Two weeks prior to the final group game against Dortmund at Anfield, Gérard took ill at half time during a home league game against Leeds.

Having missed the previous two games because of injury, I watched it all unfold from the directors' box. As the lads were in the dressing room at half time, he was being rushed to hospital. He didn't appear after the break in the dugout and I noticed that his wife, Isabel, was no longer in her seat in the stand. Nobody had a sense of how serious his condition was. Phil Thompson assumed temporary charge.

The following week at Melwood, word started filtering through that things were very bad indeed. I got the impression that his chances of survival were fifty-fifty at best. There seemed to be a real possibility that he might die as a result of heart-related issues.

To say that this news cast a shadow over the club would be an understatement. Gérard Houllier, among his many qualities from a footballing standpoint, was a fundamentally good man. When some people ask about you, or your wife, or your kids, you just know they're doing it for the sake of it. When Gérard asked, and he often did, he meant it. Not just that, the next time you talked, he'd remember exactly what you'd told him on the previous occasion.

Whether it was the schoolteacher in him or not, as much as he was there to do the job of overseeing men, there was an uncommonly human side to him that you couldn't help being drawn to. He *cared* about you – and in such a situation you couldn't help but care for him too and hope that he'd pull through and make a full recovery.

I was probably closer to Gérard than most of the lads in the dressing room. He'd often call me out of the blue to talk – to ask how I was feeling, or ask about my mum and dad. It mattered to him that my life away from the club was going well. I really respected that and every side of his character.

As far as we knew, the boss had heart surgery in late October. Thereafter little was heard. As time passed, it seemed like the imminent danger to his life was over. But there would be, it seemed, a long road to recovery.

Meanwhile, Phil Thompson continued as temporary manager. I always got on well with Thommo. There were, after all, few people who loved Liverpool more and he was never afraid to show it – sometimes to the point of out and out fanaticism.

Where Gérard Houllier was calm and measured, Thommo was the polar opposite. To say that he kicked every ball would be putting it mildly. If we won, he'd be over the moon. Equally, if we lost, he'd be devastated. There was nothing in between with Thommo – that's just the way he was.

As much as it would have been easy to let Gérard's situation derail us, that didn't happen at all. If anything, the boss's illness galvanised us. We wanted to win for him – to do him proud. For six weeks after his hospital admission, other than a few vague updates that filtered through from Thommo, there was silence.

■ ■ ■ ■

Having beaten Greece in Athens on June 6th with goals from Scholes and Beckham, Sven's England side approached arguably its first major test: Germany, in Munich, with our qualification status hanging in the balance. D-Day was September 1st, 2001.

Even a win looked like it would only keep us on track for a play-off berth. Neither the home defeat against Germany in Keegan's last game nor that bizarre 0-0 draw in Finland under Howard Wilkinson had done us any favours. In Munich, we needed something badly.

As much I'd been on the winning team with Liverpool in the Super Cup against top German opposition, going to Munich on international duty was a different proposition. Given our rivalry, Germany were hard to beat anywhere – far more on their home patch. They'd *never* lost a World Cup qualifier on home soil.

In the build-up to the game, I seem to recall the German side – particularly their eccentric goalkeeper Oliver Kahn – being uncharacteristically vocal about their chances, or rather our lack of them. None of that kind of posturing usually bothers me much but I can't deny that, on this occasion, I really did fancy giving the Germans a bit of a message in their own backyard.

On paper, we had the team to do it. We had defensive steel and attacking options all over the pitch. At Wembley in the home tie, nothing had gone right for us. Until Didi's winning free-kick settled things, it had been an evenly contested affair. They certainly hadn't dominated us – far from it.

From a striker's perspective, the opposition's formation never bothered me too much. As I've said, the individual attributes of defenders were never a particular concern of mine. I knew I could do most of them for pace anyway.

As it happened, Germany set up with a back three that night. 3-5-2, if you're good at it, is extremely hard to play against. If you get it wrong, or have players who can't fit into it, there are all kinds of gaps available for opponents to exploit.

On the night, having analysed exactly how we thought Germany might play; they scored early courtesy of a goal from Carsten Jancker that we hadn't seen coming from a tactical perspective. Nevertheless, we remained calm – while the crowd at the Olympic Stadium started chanting 'Olé, Olé'.

I remember thinking, *that's premature …*

A few minutes later, we were level – courtesy of my first goal. Looking back, Nick Barmby showed great vision to see me. He was a talented player and very unselfish so it was no surprise that he nodded it into my path. When the ball arrived, Kahn was nowhere to be seen; he'd come out to challenge Nick and was stranded.

Normally, in front of goal, the question is 'What shall I do?'

As the ball bounced, on this occasion it was purely a case of what not to do in order for us to draw level.

As long as I kept the ball down, an empty net awaited. My foot hit the ball two-thirds of the way up ensuring that the ball wasn't going anywhere high. It wasn't the purest of strikes but I had to take the risk out of the finish. It was one of the few times in front of goal where I intentionally caught the ball above the centre.

All square in Munich …

Thereafter, I sensed the confidence drain from that German team. Having weathered their initial storm and not folded under the Olympic Stadium's lights, we actually gained confidence and started doing our talent justice as the England travelling support roared us on as they always did.

Gradually, that 3-5-2 of theirs became a weakness. As the wing-backs pushed up, they left all kinds of space in behind for me to exploit. A Steven Gerrard rocket from the edge of the area, his first international goal, gave us a deserved half time lead.

As someone who always felt that they shone brightest on the really big nights, I didn't have to wait long for my second goal. Emile Heskey did well to contest and nod one down to me on the right-hand side of the area.

Despite the fact that Kahn appeared to have most of the target covered, as much as I always hated just going for power, with the ball rising like it was I had little other choice. Again, I had to keep it down, plus, because the angle wasn't ideal, it was virtually impossible to pick a side. I hit it hard, low to his left. To my surprise, he got a hand on it, but it wasn't enough to keep the ball out. I turned away to celebrate.

We were flying. But the job wasn't done.

Even at 1-3 down, we knew better than to underestimate a wounded German side at home. And remember: this was a team that had never lost a World Cup qualifying match at home.

Instead of protecting the lead, sensing that their evolving panic was making them chase the game, we continued to press as our incisive passing game started to wear them out.

My third was a fairly typical goal for me. Steven Gerrard intercepted a pass somewhere between the centre-circle and the right touchline. Just as he'd done a hundred times back in our Liverpool youth days, he looked up. Really, he barely needed to. Years of instinct told him where I'd be.

And I was – running into the channel on the right-hand side of the area, knowing his pass would be coming. And it was, perfectly weighted. Without breaking stride, I edged to the right while Kahn tried to make himself big to cover the goal. It was in vain. I thought, *I've made this finish many times before.*

Through years of experimentation I'd learned that, when you're coming in off the right-hand side as I was, in order to score in the far corner with a placed finish the natural shape of shot is right-to-left for a right-footed player. Hitting it hard with your laces straightens it out somewhat but that was never an option. Going for outright power was always last on my list of options.

From the angle I was at, the near post is often the way to go. Better still, and to give you a bigger area to hit, going high is often the correct finish. Of course, the angle of attack and the position of the goalkeeper will always determine the best finish but on this occasion I chose right.

Kahn did nothing wrong. His angles were good and he too played the percentages by diving across goal. But this was simply an angle that favoured the attacker and with my confidence high, the net was destined to bulge …

We were 4-1 up in Munich. Again, what else was there to do but dust down the somersault celebration!

Looking back on what would eventually be a 5-1 win, courtesy of a 74th minute goal from Emile Heskey, I have mixed feelings. As incredible as it was to score a hat-trick against our old rivals, in a dominant performance in their own back yard, nowadays that elation is tempered by that nagging feeling that we should have gone on to win something in that era.

Although we probably didn't fully acknowledge it at the time, we were in the midst of a truly golden era of England players. More than anywhere else, Munich epitomised that group. But more of that later …

■■ ■■■■ ■ ■

As I was preparing in the dressing room of the Stadio Olimpico in Rome before our Champions League second group stage tie against Roma, Thommo came in and made the hand sign for a phone call.

'There's a call for you,' he said, 'you can take it outside.'

'Who is it?' I asked him.

'The boss,' Thommo replied.

I walked out of the dressing room – where no mobile phones were permitted, and into a side room. There I was handed the phone, and on the other end was the familiar, if slightly delicate tone of Gérard Houllier.

'Hello, Michael,' he began, 'I just thought I'd give you a call before the game.'

'Boss, it's so great to hear from you. Thanks very much for ringing.'

'I've got some good news for you too,' he continued, 'I hope it'll give you a boost for tonight.'

At this point, just hearing the boss's voice on the phone was the best news I could possibly think of. As it stood, I would have gone onto the pitch that night with a serious spring in my step knowing that he was on the mend.

But there was more.

'You can't tell anyone,' he said, 'but you've been voted European Footballer of the year. You've won the Ballon d'Or. Congratulations!'

In that moment, I had no idea what to say.

The news, and the circumstances under which it had been delivered, was so unusual. It was all a bit surreal and the fact that we played out a muted 0-0 draw in the game later that night is now lost in time.

With retrospect, winning the award was such a strange one for me. As much as I lived for scoring goals, winning games and lifting trophies, for England and Liverpool, to be singled out as the best player in Europe for that calendar year was the kind of focus and accolade that I found hard to take, despite my usual self-belief.

When I considered it, I couldn't help thinking, *am I really the best player in Europe? What about Zidane? What about Thierry Henry?*

It seemed unfathomable to me that I, Michael Owen, should be the first English player since Kevin Keegan to win the award. I wouldn't say I went overboard with the celebrations either. If anything, outside of my immediate family, I was a little sheepish about it all. I certainly didn't want an open-top bus parade through Chester with it – although it has got pride of place in my trophy room nowadays!

Indeed, when they belatedly brought the trophy to Anfield for a ceremony on the pitch before our game against Derby in April 2002, I had long since moved on. I know people will say that to receive such a prestigious award should be something to savour and dwell on for a lifetime. For me, however, it was entirely consistent with how I approached my entire career that, as the ceremony took place and they were handing me the most prestigious individual award in European football, I was already thinking more along the lines of beating Derby County.

Get it off the pitch! I remember thinking at the time, *I need to score here against Derby* …

Again, I just could never rest on my laurels. Yes I'd won a highly sought-after individual award; it was great that I was appreciated. But all I wanted to do was score the next goal, the next hat-trick and lift the next trophy. Looking back, I was relentless in that respect and I've no doubt that that mind-set was key to my success. Nothing was ever enough.

In the boss's absence Thommo had manoeuvred us into a good place, by and large. Despite a rare 3-1 home defeat by Barcelona in November, where I'd scored first to give us the lead, we were holding our own in a tight, nervy group that also included Galatasaray and the aforementioned Roma.

With more ties to follow in February and March of 2002, we were still in the hunt for a place in the knockout stages.

As Christmas of 2001 loomed, having been top of the table in November, we sat in fourth place in the Premier League.

Really it could have been even better. With Gérard Houllier clearly pulling some strings from his sickbed behind the scenes, we had momentum. Then, first, a surprise 4-0 defeat to Chelsea at Stamford Bridge, followed by a 2-1 loss to Arsenal at Anfield, derailed us at the wrong time. At Christmas we were playing catch-up in the league and had been knocked out of the Worthington Cup by Grimsby.

As 2001 drew to a close, despite these few team wobbles, I reflected on an incredible year personally where pretty much everything had gone right. With five trophies – six if you count my Ballon d'Or, 2001 was going to be a hard year to better.

That said, what better way to end it than by scoring your hundredth goal for your club – as I did in a 1-1 draw away at West Ham on December 29th.

Towards the end of that year, I also received another phone call from Gérard.

These had become more frequent. His voice sounded less fragile with each call. I could tell his enthusiasm for the job was undiminished. It felt like it wouldn't be long before he was back in the dugout in person. Up until then, he had just been an energetic force-field of good wishes hovering above us.

'Any thoughts on Nicolas Anelka?' he said, 'I'm thinking of bringing him in on loan.'

Firstly, as I've already suggested, Gérard was the kind of boss who wasn't averse to asking players' opinions – particularly those of the senior guys that he was closest to. While he wouldn't exactly ask you to pick the team for him, he certainly valued our views. That was just one more reason to really respect him.

Secondly, I won't deny that the thought of the boss signing another striker never really thrilled me much. As a striker, you're territorial – on the pitch, and off it. As such, incomers – particularly talented, mercurial incomers of Nicolas Anelka's ilk, would inevitably be seen as a threat. 'And don't worry,' he added, 'I'm just looking for a bit of back-up.'

On paper, it was a smart move.

Following a series of fallouts with Thommo and some unsettling conversations between himself and the board regarding his future, Robbie Fowler had left the club for Leeds United in October 2001.

As much as that still left me, Jari Litmanen (who'd been signed the previous year and been continuously injured since) and of course, Emile Heskey, a bit of striker cover was certainly welcome with a full fixture list ahead. Nicolas was duly brought in on loan in December and the boss asked me to give him a call and welcome him to the club.

I don't think anyone would argue that Nicolas was something of an enigma. As his career moved on, he'd do absolutely nothing to disprove this theory. Some accused him of being disruptive and worse, but I never found him to be any of those things. If anything, he appeared to be a bit introverted and shy.

For all his supposed personality shortcomings, Nicolas Anelka could certainly play when he felt like it. On a couple of occasions in early 2002 – most notably against Newcastle in March at Anfield – he was sensational. Although he didn't actually score as part of an ultra attack-minded front three that included both me and Emile, he did everything else.

The fans really took to him. He was a genuinely exciting addition who helped us maintain a scintillating twelve game run in the spring of 2002, which included wins over Manchester United, Leeds, Ipswich, Fulham and Newcastle.

Fittingly, given the timing of his first phone call to me, Gérard eventually did return to the dugout for the Champions League return game against Roma at Anfield on March 19th.

Two weeks earlier, we'd gone to the Nou Camp and redressed our initial group stage loss against Barcelona by digging out the grittiest 0-0 draw imaginable with our backs against the wall for every one of the ninety minutes.

It was a disciplined performance when we really needed one – not that I can take any credit, I might add. I sat on the bench with a minor thigh strain that night alongside Anelka, himself cup-tied on the back of his appearances that season for Paris Saint-Germain.

Although I didn't physically play against Roma either, when Gérard returned, I know it was an emotional night. The lads told me that, until that afternoon in the team hotel, there had been no suggestion that the boss would be back that night. Apparently, a couple of hours before kick-off, he then called Thommo and gave him the news we'd been waiting months to hear – 'I'll be back.'

Anything less than a win against Roma, that in turn would secure progress to the knockout round, would have been a criminal waste of the perfect opportunity to give the boss a great welcome back present.

As it turned out, we delivered for him and us – with a goal in each half from Jari Litmanen and Emile Heskey respectively. A quarter-final appointment with Bayer Leverkusen beckoned on April 2nd.

In the first leg at Anfield, we were decent. Sami Hyypiä gave us the lead around half time and we felt that, based on what we'd seen of the Germans, a one goal lead would give us something to defend in Germany a week later.

How wrong we were.

The second leg was one of those nights where everything conspires against you. They scored first through Michael

Ballack and we equalised in the second half with a goal from Abel Xavier.

In between all that, I don't mind admitting that I spurned a few chances that I'd have taken on any other night. Two more strikes from Dimitar Berbatov and a second from Ballack looked to have buried us. Then Jari Litmanen popped up with a goal in the 80th minute that would have got us through on away goals.

Alas, it was not to be.

Brazilian centre-half Lúcio's 84th minute winner absolutely sickened us on a night where we definitely should have progressed to a semi-final tie against Manchester United. As it stood, it was a case of so near but yet so far in our first Champions League campaign. To add insult to injury and to seal the deal, Lúcio cynically stamped on my foot as the clock wound down in the BayArena.

Having threatened, at various times that season, to win the Premier League, we came up just a little short in the end. Arsenal had been irresistible on the run-in, capping a twelve game winning streak with a 2-0 win at Bolton to open up an insurmountable seven point gap on us.

Still, eighty points was more than respectable for a side that had also gone deep into European competition – it might well have won us the league in other years. Despite the lack of trophies, I still managed nineteen league goals and twenty-eight in all competitions.

Once the season was over, I thought just one thing: *bring on the World Cup …*

REBØOT_10

SCARS

The immediate build-up to the 2002 World Cup in Japan and South Korea was nothing short of a media circus.

Having qualified months previously by drawing with Greece at Old Trafford courtesy of that last-gasp David Beckham free-kick, we warmed up for the tournament (a group that included Argentina, Sweden and Nigeria) with a game against South American opponents, Paraguay, at Anfield in April of 2002.

At this point, our regular captain, David Beckham, was sidelined with a metatarsal injury. At the time none of us even knew what a metatarsal was, far less how long it would take to heal. It wouldn't be long until everyone seemed to be breaking them!

A few days before the Paraguay game, Sven called.

'I'm considering making you captain, Michael,' he told me.

'That's great, boss,' I replied, 'Thanks very much.'

'Don't say anything yet though,' he then went on, 'I haven't totally made up my mind.'

As much as I wanted to phone everyone I knew to tell them I'd just been made England captain for a game at Anfield, I couldn't. I had no choice but to sit tight until I got official word – which I later did.

It was a great honour to captain my country at senior level for the first time. Being a striker, it was even better that I scored against Paraguay after just four minutes at the Kop end. I came off at half time, feeling good about my game with the World Cup a month and a half down the line.

David Beckham's injury took forever to heal, to the extent that even when we arrived in the Far East, he was doubtful for the opening game against Sweden in Saitama on June 2nd.

It seemed as if the media were absolutely pre-occupied with the Beckham story, to the total exclusion of everything else, I thought. Granted, on the back of his heroics against Greece that got us to the tournament in the first place, he was undoubtedly as hot a property as he'd ever been in the press's eyes.

Predictably, when we touched down in Japan, eighty per cent of the banners at the airport were for David; twenty per cent of them were for me and everyone else. I just thought it was all blown way out of proportion.

There were, after all, twenty two other lads on that plane – arguably some of the best players England had ever sent to a major tournament. I felt that we were overlooked as a unit – with all the focus on the recovery plight of one individual instead. David's metatarsal was a daily, if not hourly, discussion point.

As well as being our captain, it would be insane of me not

to say that, in 2002, David Beckham was obviously a very talented player. The performance that he put in against Greece exemplified what he had. Forget about the goal too – that was the least of what he did that day. He was absolutely brilliant.

I always admired him massively because I always felt that, among a generation of players that had so much natural talent – Scholes, Giggs, Wes Brown etc. – he didn't quite have as much in the way of gifts. Yet nobody, I repeat, nobody, worked harder than David to maximise the talent he did have.

Seemingly, when he was younger, he'd spent hours and hours practising his technique, long after everyone else had vacated the training ground. In addition, while he was never the quickest, he always made it his top priority to be as physically fit as a footballer could possibly be. Throughout his career, he could get up and down like nobody's business.

By 2002 he was the finished article. He was disciplined, polished – and had perfected something quite unique in the world of football: that dipping, right-to-left delivery that was so effective from either a dead ball situation as it had been in added time against Greece, or from a wide position on the right from where he could whip a killer ball in with almost no back-lift.

Because defenders had almost no warning and therefore no time to get set, David's crosses were almost impossible to defend. For a striker like me, his crosses were like gold dust.

So, with that being said, despite the over the top, press-led hullabaloo, we all recognised David's significance in the team from a playing perspective. We knew what we gave us and we, as much as anyone, were secretly hoping that he'd be ready to play against Sweden.

As it turned out, he made it. How fit he actually was that

night in Saitama, you'd need to ask him. Regardless, he lasted sixty-odd minutes – which was long enough for him to supply the assist for Sol Campbell's first half goal, which was later cancelled out by an Alexandersson equaliser after the break. The game finished 1-1. As it always seemed to be where the Swedes and us were concerned, it was a tight, cagey affair.

When Sweden beat Nigeria a few days later, anything less than a draw in our second game against Argentina under the sliding roof of the Sapporo Dome would have been a calamity and would almost certainly have led to an early flight home.

For those of us that had been there in '98, the group game against Argentina was certainly a grudge match of sorts. For those that weren't, they still would have been aware of the rivalry, of the Argentinians taunting us by dancing on the bus after the game in Saint-Étienne, of David's sending off and so on.

Nevertheless, given that it was still just a group match, the Argentina game took on much more gravity than it probably warranted.

For David Beckham, this was particularly true. Although I'd never directly discussed it with him in the intervening years, it was obvious to everyone that he felt considerable resentment towards the Argentinians – not just for the sending off itself, but also, perhaps, for the absolute mauling in the press he received as a result.

It was a strange game, for all kinds of reasons – not least that we were playing indoors in this curious, echoing, rather airless environment.

After a few minutes, I felt as if I should have had a penalty. I was clearly, I thought, fouled in the box. But I stayed on my feet. Pierluigi Collina, without doubt the best referee I've ever met, was standing right there. I thought, *how could you miss that?*

He jogged towards me.

'Ref! Come on! I shouted, 'that's got to be a penalty!"

He came in closer.

'Michael' he said, those big, wide eyes fixed on mine, 'you know as well as I do that I can't give a penalty if you're standing on your feet.'

'But it was clearly a foul!' I protested.

'If he pushes you and you go down,' he said, 'that's different. But you've got to give me a decision to make.'

Let me be clear. At no point was the best referee in world football suggesting that I dive. Furthermore, he didn't say that, had I gone down, he would have definitely awarded a penalty either.

What he was saying was that it was almost impossible for him, or any referee for that matter, to give a penalty decision while the player is still standing on his feet.

With Collina's words still in my mind, ten minutes later, I found myself in the box at the left corner of the penalty area. As I cut inside Argentinian centre-half, and now Spurs' manager, Mauricio Pochettino, he dangled a leg out and clipped me as I went past. As slight as the actual impact had been, at least it had drawn a bit of blood on my knee.

I went down and looked back at Collina as if to say: 'Is *this* what you meant?'

Could I have easily stayed on my feet? Certainly I could have. But I didn't – I gave him a decision to make instead.

He made it.

He instantly pointed to the spot.

Normally, I would have taken the penalty at that time but

there was no persuading David that he wasn't taking that one. He drilled it down the middle to put us 1-0 up. Suddenly he was the absolute hero of the day. I found it all very puzzling.

I thought: *Come on! Don't give me that tripe ...*

It really seemed like, by virtue of the fact that he'd smashed one ball down the middle, everything that went before was forgiven. As much as it was a relief that he scored, I felt that David's attitude to its significance was different from mine.

In his mind, I'm sure he thought it laid the ghost to rest from four years prior. On a personal level, if it had that effect for him, I'm very happy that it did. While I obviously didn't want him to suffer for the rest of his life, I didn't feel that way at all. All it was for me was three points in a group game. In no way were the circumstances comparable with us being knocked out of a World Cup. His penalty against Argentina in 2002 laid no ghosts to rest for me. I'd have to live with the aftermath of his actions in 1998 for a lifetime.

I've got to say that I've rarely given that game against Argentina much thought since. As much as it might have meant something to David, for me it was unremarkable.

But given that diving, or *simulation* as it's called now, has become one of the most reviled acts in the game, something I have given some thought to many times since is that conversation with Collina.

In my work with BT Sport, I've had numerous conversations with Howard Webb, himself a top, top, referee, and he often echoes what Collina said to me that day.

The reality is that ninety per cent of players that get fouled and go down in the box could equally easily have stayed on their feet. Rarely will you see a foul that absolutely swipes somebody's legs away completely. Most penalties come as a result of tackles that the fouled player could either avoid or hurdle, or whatever, but they choose not to.

The reason they don't is so simple if a little unpalatable for the neutral: drawing a foul, particularly in the box, is a skill. Players *intentionally* draw contact. You're enticing a defender to make a bad decision. And if there's contact, a player is absolutely entitled to go down.

And then from there, and only there, the referee can either award a penalty or wave it away. Many players wait for goalkeepers to dive at their feet before touching it away and going down. This is normal. This is football.

Where it obviously goes wrong is when players pre-empt a foul before one even occurs. You'll often see players' knees buckling before any contact. Or they'll go down when there's no contact at all. Sadly, that's normal – and unforgivable. That is *not* football.

In the game against Nigeria in Osaka on June 12th, we were bang average. I don't know what it was. Whether it was the temperature, humidity or whatever – we were poor. There's no doubt too that the conditions made playing football both difficult and uncomfortable.

In the end, we drew 0-0 and when Sweden did everyone a favour by knocking out Argentina in the other final game in the group, the draw opened up for us. Denmark awaited us in the second round.

The Denmark game, which we'd ultimately win 3-0, was where my tournament was turned on its head.

After ten minutes, I was still yet to score in the tournament. Then someone fouled me. As this happened, I kicked my leg out to make it all look a bit more theatrical to make certain of getting the free kick. But in doing so, I tore my hamstring.

Or I thought I did. It was such a strange one. As much as I knew instinctively that I'd torn it, at the time it felt completely different to every previous tear I'd experienced – to the extent that I found myself thinking, *have I actually torn it?*

That alone was unusual. When you tear a hamstring in a game, your first thought is usually *I'm off* … You've got no choice. As much as you might want to, you just can't run. But with this one, as much as I knew I'd done something, I was still thinking, *well, I can still run a bit. Let's see* …

With this in mind, I hobbled along for another twenty minutes or so without signalling to the bench. While I couldn't sprint at full pelt, I could still run at three-quarter pace without it hurting too much.

Because I didn't want to expose myself, I played the remainder of the half as a bit of a goal-hanger. As it happened, a chance dropped to me and I finished it. Immediately I felt that the pressure was off me.

'I'm going to need to come off,' I told the physio at half time.

'Why?' he said.

'I've done my hamstring,' I told him.

My thinking was, *we're 3-0 up here. Why make this worse? Maybe it's something we can sort out* …

Normally when you tear a hamstring, the damage runs horizontally, *across* the muscle fibres. As such, the tear can be quite short in length, but still be very impactful. When I had it scanned after the game, the reason for my confusion became clear. The image looked absolutely horrific.

In my case, the tear was vertical, *along* the fibres – and instead of being short, it was clearly visible in the scan as being five or six inches long.

Now, on paper, a six-inch tear along the muscle was no worse than a half-inch tear going across. But, as it would turn out, there were key differences in terms of what I might or might not be able to do immediately thereafter.

The primary key, in this particular instance, was pain. Or rather, the relative lack of it. As badly as the hamstring was torn, it wasn't as painful as it could have been. With a quarter-final against Brazil in just a few days, I was suddenly thinking, *I'm bloody playing …*

The specifics of getting me in a physical state capable of taking part in that game on June 21st in Fukuroi City are something I've never discussed with anybody – including Sven or my teammates.

At no point did I train. Instead, I spent almost every moment with a Dutch physio called Richard Smith – who Sven had known since his days at Lazio and had brought along with the squad specifically for the World Cup finals.

Let me be clear and say that I was under no illusions about what was possible. To that end, I was well aware that I was never going to repair the injury in the short time I had. We were looking simply for a short-term patch-up job that would allow me to take part. After all, it was a World Cup quarter-final. I would have done anything to play.

I spent morning, noon and night with Richard Smith – two-hour session after two-hour session – with him virtually hanging off the ceiling in an attempt to put so much pressure on my damaged hamstring fibres that he'd kill the nerve endings and, by extension, alleviate the pain.

This might sound like a crude, brutal practice. And believe me it was.

At times, as he applied as much pressure as humanly possible to my leg with the point of his elbow, the tears of pain were rolling down my face. I can't even begin to describe how uncomfortable it was. My leg was black and blue with bruising.

As painful as it was at the time, when these sessions ended, I felt good. Because the nerves had been impaired, I started to feel as if there was no injury at all.

While Sven knew, obviously, that I had an issue, he had almost zero knowledge of the true extent of what I'd been going through. All I'd told him was that, come game day, I'd be fit to play.

'I'll wait for you,' Sven told me all along, 'but you've got to train the day before the game to be available for selection.'

When the day before the game arrived, I was faced with a dilemma. As much as Richard Smith's sessions had helped, I still had to protect my leg. But at the same time I had to convince Sven that I was moving sufficiently well and would be able to contribute. It was a fine balancing act.

In the dressing room before the training session, Richard was leaning on my leg again, numbing it, numbing it and numbing it for an hour. Then I jumped off, straight into a training session where I found that my leg felt much the way it had against Denmark: I could get around, at seventy or so per cent of maximum speed. Yes, it was just a short-sided game where I never had to extend myself, but nevertheless I was thinking, *this is as good as it's going to get…*

Fortunately, it was enough to satisfy Sven.

For the night before the game, we travelled to another hotel nearer the quarter-final venue. This hotel was situated right beside a golf course.

The following morning, two hours before we were due to leave for the game, I told Richard that I was still feeling my hamstring.

'Let's go for a jog on the golf course,' he said.

On the quiet, we snuck out around the back onto the golf course, just as the heavens opened. It was absolutely lashing it down.

'How does it feel? Richard asked after a couple of minutes, 'can you do this?'

'It's still hurting,' I told him. 'But the pain is lower down.'

'Point to where it's sore,' he said, 'and then lie down.'

There I was, four hours before a World Cup quarter-final, lying face down on the seventeenth fairway of a bloody golf course, in monsoon rain, while a Dutchman dug his elbow into my hamstring. It must have been quite the sight to behold. We must have looked like drowned rats.

As it happened, nobody saw us. And nobody had any clue what I'd gone through to take my place that day in the Shizuoka Stadium.

By the time the game started, I'd already convinced myself that I was going to have to play like I had for the last twenty minutes against Denmark: conservative, don't expose myself to a sprint into the channels I kept saying to myself, *just link play and get in the box.*

After twenty or so minutes, a ball from Emile Heskey flew over my head. As it did, their centre-half Lúcio, the kind of nasty, unscrupulous defender who always wanted to leave one on you, turned too.

As much as I was quicker than him, I wasn't quicker than him on that particular day.

He didn't know that, though.

He had no idea that I couldn't run past him – that I never had any *intention* of running past him. How was he to know I'd been lying face down on a waterlogged golf course a few hours prior. But, even though he had a run on me, he wasn't watching the ball. Instead of running past him, I made a half-hearted run to get in behind but then, when I saw that the ball was dropping out of the air faster than he clearly thought, I slowed down.

This was instinctive on my part. And I vividly remember thinking, as that ball died in the air, *he has no idea where the ball is. He's more concerned about me sprinting. This could hit him and drop for me.*

As it was, slowing down was a convenient, easy way out for me anyway. And just as I'd envisaged, the ball hit Lúcio's hip and dropped on a figurative plate. I instinctively took a touch and then, dink, over the goalkeeper. One nil.

I didn't have to extend – I didn't have to do much of anything. All the nagging doubts that I'd had in the build-up as to whether I was just being selfish by playing when I knew that I was only half fit were immediately justified in my mind. It was a calculated decision, and it had just paid off.

And then it was all undone.

Just before half time, with us totally dominating possession, David Beckham jumped over a challenge on the half way line. Nothing much seemed on, even when Ronaldinho took the ball off him. But this was Brazil remember. Pass to Rivaldo – 1-1.

Never in my life have I seen a dressing room as deflated as that one at half time.

To have played so well, gone 1-0 up in the baking heat and got all the way to almost the stroke of half time only to come in not leading – it was just so gutting.

'Come on, it's still just 1-1!' I remember Sven saying, to pick us all up.

But it didn't work. I was brought off after seventy nine minutes. I was struggling.

Thereafter I could only sit and watch the remainder of one of the worst performances I think I've ever seen from an England team.

Even though they went down to ten men, whether it was our system, the heat or whatever it was, we had absolutely nothing. If we'd played for another week, I still doubt whether we'd have scored.

I don't care what anyone says, Ronaldinho's 59th minute goal that ultimately won it for them was not intentional – never in a million years. As great a player as he was, there's no way he even thought about scoring from that far out.

Trust me, I'm happy to blame anyone but, as much as David Seaman had some previous – having been chipped by Real Zaragoza's Nayim in the 1995 European Cup Winners' Cup final – I really don't think it was all his fault that day against Brazil.

Inevitably, he'd get slaughtered for it, but I genuinely think that was harsh. If anything, in a situation like he was in where he was probably expecting a cross, I'd want my keeper to take a step or two out to come and command the six yard box as he rightly did. It was a total fluke – you couldn't have put that ball in a more unsaveable place if you'd placed it there with your hands. Whatever you think about it – and people still argue about it now – we were out of the World Cup.

Everyone was to blame: the manager, the players, me ... certainly not just David Seaman.

Just thinking about the 2002 World Cup upsets me now – seventeen years later. Even the night before the game, as we sat at the dinner table, we knew that, if we won, we'd be playing either Turkey or South Korea in the semi-final.

I even remember saying to Rio, 'Listen, mate. If we beat Brazil, we're going to be world champions.'

With all due respect to both of those countries, we'd have seriously fancied our chances against either of them in a World Cup semi-final. Turkey were bang ordinary and were punching above their weight. South Korea, as much as they'd beaten some good teams were – at the end of the day – South Korea. Thereafter, we'd have ended up playing Germany in the final – and we'd just stuffed them 5-1 in their own backyard a few months earlier.

As I sit here now, I am in no doubt whatsoever that 2002 was the year where all the promise of that generation of players should have come to fruition. We had everything. *That* was our World Cup.

■■ ■■■■ ■

When we arrived home, instead of commiserating with us, the press obviously thought it would be a good idea to dig out a story about our gambling habits again. How they thought this would help anyone, I'll never know. All I remember is being told about a headline that told the nation that Michael Owen owed Kieron Dyer thirty grand for a gambling debt.

As true as this was, in my eyes, it was an absolute non-story. Once again, there we were, a group of guys, miles away from friends and family, at a tournament where there was little to do between games.

As with every other previous tournament, we got the card school going and we got the book running. Just like before, it was great fun and relieved boredom. Just like before, it didn't affect our performance in any way, shape or form. Yet, here the press were again, digging this story up with me at the centre of it.

As I've said all along, I have never bothered too much about losing when I gamble. Call it irresponsible, call it delusional or call it what you want – it's just not something I ever worried about.

While thirty grand is undoubtedly a lot of money – and a figure that I don't take for granted at all, in the context of what I was getting paid at the time, it really wasn't that significant. Plus, it wasn't as if this money was lost in one reckless night. This debt was accrued over a period of six weeks. It was just the amount that was paid to settle up at the end – and it was by no means the only cheque that was flying around between us.

Once again, the press didn't get it and, despite what they'd been told in the past, they didn't even want to try to understand. They just seemed determined to portray us as reckless, entitled high-earners – rubbing the faces of the nation in our high-earnings on one hand, while disappointing them on the other with our on-field shortcomings.

Believe me, there isn't one single England fan out there who felt more disappointed than I did about our failure to win the 2002 World Cup.

And whilst most fans quickly get over that feeling, I will carry it with me for the rest of my life.

REBØOT_11

THE DECISION

After the World Cup in 2002, the Premier League season got off to a slow start for me. Apart from a penalty against Newcastle in early September, it took me seven weeks to score an outfield goal and when I did – a hat-trick against Kevin Keegan's Manchester City at Maine Road – I felt a dead weight lifting off my shoulders. As a striker, goals were my quarry. I took it badly whenever I went without.

Whether he was made available or not, I don't know, Gérard Houllier didn't keep Nicolas Anelka on beyond his loan spell. We were never told why. Off Nicolas went on his enigmatic way to join Keegan at Manchester City.

Instead, and presumably with half an eye on some attacking cover, prior to the World Cup, Gérard made a pre-emptive offer to bring in the Senegalese striker, El Hadji Diouf from Lens, along with his fellow countryman Salif Diao – a defensive midfield player, from CS Sedan Ardennes.

Gérard must have had a crystal ball. Second to the co-hosts, South Korea, Senegal were undoubtedly the surprise-package of the 2002 World Cup. Not only did they reach the quarter-final, where they could count themselves as being unlucky to succumb to a very average Turkey side, but they did it all with much enthusiasm and panache.

African football, it seemed, was on the ascendancy. Better still, one of Senegal's many stars in the tournament had been El Hadji Diouf. Although he didn't actually score (Salif Diao did) Diouf's enterprise and energy made him undoubtedly seem like one of Gérard's characteristically shrewd acquisitions.

He confirmed the early promise by scoring twice on his first appearance in a 3-0 win against Southampton at Anfield. Thereafter I'm not sure that many people around Anfield would consider him to have been a really successful signing.

On the whole, 2002/2003 was a season of two distinct halves from a club perspective. We made a fast start with two wins, which we followed with three successive 2-2 draws against Blackburn, Birmingham and Newcastle.

Thereafter, we went on a seven game winning streak that took us to the top of the Premier League in early November, four points ahead of reigning title holders Arsenal.

In the Champions League, our group – which consisted of Valencia, Spartak Moscow and Basel – didn't look as if it was the toughest. However, a 2-0 loss in Valencia soon had us on the back foot and this, not unlike the Worthington Cup final against Birmingham in 2001, was a game that I was really irritated to be left out of.

Given that I was a proven big game performer, I just couldn't see why Gérard, having originally told me I was starting, left me on the bench. It made no sense whatsoever – particularly as he'd rested me the previous week against Bolton because he said he said wanted me fresh for the Mestalla. Milan Baros, who had scored two against Bolton in my place, didn't even get picked!

I just thought *it's one of the biggest games of the season. Surely I should start?*

Instead, the boss went with Emile Heskey and El Hadji Diouf on the night, despite me charging into his office and remonstrating with him about it. It had no effect. As I mentioned, we got turned over 2-0. Valencia gave us a footballing lesson that night.

The following week, we drew 1-1 with Basel in a nervy affair at Anfield. Thereafter we put eight past Spartak Moscow over two games (including a perfect hat-trick from me in the away leg) to haul us back into a reasonable position in the group with two games left. A defeat to Valencia at Anfield, who booked first place in the group in the process, left us needing a win against Basel to qualify in second place.

On paper, it should have been doable. In reality, the tie was effectively over after half an hour. They threw everything at us. We had nothing in response. Soon we were 3-0 down and in desperate trouble. That we salvaged a 3-3 draw on the night is immaterial. It wasn't enough. We bowed out of the Champions League at the group stage and parachuted into the UEFA Cup.

Whether the game in Basel triggered something as far as our confidence was concerned, we'll never know. But we were never quite the same again in that 2002/2003 season and to prove it we embarked on a twelve-game winless run that was only halted on January 18th when we finally ground out a win in a turgid encounter with Southampton at St. Mary's.

2003 was disappointing by and large. The team lacked confidence and it showed in our lack of consistency in both the league, where we ultimately toiled into fifth place, and the UEFA Cup, where, having dispatched Auxerre and struggled past Vitesse Arnhem, we were bundled out of the tournament by Celtic in the quarter-finals.

The sole team highlight of the season was lifting the Worthington Cup having beaten Manchester United 2-0 in the final courtesy of a goal each from Steven Gerrard and me. As sweet as that day was, it felt like a mere consolation. After such a promising start in the league, we'd failed to capitalise.

I finished the season with twenty eight goals in total with nineteen of those in the Premier League. One of them, against West Bromwich Albion on April 26th, was my hundredth Premier League strike. Alas, that stat, and my overall haul, wasn't enough to allow me to wrest the PFA Player Of The Year award away from Thierry Henry.

■■ ■■■■ ■ ■

From the beginning of 2003 onwards, I think Gérard was more conscious than ever of the fact that I had a susceptibility to muscle injuries. The evidence was plain to see. After a shaky start to the 2003/2004 league season, we got our act together well enough to drag ourselves up the table.

I'd been scoring goals as regularly as ever both in the league and the UEFA Cup, as I passed Ian Rush's record of twenty goals in European competition with a late equaliser against Slovenian outfit, Olympija Ljubljana.

Then an ankle injury, sustained against Arsenal in October, completely derailed the majority of my season. While the ankle itself would ultimately heal, between October 2003 and February 2004, I just couldn't shake off what felt like continually occurring thigh and hamstring niggles.

As one healed, another appeared. It was a frustratingly vicious circle that really got me down. I wanted to play, to contribute, but I just couldn't. Not just that, I genuinely believe that Gérard felt that my issues were as much mental as they were physical. To me, that suggestion was confusing to say the least. From my pragmatic point of view there seemed to be no argument. After all, you could look at a scan and *see* that a particular muscle was torn at any given time.

I know people in football sometimes say 'Never treat a scan alone.' There is some truth in that, I agree – a scan doesn't always tell the complete story. But I'm still not sure why Gérard found it hard to accept the existence of hard, medical evidence – particularly in the case of someone who'd obviously been affected by muscle injuries in the past. Maybe he thought I was nervous, tight – whatever. And maybe he believed I needed to free myself of fear. I don't know this, of course – I'm just surmising with hindsight.

Possibly because he'd never really kicked a ball himself, he didn't know what a hamstring pull felt like, either. He, or any other guy in the street, might think, 'I've had a hamstring that's a bit stiff and sore. I just pushed through it.'

If that's the case, fine and good luck to you.

But unless you've had regular, debilitating muscle injuries when playing sport at an elite level, you can't possibly understand how hard it is to recover and get back to playing as you were before.

Regardless, at various times when these hamstring niggles would resurface, Gérard suggested that I spoke to a psychologist to talk it all through. I only agreed because I respected him. But cynical as I am, I just thought, *this is pointless*.

And it *was* pointless.

I went into the consultation room, sat down and stared into the blacks of the eyes of the specialist whose name I can't recall. I'm sure for some people these psychologists really help. I'm not ridiculing the approach at all. But for me, I think I subconsciously resist their efforts. Deep down, I think I'm too mentally tough to let them in.

'I'm not sure I can help you,' he said. 'I've never encountered anyone with such a strong mentality.'

This guy was regarded as one of the best. He'd worked with champions, Olympic gold medallists and championship-winning teams of all kinds. Along the way I'm sure he'd encountered a few nuts that were initially tough to crack.

Subconsciously, I'm certain I didn't want him to help me. After all, the reason I was asked to meet him was because Gérard thought my injuries were a mental thing. I knew that they weren't.

Another reason it was never going to work is that I've always taken badly to instruction. It's a trait that I don't even like about myself. I don't even understand why I'm like that. For example, I'd like to get my golf handicap down but the thought of spending an hour getting lectured on what I'm doing wrong puts me off. All very strange, I know...

'Your mental strength seems fine,' he said after a few sessions, 'I'm not sure I can offer you anything.'

The problems were most definitely not in my mind. Through time and experience I'd just learned to understand and trust my own body. I knew beyond doubt what injury felt like. No amount of psychology could change my intuition.

Since then, I've lost count of the number of people who have rung me up – a manager or a teammate who was having experience of someone getting recurrent hamstring injuries and said, 'How did you do it? How did you get over them?'

What was clear was that, in all these cases, these players felt that nobody understands them and their manager thinks the injuries are all in their head. I can, of course, relate to that totally. And I also know that it's not in the mind – more a case of, if you haven't personally experienced recurring hamstring or other muscle injuries, it's very difficult to understand how hard they are to overcome.

By the mid-point of the 2003/2004 season, my contract at Liverpool was winding down to that critical stage where club and player's agent might expect to start engaging in a bit of contractual cat and mouse. Both are concerned about the value of the asset, but for entirely different reasons. There was just a year to go.

In such a situation, the agent's job is to protect the player. And a lot goes on in the background to make sure that happens. Rarely is it a case of simply running down a contract to force a club's hand. That's the kind of pub talk that fans engage in when they're not privy to what's actually going on and, more often than not, it paints the player in a bad light.

The reality of the situation is that it's a chess match between the club and the player's agent. Knowing that the time left on the contract is reducing, the agent knows that the potential interest of other clubs can act as leverage.

Equally, the club knows that, with only a short time left on the contract, they need to secure that player's value going forward. Inevitably, it gets complicated. Furthermore, the fans always want to believe that their club is acting fairly. Never would they consider that the player might be backed into a corner.

By this point also, Gérard Houllier had been under quite a bit of pressure himself. Even though we eventually limped into fourth place and secured the last Champions League berth, there was lingering dissatisfaction with not just the boss's recruitment policy, but also his style of play in general.

The upshot of it all was that, by the end of the season, none of us knew whether he was staying or going.

As it turned out, he was going, and during this changeover period during late May of 2004, I remember being one of a few senior players who got a call from Rick Parry, our chief executive, courting our opinion on a few names for potential management candidates that he was thinking of.

I got a call. Jamie Carragher got one, as did Steven Gerrard – 'What do you think, lads?'

One of the names on Rick's list was Rafa Benitez, who had been managing Valencia with no shortage of success.

In just three years, Rafa had worked nothing short of miracles at the Mestalla – first winning La Liga for the second time under his management, this time by five points, and then beating Marseille in the UEFA Cup final in Gothenburg. Any club in Europe would have wanted Rafa at that time. Any club apart from Valencia that is…

Seemingly, despite unprecedented success, he and the club's director of football didn't exactly see eye to eye on matters of recruitment. The start of a pattern with Rafa, you could argue.

Rafa left his post in early June. Meanwhile manager-less Liverpool were in prime position to capitalise.

As fate would have it, after all of these conversations about managers, we went to Portugal with England for the European Championships in mid-June, whereupon Rafa – who had indeed been appointed Liverpool's new manager only weeks prior – came over to our hotel to meet us.

Immediately, I remember getting a whiff of an ill wind. Even then I was thinking, *maybe he doesn't rate me?*

The 2004 European Championships in Portugal under Sven were a very strange tournament, for me personally anyway. On reflection, it's about as close to a personal crisis I ever got in my playing career.

It all started so well, too.

Prior to the tournament, we went to Vale De Lobo in the Algarve for our training camp. We took our partners, stayed in villas around one of the main hotels, and the squad – which had pretty much picked itself with no Gazza-like selection fall out issues – trained on a pitch within the complex. It was a relaxed week. Thereafter, we flew to our base in Lisbon.

Portugal was where a young Wayne Rooney popped his head above the parapet in a major way. Prior to the tournament he'd played two or three games and in doing so had quickly become the new darling of English football in the process.

Among us, Wayne was a really cheeky Scouser who didn't adhere to the accepted rules of hierarchy.

Even as a kid in my early days in the England squad, I would never have nut-megged someone in training, or tried to chip the keeper – even if it was the right thing to do in the circumstances.

Wayne didn't give a damn about anything like that. I remember one of the first shooting practice sessions where he nonchalantly chipped David James with his first kick of the ball. Meanwhile I'm thinking, *oh my God, he's brand new into the squad...*

Of course, everyone always wants to big up the latest prospects – a Theo Walcott or a Franny Jeffers-type of player. But of all the lads that come through, there are very few that you think could be something very special. From what I've been told, I was one of them and Rio Ferdinand was clearly another – it was obvious that he was like a Rolls Royce right from the start.

Well, Wayne Rooney was so good that – when you first squared up to him on a training pitch – you were pretty much certain he was the best player we had. When he did his stuff, people honestly didn't know whether to laugh and think it was brilliant – or instead think that he needed a clip around the ear.

As much as I personally wouldn't have done the things he did, Wayne was that much of a street-wise footballer who did what his instincts told him, that everyone's overriding view quickly became one that accepted that the kid was quite simply a genius. And he proved it in the tournament.

But as Wayne's stock rose with every goal and every headline, my self-confidence, which had always been rock solid, steadily ebbed away. It was so unnerving. I'd always thought I was mentally invincible. I'd done well in qualifying. Unlike the previous Euros, I was in a really good place when I arrived in Portugal.

Wayne walked straight into the team alongside me, the main striker at the time. In the first game against France in Lisbon, Frank Lampard gave us the lead in the first half. Then they scored twice in the last minute to beat us 2-1. Wayne and I both started and were both substituted in the second half, replaced by Emile Heskey and Darius Vassell respectively.

We then beat Switzerland comfortably – 3-0 in Coimbra. Wayne scored twice and I assisted with both of them. After the game, the atmosphere changed. As much as I still felt like the primary goalscorer, the main man, the hysteria around Wayne Rooney was incredible. Every paper I picked up was singing his praises.

When it came to selection conversations about the third game against Croatia, the emphasis had completely switched. Even though I was still confident in my ability and was playing quite well, I started doubting my status.

Suddenly, Wayne was the main striker. And it was between Darius Vassell and me for the supporting role. It wasn't jealousy I was feeling – perhaps just the first dawning that a changing of the guard was under way. To me, being in my mid-twenties, that felt like a very premature shift.

I severely doubt that Wayne had any concept of what I was going through. I saw in him a reflection of what I was in '98: a young kid, oblivious to the world around him. Added to that he was an extremely free spirit who didn't worry much about anything.

Little did we know at that time, but those four games in Portugal 2004 would be the peak of his international career. As much as he had a great career and broke records, if you're knocking Wayne's legacy at all it would be because he never really caught fire in major tournaments thereafter. As much as one player is only as good as the guys around him, he undoubtedly had a couple of no-shows. Nevertheless, I started in the final group game against Croatia in Lisbon. We won 4-2 and Wayne scored *another* two.

Again, I didn't score, but supplied assists, as the supposed main striker, to a guy who was essentially playing behind me in a number 10 role. I was really struggling with the fact that – as much as I believed that I still represented England's best chance of a goal – I just couldn't put the ball in the net.

After the Croatia game, for the first time I felt like I'd lost my sense of purpose. I was feeling really bad about myself. The shit filter was malfunctioning for once. I was used to walking into the canteen and hearing people whisper, 'Here he is, the main man. We need him fit or we're in trouble today,' type of thing.

I was accustomed to getting off the team coach and hearing fans shout, 'Come on, Michael. Let's have a goal from you today!' I felt relied upon, and responsible.

Now, anytime I got off the bus, all I heard was, 'Rooney, Rooney!' I thought, *God, in everyone's eyes, he's now our best chance of scoring …*

In the week building up to the quarter-final game against Portugal, I went to Sven after training one morning.

'Boss, my parents have arrived,' I said, 'Do you mind if I go into town to meet them this afternoon?'

'Sure, no problem,' Sven said.

At this point he had no idea that my head was about to explode. I jumped into an FA car and went down to meet my mum and dad. I just wanted a total change of scene for a few hours – to be in the company of people who unconditionally loved me and wouldn't judge me.

I met my parents in a little café and we just sat and talked like we would at home. Nothing was specifically said. I certainly didn't tell them how I was feeling. It was one of the only times in my life where I thought, *Jesus, I need my mum and dad right now.* An hour later, I got back in the car and went back to the team hotel. I kid you not, when I walked in the door, I swear I'd grown two inches.

I started against Portugal in the quarter-final on June 24th in Lisbon. I was a different person than the one who'd played in the previous three group games. As soon as we kicked off, I knew I was on fire.

After three minutes, David James's goal kick flicked off the head of one of the Portuguese defenders. As if it was an intentional ball over the top, I instinctively sprinted onto the loose ball and flicked it in with an unusual kind of pirouette movement. As it hit the net, I honestly thought, *I've never scored a goal quite like that...*

I just can't stress how important that goal was. I knew Wayne was on fire. I wanted him to be. But I also wanted to contribute and the only way I could do that was by scoring.

From that moment forward, I felt that we were a legitimate partnership – and the heartbreak about it was that Wayne broke his foot after twenty-five minutes and basically had to go home.

Thereafter followed an absolutely shocking tactical decision from Sven. Nobody could believe that he went like-for-like and brought Darius Vassell on. We were 1-0 up! We should have brought on another midfielder – someone like Owen Hargreaves – and just kept things tight. Portugal had just one up front and had packed the midfield themselves – they were already outnumbering us as it was.

Anyone that understands the game will tell you that you can get away with that in football for twenty minutes or half an hour – maybe even a half. But eventually, as people get tired, that extra body in midfield always tells in the end. And it did. They dragged one back in normal time and then we scored one each in extra-time in a topsy-turvy affair that ended 2-2.

Obviously, we then ended up going to penalties. Sven pulled us all together to decide who was taking them.

'Michael, penalty?'

' Yes, boss.'

'Lamps?'

'Yes, boss.'

Darius Vassell was stood next to me.

'Penalty Darius?'

Silence.

'Darius?'

'No.'

I laughed, I probably shouldn't have. I couldn't think what else to do. I just couldn't believe my ears.

'Fine, no problem,' Sven said, and moved on to the next person.

The minute it went to sudden death, and when Darius Vassell was next in line, we all knew what was going to happen. I bloody *knew* he'd miss. And he did miss. And we were out.

I don't want Darius to pick this book up and think I'm having a go at him for the sake of it. It's hard enough to miss a penalty in an important game. Ask David Beckham. He ballooned one that night too.

Looking back now, the events of that night were entirely consistent with Darius's personality – as far as I could see. He was a really nice kid who wouldn't say boo to a goose. He was fast – almost a ready-made impact player. But it almost seemed to me that he was one of those confidence players that you come across regularly – guys that don't have much self-belief and therefore don't like much responsibility. In fairness to him, that's fine – and his lack of confidence on the night would be justified.

Regardless of his reticence, as a centre forward it's almost an unwritten rule that – when half of your outfield team has to take a penalty in a shoot-out – you have to volunteer. I don't care how much you don't want to take one. I didn't want to take one. *Nobody* wanted to take one! It's an absolutely thankless task. But as a striker you *have* to step up. Darius wouldn't do it. I'll never forget that.

We left Euro 2004 with that familiar nagging feeling of what might have been. Portugal went on at our expense and lost in the final to Greece. Greece won it. *Greece?!*

As much as there were tactical question marks with Sven, there's no doubt in my mind that, had we beaten Portugal in a penalty shoot-out and hadn't lost our main player at the time, with a little bit of nous and luck, we could have won that bloody tournament. Instead, it was just another we let slip away.

I can never really understand what I was feeling when I returned to Liverpool after Euro 2004.

It was a strange time at the club – simply because I had little experience of managerial changes. Having only had experience of Roy Evans when I first joined, Gérard Houllier was all that I really knew.

Rafa Benitez clearly came with a few agendas in mind. Right from the off, to me it felt as if one of them was to make totally sure that, whatever happened, Steven Gerrard would stay at the club. He wanted him to be the pivotal figure at Liverpool going forward. That, I suppose, I could hardly blame him for. Steven's talent – and potential, was clear to see.

What he thought about me in 2004 was much harder to figure out. Was I part of his plans? Did he want to move me on? I have no idea.

But one thing was for sure. At a point in my contract, one year left and counting, when we'd be expecting to resolve my contract stalemate, I think I just wanted the new manager to tell me, or show me, that he wanted me. I wasn't getting that from him.

What was more unnerving was that Rafa didn't seem to want to even *talk* about my contract situation, far less resolve it one way or another.

Even Jamie Carragher picked up on Rafa's apparent reticence. He referenced the situation later while suggesting that it was this vacuum surrounding my future that might have ultimately forced my hand to leave in a 'right, if he's not that bothered about me, I'll look elsewhere' type of way.

On reflection, that wasn't the case.

The truth is, Rafa was just being Rafa. He has, I now know, the reputation of being cold and implacable at the best of times. You're never too sure what he's feeling or thinking. I've never seen anything like it in a football manager.

I've since been told that when Steven Gerrard basically won the FA Cup on his own in that thrilling final against West

Ham in 2006, Rafa still said next to nothing. I remember asking him at the time, half-joking: 'Surely the gaffer gave you a pat on the back after that?' 'Nope,' he said. At various times afterwards, both Carra and Didi Hamann have corroborated what Stevie said.

Therefore, with hindsight, it makes total sense that, in the few pre-season games that I played in later that summer in Canada and America, Rafa remained mostly impassive and aloof – even when things were going well.

Against Celtic at East Hartford, I had what I considered to be one of my best games in a Liverpool shirt. We won 5-1; I scored a really good goal and played very well. All uncertainty about contracts goes out the window at moments like that. All I was thinking was, *I'm loving this…*

After that game, at the very least I was expecting Rafa to say something like, 'well played today' – even if he'd done so in private and not in front of the rest of the lads.

Instead, when he did speak with me, he went off on what I considered to be bizarre tangents – telling me that I needed to do this, that and the other to be even better. None of it seemed in any way relevant to what had just happened on the pitch.

I was left scratching my head. And I continued to scratch it when, after scoring the winner in a 2-1 victory over Roma at Giants Stadium a week later, Rafa again offered little in the way of affirmation.

Then, when he decided to split established rooming arrangements up (Carra and I had shared rooms together for five or six years) I clearly remember thinking, *this situation really might not be very easy in the long term.*

And I wasn't alone.

Everybody seemed to be resistant to the jarring changes that

Rafa was ringing at the very beginning of his tenure. Almost overnight it seemed like a prevailing undercurrent of disquiet swept in. In general, Rafa seemed unconcerned about what anyone thought. It was clearly his way or no way.

With hindsight, even though I was questioning some of Rafa's judgement in these early days, the reality is that I would have, just like everybody else, accepted that this was simply a common scenario whereby an incoming manager just wanted to put his imprint on his new club.

And to do that, if it meant that he had to shake some of the guys who were accustomed to a cosy status quo from their comfort zones, then so be it. Nobody likes change at the time, but soon everyone forgets what used to be normal.

Truthfully, though, none of Rafa's behaviour or personality traits had anything to do with my decision to leave Liverpool. What did influence my decision to leave was a phone call from my agent towards the end of the pre-season trip to America.

It's important to say that, honestly, I hadn't given any consideration to moving at that time. The Bosman rule had only just come into effect and therefore the further you were into your contract, the more powerful you were in theory – even though at the same time you were taking a risk if your form dipped or you got seriously injured. By and large, players had more power.

In that context, I know that Tony Stephens was pretty keen on me holding fire for a better deal. That's the agent's job: to position the player as well as they can possibly be in every sense – and for me it certainly wasn't about money. I was earning more commercially than I was from club wages at that time anyway.

What is true is that few would argue that Liverpool hadn't

really made enough progress under Gérard Houllier. It had felt like we'd been treading water somewhat off the back of a really successful period – and that was illustrated by the fact that we hadn't really closed the gap in the league.

As time passed, I suppose part of me often wondered if I'd ever be part of a league-winning team at Liverpool.

So, looking back now, knowing full well that it's a bit of an Owen family trait to do a bit of 'is the grass greener on the other side?' stargazing, maybe a part of me really was inquisitive and thinking, *I wonder what it would be like to play abroad...*

'Real Madrid are interested in talking to you,' I was told by Tony Stephens.

The first thought that crossed my mind was that Tony had brokered David Beckham's move to Madrid the previous summer.

In doing so, it occurred to me that he must have also cultivated good relations with the key decision makers at the club. Not just that, given that I knew that he'd kept in pretty close contact with David ever since, the lines of communication, I thought, would be wide open.

'I'm interested,' I told him. 'Can you find out more?'

Whether Tony suggested me to Real Madrid or not, I didn't know at the time. Had he, like any good agent might, been courting them by saying: 'Michael's got a year left on his contract'? Again, at the time I wasn't aware, but obviously am now – especially as he says as much in his foreword!

All I knew for certain is that interest in me was expressed – and that interest had come directly from Florentino Pérez, Real Madrid's President, and not from José Antonio Camacho, the coach at the time.

I've read and been told about rumours that claimed Madrid

had been pursuing me for years prior to 2004 – possibly as far back as 2002. That, I severely doubt. If it had happened, Tony would have been straight on the phone to me, believe you me. The first I ever heard was the call from Tony in the summer of 2004. A conversation had been had with Real Madrid. They wanted me – that was understood. I needed, I told them, some time to think it all through.

It wasn't just my life that would be turned upside down by a move abroad. There was Louise, my daughter Gemma who was very young at the time – and then there were the friends and family members that we'd be leaving behind.

After the call ended, I just couldn't keep a lid on it. The first thing I did was ask my mate and confidant, Carra, what he thought.

'Madrid are in for me, mate,' I explained, 'what do you think?'

'You're delusional,' he said – in typically blunt Carra style. 'Ronaldo, Morientes, Raúl – they're all crowd favourites. You won't play.'

I felt my eyes turn black.

Really? I thought.

I'm sure that by saying what he did, Carra thought he was doing me a favour. He probably thought I'd agree with him after the initial excitement of the approach passed. Instead, his comments just made me want to go even more. After all, it's human nature to back yourself when you're being doubted.

That said, because of my deep affiliation with Liverpool and the life Louise and I had in England, it wasn't exactly a no-brainer. I swung agonisingly to and fro on the idea for the remaining days until we travelled back from America.

Then we had to make a decision.

But I still couldn't do it.

I tossed and turned in my own mind for a couple more days. I never wanted to leave; I had no intention of leaving Liverpool. In my own mind, I think I expected myself to be at Liverpool for my whole career.

However, the one thing I just couldn't get out of my head was that if I said no to Real Madrid, it might be a regret that would linger for the rest of my life. These were the *Galacticos* after all. If I didn't want to be part of a team like that, why did I even play the game?

I suppose part of me thought – stupidly with hindsight, *just do an Ian Rush. Sample it for a year or two. Then you can always come back…*

At some point, Rafa called me into his office. I didn't sit down. I got the impression that he actually wanted to hear very specific words exit my mouth.

'So you really want to go to Real Madrid?'

I said nothing, as my mind frantically searched for a response. Rafa knew exactly what was happening. It felt like he wanted a confession.

'Are you telling me you want to *leave* Liverpool?'

As he stared, waiting to hear me confirm it, I just couldn't do it. Instead I piddled around a while longer.

'Well, I do think that I might regret it if I say no…' and various other deflections that didn't include the words 'I want to leave Liverpool.'

I couldn't say it to either Rafa or myself – because at the heart of it, I really *didn't* want to leave. Rafa seemed to want closure on me. I didn't want closure on Anfield.

Golden memories: Receiving the Ballon d'Or at Anfield with Gérard Houllier in the background

Class act: I played my part in bringing Didi Hamann to Anfield! A great player and still, to this day, a great friend

Centurion: Celebrating with Patrik Berger after my 100th goal for Liverpool against West Ham in December 2001

What a night: The future looked bright for England after we demolished Germany 5-1 in their own backyard in September 2001. I scored a hat-trick and my club colleagues Steven Gerrard and Emile Heskey also netted

Leading my country: A proud day as England manager Sven-Göran Eriksson passes me the captain's armband in April 2002

Flying the flag: Posing for the press ahead of the 2002 World Cup and *(left)* counting down the games to Japan and South Korea with Steven Gerrard

Learning my lesson: Pierluigi Collina – the greatest referee I've ever known – gave me some valuable advice during the World Cup group game against Argentina – and I took it...

So near, yet... My goal against Brazil in the World Cup quarter-final – but it wasn't to be. With the squad of players we had, we missed such a great opportunity and it still haunts me now

Night to remember: It may not stand out in the memory of Liverpool fans but this game against Porto was when everything clicked into place

Lights out: Carried off with a nasty head injury after a painful collision with Derby County's Chris Riggott. A scary experience

Another trophy: Leaving Roy Keane in my wake as I score in our Worthington Cup triumph over Manchester United in 2003

Fast start: Celebrating with the fans after my third minute goal in the Euro 2004 quarter-final against Portugal

Driving seat: Go-kart racing ahead of the tournament with new kid on the block Wayne Rooney

Every striker's duty: Scoring from the spot in the penalty shootout wasn't enough to see us through

Over to you: Passing the Ballon d'Or to the next winner Ronaldo. Looking on is the Brazilian Ronaldo – someone who would go on to become a good friend during my time in Spain

Big move: With Mum, Louise and Dad after agreeing my transfer to Real Madrid

One of the Galacticos: Lining up with the likes of Ronaldo, Guti, Roberto Carlos and Zinedine Zidane was surreal

Friendly face: Celebrating with David Beckham *(below)*. But we lived different lives and didn't really see that much of each other socially in Madrid

White hot: Celebrating scoring the winning goal against Dynamo Kiev in the Champions League in 2004

Black and white: Putting pen to paper on a contract with Graeme Souness and Freddy Shepherd. Right up to the last minute I was uncertain about the move to Newcastle

Fan fever: It was reported that 20,000 supporters turned up to see my unveiling at St. James' Park

Off the mark: Celebrating my first goal for Newcastle against Blackburn with Alan Shearer

REBØOT_12

A NEW DYNAMIC

Yet I *did* make the decision to uproot the family and leave Liverpool for Spain. The magnetic draw of the continent, and arguably the best club in the world, was just too strong.

And once the wheels were in motion, I just went along with it all – which included sitting on the bench for Liverpool's Champions League qualifier in Austria against Grazer AK because, by this point, Real Madrid's representatives had been to Liverpool to finalise the deal.

Part of that conversation inevitably included an undertaking to make sure that I wouldn't be cup tied for my new club. As much as that made sense to everybody, it only served to make the reality of my decision even more real.

Even on the way to the airport to fly to Madrid, I was still very much on the fence as to whether I was making a decision that I'd regret for the rest of my life. One part of me was excited by the opportunity that lay ahead. Another was absolutely tortured by the life we were leaving behind. As much as I'd talked it all through with as many friends and family members as I could and received mostly support, the whole concept still felt like the most enormous wrench. Reality had now set in. There was no turning back. I know I cried for a good part of that journey to the airport.

Bizarrely, something that was really worrying me about arriving in Madrid in the short term was the keep-up routine every new player has to do in the Bernabeu centre circle! As a prospective *Galactico* you're expected to perform, do tricks, to *dazzle.*

The problem was, while I knew I could basically keep a ball in the air as long as anyone, I've never had any tricks whatsoever! I was a no-trick pony whose formative years had been spent perfecting the art of putting the ball in the top corner, not balancing it on the back of my neck or doing 'around the worlds'. I was so nervous about going on the pitch, maybe dropping the ball and everyone thinking I was crap that it nearly swayed my mind about going through with the commitment to sign.

When it came to it, I went on the pitch and had all the customary photographs taken. And then, inevitably, that moment came when they threw a ball at me – and then every camera in the place trained in on whatever I was going to do with it.

Panicking, I thought, *I'm just going to volley this…*

Hoping the crowd would think I was doing a nice thing by gifting them a souvenir, I volleyed the first ball as hard as I could into the crowd!

Then another ball came and I volleyed that into the other end. A succession of balls arrived and I just smashed all of them into the crowd. It seemed easier. I couldn't face the idea of having to do any tricks. And I think it was convincing; I never really had to wow the fans. The players were a different matter altogether…

As a footballer going into a new club – particularly one that was bursting with superstars like Madrid was in 2004 – I knew I had to gain the players' respect very early on.

After all, I wasn't exactly coming in as a silky number 10 with great touch, great link-up play and lots of skill – the kind of player everyone drools over. I was a fast centre forward that liked to run over the top. They knew I was fast, and they knew I could finish. They knew I could play. But I needed these Galacticos to know that I could *really* play.

For example, I needed these top lads to know that, in a tight area, they could give me the ball and I'd keep it. Wherever you go, giving the ball away is the ultimate sin. It had been ingrained in me since my earliest Liverpool days that, if you lost the ball, you were letting the team down. Real Madrid was no different.

With that in mind, I made it my business to demonstrate, in my very first training session, where a lot of the focus was on possession games, that I wouldn't lose the ball and make my teammates expend energy by chasing to get it back.

I also wanted them to know that I had loads of courage when things got tough. At the top level, sometimes a player finds himself going down a cul-de-sac near the corner flag of his own creation.

In such situations, you've got to be able to offer yourself up, make yourself available to take the ball – and to potentially put yourself in an even bigger hole for the team cause. That's the kind of selfless courage that other good players recognise straightaway.

These less tangible qualities are the attributes of a player that are perhaps more apparent to the players than the fans. From the stands, they can't see what players see.

The pressures of trying to impress aside, the pace of everything at Madrid was much more sedate than I was used to.

Being truthful, training sessions were very lax. After all, when you've got a couple of Brazilians in the squad, the atmosphere tends to be quite jovial. It reminded me of how Liverpool was before Gérard Houllier arrived in that, because there were so many big names, the coach was never really going to bollock anyone.

Don't get me wrong – it wasn't a total piss-take. He'd put on a possession game; he'd put on a bit of five-a-side. On paper, these would be disciplined. But if Roberto Carlos felt like playing up front one day on a whim, or Ronaldo wanted to go and play right back because he'd had a couple of drinks the night before, they'd just do it. It almost made a mockery of things. In Spain, the coach has far less power than in other countries.

The upshot of this environment for me personally was that it was quite easy to shine in these early training sessions. Because the coach was so lenient with this band of superstars, those who really put the effort in really came to the fore. And in Spain, it wasn't just the coach and players taking note.

The press and an accompanying army of camera crews attend every training session and report the details in the following day's newspaper in glaring detail.

You'd pick up the paper and it would say: *In shooting practice yesterday, Michael Owen had ninety four shots, scored sixty three, twenty eight with his left foot, the remainder with his right.*

It's one thing to be marked for your performance in a game, but entirely another to have your training assessed in such specific terms. Not good, not bad – it's just a different way of doing things.

The Bernabeu itself is an odd place, too. As much as it's huge, austere and iconic, on match days it's much more like a theatre – where people go to be entertained.

At Anfield, although it held half the amount of people that the Bernabeu did at that time, it felt like the crowd could physically lift you. It also felt like they could change your mind. If you had the ball and heard the Kop roar you on, you'd think twice about passing the ball sideways. The crowd felt alive, and it made you more alive.

In Spain, certainly at Madrid, the relationship between the fans and the players is different altogether.

Fans – with the exception of the small group of Ultras behind one of the goals – don't really chant or respond much to what's happening on the pitch. As a player you're aware of the disconnection.

As much as there might be 80,000-plus in the stadium, you'd never really know it unless a goal went in. Obviously some weeks are exceptions. El Clásico, for example, is white-hot. But in general, the fans sit quietly, eating snacks, expecting to be entertained.

On the pitch at Madrid, I still felt that I had a lot to offer. While I wasn't as fast as I had once been, the expansive style of football that we played (and we had the ball a lot) meant that many of my qualities were applicable week in, week out.

And what a group of players it was.

Zinedine Zidane was the silent type – and that's not just because his Spanish and English were just average and my French similarly so. There wasn't much we could do other than the occasional 'good morning' and the odd nod of approval.

Language barriers aside, I'm not sure if chatting was Zidane's style anyway. When we were in the dressing room, some guys would be talking; others would be on their phones. He was just one of those people who seemed more comfortable to sit, listen and to take everything in.

Looking back, he and Ryan Giggs are very similar in that respect. They don't always say much, but absolutely nothing gets past them. Funnily enough, if you'd asked me at the time if I thought he'd later go into management, I'd have said not. But obviously he's done it – and in no uncertain terms.

On the pitch, there's no doubt that Zidane is the best player I've ever played with. He's one of those players that, when you watch them, you just know they were born to have a ball at their feet. He never pushed it too far ahead and it was always in perfect control. His ability to turn with both feet was exactly the same.

He was a big lad too. While he didn't have rapid pace, he had power in that he could burst from a standing start beside you and would be five yards away from you in the blink of an eye. Technically, he had everything – and the only person that comes close to him in my eyes is Steven Gerrard. Zidane was more comfortable with the ball at his feet, but Steven was very, very close.

Ronaldo was something else entirely – and probably my favourite lad during my time at Madrid.

He was friendly, kind; we socialised quite often after training. He was without doubt the life and soul of the dressing room too: always laughing, always joking – he couldn't sit still and was a bit like Paul Scholes in that respect. He couldn't just put on his training kit and sit down. He'd juggle the ball – set up a mini head-tennis court in the middle of the changing room whether we were playing home or away. Then you'd have him, Santiago Solari, Roberto Carlos and a couple of others playing head-tennis while I just sat there and watched them. A hierarchy even existed at Madrid.

On the pitch, I observed Ronaldo with a combination of curiosity and admiration.

What first struck me, in one of the earliest training sessions, was just how inflexible he was.

When we were doing quad stretches, I looked over and noticed that he literally could barely get his knee to ninety degrees – far less any further. He'd had major knee surgery twice – once unsuccessfully, another time to redress the first surgery – and it had clearly taken its toll by this later part of his career. I used to think, *if he can hardly bend his knee, how the hell can he run?*

But he could still run and play – albeit he'd had to adjust how he played. If you watch, he had a shuffling type of running style.

Similarly, whenever he needed shooting power, he'd often toe-poke it – simply because he couldn't bend his leg far enough to give it a proper smack.

Yet, there he was, still playing for Real Madrid at the top level of the game – totally compromised by his failing body. I've got huge admiration for him; he was amazing.

A popular misconception is that I mostly came off the bench in Madrid. That's not true. In fact, if you look at the stats, I started more games than I didn't. I was never sure why that myth was perpetuated.

I'd gone into my spell in Madrid having identified what the competition was from a personal perspective. As a striker, you have to. You had Raúl, Ronaldo and Fernando Morientes – all three of them top, top players in different ways.

Along with his mate Iker Casillas, Raúl was the undisputed darling of Madrid. He could do no wrong and would be hard to remove. On paper, if we played two up front, which we mostly did, it looked like he and Ronaldo would start. I thought that I was probably third or fourth in line.

In training, this hierarchy often leads to a few mind games. As a striker, you want to play. And to play, you've got to impress the coach. Nobody will admit this, but, in this kind of situation, you do also hope that your rivals train and play crap – especially if you're not in the team.

As much as you always want the team to win, I think a striker is in a unique position in that there's more scope for selfishness. You've got to do your job, first and foremost. To be a really top striker, you have to feel that way. If we lost 3-1 I'd be absolutely gutted that we'd lost. However, there was always a part of me that felt, even in a 3-1 defeat, if I scored the one goal, I'd still think, *well, at least I did my job.*

It's not easy to admit that – but I'd be lying if I didn't. On reflection, wherever I went, I was as self-centred as a player could possibly be – while still being a team player. It wasn't because I was selfish – but because, more than most, I was driven to be the best.

However, in the very first La Liga game of that season, away at Real Mallorca, I got some assistance when Raúl got injured. The coach signalled to me to get ready while Morientes sat there. I thought, *aye-aye – looks like I am third in line, here.*

Better still, having got on for my Real Madrid debut, I set up Ronaldo for the winner in a 1-0 win. A bit of misfortune for someone else gave me some much-needed momentum – sometimes that's what football is about. And when these chances come along, you grab them with both hands.

And I did.

As much as I played, I also scored more regularly than people remember also. At one point I seem to remember that I had a club record for goals in consecutive games under threat. I scored against Dynamo Kyiv in the Champions League, followed by goals against Valencia, Getafe, Málaga, and Albacete in La Liga. I added one more against CD Leganés in the Copa Del Rey. I was banging them in.

My enduring memory of my first experience of El Clásico, away in the Nou Camp in November, was travelling to the stadium. Never in my life had I navigated such a hostile atmosphere. Anything that happens in England before derby games pales in comparison to Spain. I quickly got a sense of the scale of the dislike between the two clubs.

For at least the last two miles before we reached the stadium, it would be no exaggeration to say that twenty bricks and fifty bottles were lashed into the windows. Inevitably the glass shattered and half the players ended up huddled into the centre aisle of the bus. It wasn't just boos and whistles – it was really serious stuff.

At that stage, Barcelona, under Frank Rijkaard, were starting to become dominant. Among others, they had the likes of Ronaldinho and Samuel Eto'o in their line-up. There was also a young lad called Lionel Messi. Of course, in 2005, there's no doubt that Lionel wasn't quite the finished article he now is. He was small and skilful no doubt, but by no means were teams being forced to compose a strategy specifically to negate him at that time. He was just one of several very good players in that Barcelona team.

Obviously, we all know that that situation changed with time. I have no doubt in my mind that he and Cristiano Ronaldo – the best two players that have ever played the game – changed football. What's more, because they played in the same era, I think they have spurred each other on to greater things each week.

Who's the better of the two? People ask me that question all the time and it's not an easy one to answer. If pushed, I would probably say that, as amazing as Messi is, Cristiano Ronaldo perhaps ticks a few extra boxes.

Firstly, he clearly has the edge in physicality. Secondly, he's won major honours internationally by dragging an average team across the line. And finally, he's succeeded in multiple countries whereas Messi has only dominated in Spain. Could he have gone to Italy or England and done the same thing? We may never know.

Regardless, we're really splitting hairs. They are two absolutely outstanding players – and their achievements and status only make my Ballon d'Or spin that little bit slower in my trophy room. I'm honoured to have won the same award when I consider what those two have done.

Anyway, we got a 3-0 thumping that night in the Nou Camp. I remember coming off the bench to replace David Beckham after fifty five minutes at which point we were already 2-0 down. I had an effort that hit the roof of the net but that was my sole contribution in a game that Barcelona absolutely dominated.

The second game that season – months later at the Bernabeu – was altogether different. Leading up to the game, a decision was made by our coach at that time, Vanderlei Luxemburgo, to change our shape. Shape, in general, wasn't something we spent much time on at Real Madrid. Our shape didn't really change from game to game.

Furthermore, it was understood that the lads knew this shape inside out anyway and at the very most, there was usually only one or two changes to the team each week. We had eight or nine Galactico players that would never be dropped.

Early in that week, however, the coach told us the starting team. And to my surprise, I was in it. The strange thing was, he had me in there as a sort of right-winger/right-sided midfielder. To say that I was a little bit sceptical would be an understatement. Aside from the occasional time as a kid, I had never played that position, nor did I particularly understand it.

'Go and join the centre forward,' coach Luxemburgo told me, 'but *start* on the right-hand side,' he added.

As much as I understood the enormity of the occasion, and as much as I'm not normally a nervous person, it might have helped that, at the start of the game, a lot of my headspace was being occupied by the act of thinking about the position I was playing and where I needed to be at different stages.

I needn't have worried. The game itself was just fabulous. We had so much energy; the system was working. We were closing down; I was able to pin my side down. In general the change of shape was a great move by the coach and we ran out comfortable 4-2 winners. I scored the fourth after a ball over the top from David Beckham.

I had a significant moment after the game as I sat in the players' lounge after the match with the family. As much as scoring in a game like El Clásico was a highlight, the image of the scoreboard on the wall with the six goalscorers' names on it felt even more satisfying: Zidane, Raúl, Ronaldo, Ronaldinho, Eto'o and Owen.

I've never been one for being overawed by a situation I've found myself in. I've never felt that I don't belong in one either. Whatever level I reached, I always felt confident that I should be there and knew how to carry myself as if I expected it.

There were doubts in my mind when I left Liverpool to go to Madrid – I've never minded admitting that. But when I saw my name up there alongside arguably five of the world's greatest players, I couldn't help feeling very satisfied, even vindicated. It wasn't a giddy happiness I was feeling. It was much more of a 'have some of that!' emotion. There I was in the Bernabeu players' lounge having just scored in El Clásico. All I could think was, *that's why I came here…*

Not everything was perfect in Madrid, however. On the family front, life was continually very trying.

As strange and perhaps defeatist as this might sound, almost as soon as we arrived in Spain, I instinctively had this sense that my time there was going to be short. Sometimes you just *know* – and I should stress that none of this is any reflection on Real Madrid as a club or the people of Spain. Everybody bent over backwards to help us right from the start.

The thing is, we had gone out to Spain with a set of preconceived expectations: beaches, palm trees, swimming pools and so on.

I remember thinking, *how could we not love it?*

That, of course, was just idealistic fantasy. The reality was somewhat different. Our Madrid existence was functional.

From mid-August, the club put us up in a hotel while we tried to find a house. It was a business hotel, which I've no doubt that Real Madrid got great rates on, and we were obviously given a very nice room.

But the two of us existing in one room, with a young daughter who was at the age where she needed to be entertained, would have been difficult enough for one month. But one month became two, and then two became four.

Our typical day would be to get up at seven, go downstairs for breakfast, and then I'd leave at eight for training in the one car we had in Spain.

Thereafter, Louise was stuck in this hotel in a business district, in the middle of summer, with a young daughter, not speaking the language, until I came back from training at around two.

I can't even imagine how tough it was – but the ten missed calls and the texts saying 'are you on your way home?' on my phone when I finished training every day, was enough of a clue. It quickly became a strain on everybody, me included.

At Liverpool I'd been focused entirely on football. I lived and breathed it, every day of my life. The most important decision that entered my head was, *how am I going to play my best for Liverpool tomorrow? Or in a week's time. Or next month…*

In Madrid, the dynamic was completely different. I was trying to please everybody. On one hand Ronaldo would be saying: 'Let's go for nine holes of golf after training …'

Obviously, for me it was important to sometimes say yes and to get in with the lads. On the other I'd be feeling awfully guilty because I knew that, while I was making plans, Louise and Gemma were stuck without transport in the hotel.

More often than not, I'd be frantically speeding back to see them and, of course, they'd be sitting on the hotel steps waiting – 'Daddy's back!'

On the days where I didn't do anything with the other players, having already done a full day of training, I might have wanted to put my feet up a bit. But because they'd been cooped up in my absence, my day was just *beginning* when I finished my work at Real Madrid.

So we went out, went to the zoo, drove to parks, drove to carousels, ice-cream parlours and whatever else. I must have been to that zoo fifty times – and that was just in August!

Given the well-known Spanish mentality of mañana, by the time we found a house and moved into it, Christmas was upon us. The problem was, having endured the sickening mundanity of hotel life for so long, Louise was ready to chuck it all in and go back to England before we even started actually living in Spain like a normal family!

As much as we ended up living close to David and Victoria Beckham and were two English families living abroad in the same city, there wasn't much in the way of social life as far as them and us were concerned.

Given that both Louise and Victoria were quite lonely and were both looking after young kids, they'd occasionally see each other while we were training. That was the extent of the friendship, however. It never evolved into a situation where we'd do something together as two complete families. There was always a distance.

This perhaps wasn't a surprise given that, by the time we found ourselves at Madrid together, David and I had even less in common than we ever had. I was a footballer and a family man who was reluctant to put myself in the public spotlight unless I absolutely had to. I certainly didn't like wearing the latest trendy gear or mingling among socialite company. Louise was exactly the same.

David and Victoria on the other hand, were *both* bona fide superstars in their own right. They'd be flying to premieres in London, he'd be modelling – they were operating on a completely different stratosphere from a social perspective. As much as he and I talked and would sit together on the team coach, I never once got the impression that I was on the inner, inner circle of David's group of friends.

I also knew that the same applied to many of the lads he'd left behind at Manchester United. As much as David could be with the Giggsy, Scholesy and Nev types whenever he needed to be, he was always the odd one out in those latter days at Old Trafford.

Where they'd be going out for a few pints after a game, David would quite often be getting on a plane to France or such like. They all liked him, and vice versa, but they lived completely different lives – a fact that wasn't lost on Alex Ferguson at the time, who seemingly grew frustrated with the lifestyle David was living.

Looking back on my time in Madrid, as much as it was only a year, it often didn't feel like it. On some levels, primarily because of the off-field tension, that year felt much longer than it actually was.

Everything took longer in Spain – even getting paid. This strange feature of Real Madrid was one that I wasn't aware of when I first arrived. In England, and I believe in most other football countries, players are paid monthly. Although the salary is described as being weekly, four multiples of that weekly number would appear in your bank account at the end of each month.

In Madrid, they paid us six-monthly. So for six months, literally no euros appeared in your bank account. You played, you trained, you lived, you ate; you went to the zoo a hundred times – while literally no money arrived.

Then, around Christmas time, a couple of million quid lands in your bank account in one fell swoop. This was apparently the Madrid way – and it had been for many years. Nevertheless, it was a little disconcerting.

Equally disconcerting, and simultaneously one of the funnier/sadder things that happened in Madrid, was the appearance of a certain somebody I knew.

Before training one morning, one of the Madrid office staff came back to the dressing room to find me.

'There's somebody out front to see you,' I was told.

'Oh, yeah?' I said, 'who's that?'

'Paul Gascoigne.'

Initially, I thought I was being wound up. I thought, *why on earth would Gazza be here in Madrid?*

To rewind slightly, back in 2002, while I was still at Liverpool, I remember receiving a call from an unknown number when I was driving back home from Melwood. I thought about ignoring it, but I answered anyway.

'Alright Michael? It's Gazza speaking,' the voice on the other end said.

I'm quite gullible as it goes, but even I was still doubtful whether this was, in fact, Paul Gascoigne. As it turned out, it was indeed him – and he had a favour to ask. He was an Everton player at that time.

'It's my daughter's birthday,' he explained, 'and you're her favourite player. Could I come round later tonight so she could meet you?'

As bizarre a request as it was, I agreed and told him to come around in a few hours. Meanwhile, I phoned my mum and dad and my brothers and sisters. 'Gazza's coming round later,' I told them, 'You should come round as well!'

Sure enough, later that evening, there was a knock on the door and there stood Gazza with his whole family. I invited them in for a cup of tea and offered to sign something for her birthday and take a photograph or two.

Six hours later, his daughter was sound asleep on the sofa. Meanwhile, Gazza and I were still playing table tennis and snooker into the early hours of the morning. I couldn't have got rid of him even if I'd wanted to. He was hilarious company. None of us could believe what was happening.

So, fast-forwarding a couple of years with that late night bonding session a pleasant but distant memory, I walked into the reception area at Real Madrid and there, in front of me, was Gazza. When I looked closer, he was carrying a pair of football boots.

I won't deny that, given how slow I can be on the uptake, I thought, for just a split second: *What? Have we signed him?*

Then reality kicked in again when I rationalised with myself that, as good as he had once been, there was no way that Real Madrid would have signed Paul Gascoigne in 2005.

Then I thought, *maybe he's here to just train with us?*

Really, that made no sense either. The club would not have entertained that either.

I thought, *so why is he here?*

Sadly, I still don't really have an answer.

All I can say is that Gazza didn't seem to be in the most stable frame of mind. As much as it was great to see him, in such odd circumstances, there was something incredibly sad and poignant about the image of one of my all-time heroes standing there in the front reception of the Bernabeu holding his football boots.

We had a brief conversation and I could tell that he perhaps wasn't thinking too rationally. I could be wrong but it felt to me as if he just wanted to show the other people in reception that he knew me. Maybe he felt that by doing so he'd be legitimising himself and that they would allow him to train? I really don't know; I'm just surmising. I had to then go back to the dressing room and I left saying that I'd see him when I came out later. As it turned out, when I re-emerged, Gazza had gone, leaving no explanation.

I'm sure I've seen him since and I certainly didn't mention that day to him. He never mentioned it either. I still have no idea why he was in Madrid.

REBØOT_13

LOSING CONTROL

Newcastle manager Graeme Souness called me roughly every two weeks for almost the entire year I was in Spain and I can't deny that I liked the attention – particularly from someone with such standing within the game. Whether he thought I was unsettled or not, I have no idea.

But there's no doubt that, being away and being told that someone back home thought so highly of me, gave me a real feeling of comfort – particularly while the atmosphere was a little tense at our home at the time because we all missed England.

Looking back, I honestly just think that Graeme was taking a punt. He would have probably thought, with a World Cup at the end of the following season, that I'd want to be playing regular games. That was a reasonable enough assessment given that I was starting probably just more than fifty per cent of the time at Madrid.

As the year wore on, he'd call me and say things like: 'Michael, I see you didn't start last weekend. Would you think about coming back to Newcastle?'

Now that I've lived life a bit and done business in my post-career, while I don't think I led Graeme on, with hindsight I might have handled his first phone call differently.

Instead of straight-out saying: 'If I come back to England, I'll only be going back to Liverpool' – which was how I felt – I think I said: 'I'll come back to the Premier League and I'll look at my options when the time is right.' If I have any regrets in my career, declaring this stance at that moment would be one of the major ones.

By saying what I did, I suppose I gave him a chink of light. Graeme had been around football long enough to recognise when someone was hedging their bets. To him, I'm sure there was a sense that I was more open to other possibilities than I actually was. I put that entirely down to my dislike of giving anybody bad news.

Although I didn't know him personally, I respected Graeme Souness hugely, not only as an experienced manager, but also as one of the greatest Liverpool players ever. To that extent, I could never have just cut him off and said: 'Sorry, I'm not interested in playing for you.' I just wanted to be polite.

The reality was, towards the end of my year in Madrid, I'd made up my mind that I was coming back to the Premier League. I'd loved most aspects of my time there. I'd played well and really enjoyed the people, the club and Spain generally. But as a family, we were homesick. Mentally, I was leaving. Contractually, we still had to make it happen.

To that end, the wheels went into motion for me to return to Liverpool as the season in Madrid ended. I flew over at some point in the closed season to discuss the options with the club and I'm pretty sure that the press had got wind of these plans in advance. How, I have no idea.

Obviously then, I couldn't just waltz into Melwood for a meeting as the press would have cottoned on and descended upon us. Instead, we decided to meet at a neutral venue, which turned out to be Bruno Cheyrou's home in Liverpool.

In my absence, his wife had become friendly with my sister, Lesley, so we arranged a meeting at his house – a private place with gates – and unknown to the press, that included me, Rafa Benitez, Rick Parry and Tony Stephens.

Initially, we all chatted like friends in the lounge. Then I stayed and sat with Rafa in the lounge while Rick and Tony split off to talk independently in the dining room. We spoke about football; they talked about how the numbers could work.

As far as I was concerned, both conversations went very well. Rafa said he wanted me and we left on the understanding that Liverpool would take me back on considerably lesser personal terms than those that I'd left on a year earlier.

It's important to say that, when Tony double-checked this detail with me, I was absolutely fine with it. I just wanted to go back to Liverpool and for everything to be how it used to be. It wasn't about money. *Whatever it takes,* I thought. The transfer fee itself would be left to the two clubs to agree at a later date.

Then you could say that my diplomatic response to Graeme Souness's spirited pursuit came back to bite me.

Right at the beginning of the 2005/06 season in Madrid (the English season had already been running for a few weeks by this stage) the President of Real Madrid, Florentino Pérez, knocked on my hotel room door one day while we were preparing for a game.

'Newcastle has made a bid in the region of sixteen million pounds,' he told me, 'If you want to go, then you can go. If you want to stay, you can stay.'

For all the reasons already mentioned, my staying at Madrid really wasn't a viable option. I would have been very lonely and Louise wouldn't have been able to endure being away from friends and family any longer.

'But I want to go to Liverpool,' I told him.

I'd be being dishonest at this point if I didn't admit that the heroics of Istanbul were weighing on my mind. As much as I was delighted for all my mates that had lifted the cup, on a personal level I wasn't just disappointed – I was jealous. I know that doesn't sound great, but that's how it felt. Had they won it five years after I left, that would have been one thing, but the very next season? That was tough to take.

'That's not possible unless they match Newcastle's offer,' he said.

At the time, that statement was a dagger in the heart. I was being presented with two options – neither of which I particularly fancied.

Looking back now, Madrid's position was perfectly understandable I suppose. Football is business after all. But for the naïve people out there who think footballers always call the shots, this is an example of a scenario where I just didn't have a choice.

The truth of the matter is that once someone employs you, and as much as you always try to do things by the book, sometimes you're at the mercy of whatever business move your employer has to make for the best interests of that club. I totally accept this to be fair.

Football fans, however – particularly those who always

blindly side with their club regardless – need to realise that things aren't always rosy for a player. Sometimes the tide is against them, but that side of the story isn't always heard.

For example, in this case, I knew that Real Madrid needed the proceeds from my sale to buy Sergio Ramos from Sevilla. Knowing this, I felt that, with the right offer for me on the table, I might have a bit of leverage with Pérez. I also knew fully well that the gap between eight and sixteen million was just too big.

I needed Liverpool to come a little closer to give me some kind of bargaining position with Madrid. At say twelve million, I thought that I'd have some kind of playable hand in what was becoming a game of poker.

In my mind, I figured that if Liverpool could have gone to twelve million, I could have sat tight at Madrid, knowing that they needed the proceeds of my sale, and said: 'It's Liverpool or nothing.' I would have, I suppose, risked staying at Madrid for another season but that was a chance I was prepared to take.

Thinking, *I can't go to Newcastle; I can't stay here. I've got to go to Liverpool,* I phoned the main man himself, Rick Parry, in a state of absolute panic.

I had to hear it from the horse's mouth.

'We can't, Michael. We sold you for eight million, we simply can't go higher than ten,' he said.

His words absolutely sank me.

That, I suppose, was that.

Although the news felt like a second, longer, dagger in the heart, again, looking back, I see why he took this position. Liverpool were already making something of a concession by offering more than they'd sold me for a year prior.

Furthermore, with the benefit of even more hindsight, it actually feels like Rick helped me in a way. Receiving the news was a bit like how I'd imagine someone might feel when an ex says that they don't want him or her any more. It hurts, but at least the rejected party can move on.

For me, it removed lingering doubts and gave me clarity. At ten million, I knew I had no hand to play. And I'm not even certain whether Madrid would have accepted twelve. I'll never know.

Meanwhile, in the background, my agent was telling me that he thought a move to Newcastle was the right thing to do. I wasn't so sure.

At the time, I just couldn't escape that fact that Newcastle weren't a top Premier League team. From a career perspective, there was no doubt in my mind that a move to the North East was a downward step.

The way I saw it, I'd played well for one of the world's biggest clubs. Now I was faced with the reality of going to a club that had never won anything and was in the relegation zone in the Premier League after four or five games. By going, I was undoubtedly lowering my level. As unpalatable as that opinion might be to Newcastle fans, that's more or less what I felt.

Inevitably, there were also aspects of a move to Newcastle that did appeal to me. Life isn't always black and white – no pun intended.

Firstly, I saw my relationship with Alan Shearer as one of the positives. Knowing about Graeme Souness' contact with me, Alan himself had weighed in by encouraging me to consider coming to St. James' Park to continue what had been a successful strike partnership with England.

I could see that point – and I also liked the idea of going up there to potentially be a hero at a club with a loyal fanbase not dissimilar to that of Liverpool's. The move wasn't devoid of attractions. And it's important to say, again, that money was not at the forefront of my mind.

'This is such a strong position from which to negotiate,' Tony Stephens told me. 'We can build a buyout clause into the four-year contract that says, after each year, you have an option to go back to Liverpool at a price that reduces incrementally each year by four million pounds.'

That concept pricked my ears. In my mind, I saw myself as probably having to spend one year at Newcastle in order to get back to Liverpool. And no part of me felt bad about going there on that basis. As I've said, football is business – and the aim is to structure everything to work in the player's favour. That's why agents exist.

I just thought, *this is the only way…*

A fee was then agreed, after which I flew back to the UK to my home to do a medical, which was arranged to take place at Nuffield Hospital near Newcastle with only a day or two left in the fast-closing transfer window.

Meanwhile, Newcastle wanted to send their chairman Freddy Shepherd and the chief executive down in person to my house to sign the contract – with the club photographer in tow to document it all, with me wearing a club shirt with Owen on the back of it. Everything was moving unsettlingly fast.

Having landed on one afternoon in early August 2005, there I was, with a Newcastle convoy due to make its way down south the following morning. I thought to myself, *it's going to happen tomorrow …*

Let's just say I was getting increasingly cold feet about the whole idea. That evening, I sat there on the sofa, mentally pacing the room in turmoil, surrounded by my wife, my mum and dad, my tax advisor and Simon Marsh from Umbro.

It should be said that Simon had never wanted me to go to Newcastle in the first place. Purely from a business standpoint, with me as their lead asset, it did less for the Umbro brand if I was playing at a club with no European involvement.

At one point previously, Simon had even gone to the length of calling Liverpool and offering to cover a couple of million of the shortfall in the form of a loan, but Liverpool wouldn't accept it – who knows why not?

Sitting there in this group, the night before I was due to put pen to paper, we basically took a vote between us around the table. And the general consensus was that going to Newcastle was the best career decision. Unfortunately, by this stage, I was not one of those in favour of the move. I'd changed my mind in line with Simon Marsh. But Louise, my mum and dad, my agent and my tax advisor were all for it.

As much as I had said yes and flown back with the contractual caveat in place stating that I'd have various opportunities to leave, once I actually got home and had to face the cold reality of the situation, I simply couldn't ignore the voice in my head that was telling me that I was just too good a player at that time to sign for Newcastle United. I strongly felt that I belonged at Champions League-level clubs.

Faced with this potentially embarrassing U-turn, I went to bed conflicted by my own reservations, offset by the fact that many of the key people in my life disagreed with me.

Suffice to say, it was not a peaceful night. At three o'clock in the morning, having tossed and turned around fitfully for a while, I got on my phone to Tony Stephens.

'I can't go through with it. It just doesn't feel right,' I told him. I'll always remember what he said in response.

'Michael, I hear what you're saying. I will tell the car to turn around, but it's going to kill me in a reputational sense. I've given them my word because you told me you would go. I think you're making a big mistake.'

As if to punctuate everything, he then added: 'And it's a massive deal.'

If I was thinking only of the money, Newcastle blew everyone out of the water. That was indisputable. They were offering me a hundred and twenty grand a week. Nice work if you can get it, people will think. I believe Andriy Shevchenko and maybe Frank Lampard were the only other players on six figure salaries at that time. In addition, they were offering me a box at St. James' Park and a house with full staff.

But, as strong a position as I was in, it wasn't about the financial perks. For me, it was never about cash. I'd moved to Madrid for less than I was on at Liverpool. It was always about career for me.

After talking to Tony and going back to sleep, when I woke up again at around eight I was still adamant that I wasn't going. Meanwhile the convoy was halfway down the road apparently. I picked up the phone again.

'Tony. *Tell* them to turn around. I'm not signing,' I said.

It wasn't as if I was thinking that I'd just have to go back to Madrid at this stage. In fact I wasn't thinking clearly about any repercussions or alternatives at all – only that I couldn't go through with signing for Newcastle.

Maybe part of me was thinking subconsciously, deluded perhaps, that someone else would come in for me. But the harsh reality was that nobody else was even on the radar.

By this point I was sure I was just pissing Tony off – I could tell that by the strain in his voice. All he could do was reiterate what he'd told me already by reinforcing the clauses on the contract that worked in my favour.

At nine-thirty that morning they arrived. While they were in transit, there was still every chance that I'd pull out. When they physically *arrived* at my house, I was resigned to the fact that it was happening. No Newcastle fan will particularly want to hear this but, as this book is about truth, that's the honest truth. This, I should say, was not a reflection on Newcastle United specifically. I would have found a reason not to sign with any club that wasn't Liverpool.

As if I needed any more confirmation that this less than ideal career move was happening, they gave me the shirt and the photographer positioned me in my back garden. Once that first snap of me in a Newcastle shirt was taken, it was over.

I thought *that's it…*

The irony of all of this is that, once I actually arrived in Newcastle for the first time, all the excitement that came with being a record signing at a club with such a passionate fanbase started counter-balancing my earlier reservations.

The day after signing, the club flew me up to be greeted by twenty thousand delighted fans at St. James' Park. Instantly, I felt like a hero. There was a warm-up game not long after my arrival and there was a league game ten days away at home to Fulham. Everything felt so imminent, so exciting.

As match day approached, I could feel a level of expectation being heaped on me that I hadn't experienced for a while. I wanted to prove to the fans that I was worthy of being their record signing. Before long, I felt that – although it wasn't my dream move – things could potentially be great at Newcastle on a number of fronts.

As it turned out, I didn't score on my debut, a 1-1 draw at home to Fulham. But the following week, both Alan Shearer and I scored in a 3-0 win away at Blackburn. Five more goals followed in subsequent away games at West Brom and then at West Ham. I felt wanted and I liked it. And I was off to an absolute flier.

Meanwhile, it was great to see Louise so happy too given how miserable she'd been during the previous year in Spain. Newcastle initially offered us an enormous stately home, owned by the Shepherds, I believe, somewhere on the outskirts of the city. I can't recall exactly where. It was stunning – and the club would be picking up the tab for everything, we were told.

While I could possibly have seen myself as the pseudo country gent, out in the woods, Louise was considerably less enamoured. We both eventually admitted that the house was a beautiful but nevertheless very creepy place to live – with various stuffed animals staring at us from every wall being one of the more off-putting features. In a nutshell, it just wasn't what we were used to and there was no way Louise would have stayed there alone.

So, in the short term, we moved in with Alan Shearer and his wife for a couple of weeks while I trained and Louise did the rounds with the estate agents, looking for somewhere more to our liking to rent – that's how matey Alan and I were.

I'd grown up admiring Alan as a player. When I was

developing as a player between the ages of ten and sixteen, he was the main man – banging goals in left, right and centre.

Then, before I knew it, he and I were England strike partners. Thereafter, our friendship only flourished. We both liked golf and racing – he'd even eventually own horses at my racing stables. In 2005, we got on really well; me being at Newcastle was perfect.

However, not wanting to outstay Alan's kind hospitality, we then moved into a hotel for a short while until Louise eventually found a house to rent – which was again, a little remote, ten miles past Darras Hall village up a track that led into the wilderness.

The house itself was huge, and was surrounded by a mini-estate of a few smaller properties, once of which was Steve Stone's place. For Louise and me, with Gemma being almost of infant school age and us having dogs, it worked out fine. And remember, in the back of my mind, I was probably still thinking, *I'll only be here for a year before I can go back to Liverpool.*

What appealed to me also was that this came with quite a bit of land. I immediately thought, *that'd be perfect to land a helicopter. We could fly virtually house to house from our home if need be.*

I knew when I agreed to write this book that there would be a few issues I couldn't avoid discussing. And that bloody helicopter was one of them! It was, after all, one of the main sticks that Newcastle supporters have enjoyed beating me with over the years.

With hindsight, it probably didn't look great to fly around in a helicopter – or land it on Newcastle's training ground on Christmas Day, as I once did in response to a dare by the lads.

I landed it right in the centre-circle of the artificial pitch because a bunch of them said it would be a laugh. I felt like an idiot; stunts like that weren't my style.

But the truth is, the whole idea of a helicopter was completely innocent and entirely designed to make it easy for Louise, Gemma and my parents to come up and see me and watch games – while still retaining the day-to-day relationships they all had back at home. It was a *family* decision.

In no way was I trying to be a flash prick by flaunting the considerable salary I was getting in the faces of the hard-working fans. Nor, as some have speculated, was it because I didn't want to live in Newcastle. That's how it was taken, but none of that was the intention. I loved Newcastle and the people, and I still owned a house there until relatively recently. I rented it to Hatem Ben Arfa until he left the club!

The helicopter just made sense at the time. Having come back from Spain where we'd missed family and friends, I was probably moaning to Tony Stephens at some point before I signed about how difficult it would be for the family to travel back and forth to the North East to see me play once or twice a week. Tony said: 'If it's such a big deal why don't you just buy a bloody helicopter?' *Fair point,* I thought.

And that's what I did. The helicopter was the perfect compromise, and we all used it at various times to travel up and down whenever it suited.

If I had time off coming up, I might call the pilot, Mark, twenty four hours in advance, to arrange to go home for a day and a half – particularly after Louise and Gemma moved back home permanently after two years when the time came for Gemma to start school. It was a forty-five minute trip, usually with the wind at our back on the way east to Newcastle.

The funny thing is, not only did my family and I use this helicopter, various other players were very happy to have access to it too throughout my time at the club. Strangely, none of that made the headlines, or riled the fans.

Alan Shearer seemed to be very happy to rent it to take his mates up to Loch Lomond to play golf a few times a year. All very convenient. Kieron Dyer used to fly home on it; Nicky Butt used to get a lift home with me on it. I used to drop him at a little aerodrome at Barton near his house regularly!

We used to joke about him never getting any stick about it when all I heard was, '*Oh, Michael Owen's got a bloody helicopter.*' I love Nicky, but he was in that helicopter as much as I was.

I don't know what I would have done without that helicopter but it's just one of those things that, when things are going well, it doesn't get mentioned. However, if anything goes wrong, it's inevitable that it becomes a stick to beat you with. That's really all there is to say about it.

■■ ■■■■■ ■ ■

Meanwhile, back on the pitch, my and the team's good form continued up until the Christmas period of 2005. I banged in goals, we climbed the league table; the manager Graeme Souness, who I liked a lot incidentally, worked his magic.

As soon as I signed, I knew immediately that he was my type of manager. He was hard, he was a good judge of character and he didn't suffer fools. Better still, he liked me and was always willing to share stories about his colourful career – usually in the medical room after training.

For some reason, medical rooms at football clubs are often the focus of social activities. At Newcastle there always seemed to be half a dozen lads in there. After training you'd have a shower, maybe go into the canteen and then on the way out you'd poke your head around the medical room door to get anti-inflammatories or such like.

Inside, something resembling a mother's meeting would usually be in progress – normally involving Souness, Dean Saunders (cracking lad, I should say too) and the team doctor, Ian McGuinness, who was also a top man. I just loved going in there, passing a bit of time, cracking a few jokes and hearing Graeme talk about events and characters from the past.

On reflection, as much as the game and players are always changing, I really welcomed Souness's old-school approach. Was he as intimidating as is often said? I'm sure he could have been. But I personally never really saw that side. The only hint I ever got was at a game away at Wigan once when he was so incensed with our first half performance that he launched an entire tray of plates at a wall in the half time interval. Suffice to say, we paid attention afterwards.

In general, though, between us I think there was a mutual, unspoken respect that perhaps only players who have both reached the top of the game can share. I liked Graeme; he liked me. That relationship really smoothed my first few months in the North East.

By the time we came to play Tottenham at White Hart Lane on New Year's Eve, 2005, life couldn't have been better. Then I went into a challenge with goalkeeper Paul Robinson and my world collapsed.

Looking back on it, part of me thinks I should have hurdled him. I was probably never going to score anyway because he was smothering the chance. I could have thought, *don't risk it, Michael. Don't get injured…*

Instead, because I got to the ball a fraction of a second before he did, I went through with it thinking, *can I score here?*

That was my striker's instinct at work. The only conceivable finish in such a situation would have been to dink him. I couldn't possibly go round him; he was right on top of me. And so with a small part of me still thinking I could somehow score, I then toed it into him whereupon he landed on my right foot, I think with his knee.

I felt a crunch straightaway. I knew my foot was broken. The ball, meanwhile, had skewed away sideways somewhere and/or somebody cleared it. The next sound I heard was the half time whistle. Walking off with a limp, it was clear to everyone, our physio included, that I was badly hurt.

When I made it into the dressing room and removed my football boot, the side of my foot had swollen up significantly. Before I knew it, my foot was in a protective boot and I was being taken for an X-ray that would ultimately reveal a fracture in my fifth metatarsal.

Even before that confirmation, everyone knew what this meant: two months out of the game at the very least. In the context of the club's resurgent situation and my cracking start scoring goals, this news was a disaster.

As much of a momentum killer as it was, I was reasonably philosophical about the injury itself.

I'd never had a bone injury before; it wasn't like I had weak bones that were prone to breaking. It was just a totally freak occurrence that could have happened to anyone.

Plus, I'd done it playing for Newcastle, going in where it hurts while trying to score a goal. It was just one of those things, and there was no criticism from the fans whatsoever that I was aware of.

In January, with the World Cup in Germany in June, it didn't even enter my head that there was a possibility of missing the tournament. In fact, at that point, I was only thinking about getting fit to play for Newcastle as quickly as possible and I worked out that I'd probably be back some time in March.

When we looked at the injury in detail with John Hodgkinson, my specialist, we were told that there were a couple of options by way of treatment. I could have it screwed, which simply brings the fractured pieces together with a two-inch piece of metal. Alternatively, we could leave the fracture to knit together of its own accord.

The problem, I was told, with the latter, less invasive option was that there was no way of predicting how long the healing process might take. The speed depended on how long the two fractured parts took to calcify and reconnect. How long is a piece of string, basically.

'I can't tell you if you'll be back in two months or four,' John told us.

Although having an operation to have it screwed came with the usual risks attached: it was intrusive, painful, could cause a potential infection and all the rest of it, there was at least a guarantee that I'd be back playing in a set time period – probably three months to be on the safe side. At least it wasn't open-ended guesswork.

After discussing it together, the club and I, we decided to go for the safer option of getting it screwed – a procedure that I had done not long afterwards down in Manchester. Thereafter, I had to go to back to Manchester for X-ray check-ups every fortnight to measure the stability of the healing process.

Six weeks in, I was supposed to be at a stage where I could jog comfortably. The problem was, it was really uncomfortable. I understood very well the challenges of coming back from a metatarsal break.

These bones, particularly the fifth (outside) one, are naturally very flexible. After surgery, however, having been strengthened with metal, there's obviously an expectation that there might be a feeling of rigidity and some disconcerting discomfort because of that.

But this felt different. I was getting the kind of pain that made me stop and think, *this isn't right*. Although all the medical experts were saying that some pain was to be expected, I knew that there was something wrong, but still pushed through.

One day I was at an open training session for fans at St. James' Park. I'd just started my recovery proper; I was jogging at half pace and going through the warm-up with the other lads before they went into the harder stuff without me. We were playing a game of keepy-ups: 'whoever drops it gets a flick on the ear' type of thing.

The ball came to me and I dropped it. But I didn't agree that it was my fault – more that it was a shit ball! As everyone walked up to me to give me my punishment, I pushed off for two or three strides just so I could buy myself some time to protest my case – 'I'm not having that, lads!'

As I did, I felt another clunk in my foot like the one I felt at White Hart Lane. Immediately I thought, *I've done it again …*

I said to the physio, 'I think I've done my bloody foot again.'

The following day, we went down to Manchester for a check and, to everyone's surprise, visually there was nothing really amiss. All we could see on the X-ray was that there was still a tiny gap.

The injury certainly hadn't re-fractured in training but perhaps something had just shifted. At this point we were all starting to panic a little. With the season ending in May and a World Cup looming, I was keen to get a sense of how long it would be until I could get back into full training.

'Listen,' the doctor said, 'this is going to heal. But again, looking at it here, it could still be another three months.'

This wasn't what I wanted to hear. As it stood, I was probably missing the World Cup.

There was, however, another option. They could go in again, remove the existing screw and then tighten a new one in its place – the aim being to achieve a bit more grip on the bone surface which would, in turn, pull the break closer together.

If we did this, I was told, I'd be back playing in something like eight weeks. Doing my calculations on that basis, I figured that I could be back in time to play the last couple of games of the season.

At this point I thought I should call Sven-Göran Eriksson to keep him up to date with what was happening. Given that I was in the guts of my England career and doing really well, I thought I owed it to him to keep him informed. I certainly didn't want him to find out that I'd had operations without telling him.

I called, explained the situation and the options that had been laid out in terms of how they might affect my availability for England. He was in agreement with the idea of a second operation. 'As long as you're fit and healthy, Michael,' he said, 'There'll be pre-World Cup games to break you back in.'

I thought, *I've just got to do it.*

Newcastle United agreed. They were as concerned as I was and wanted the best outcome for me. I had the second operation in late February or early March, and then my foot was back in a plaster cast/pot again for another six weeks.

By this time, after a string of what were considered to be poor results, Graeme Souness had been sacked and replaced by Glenn Roeder (with the recently retired Alan Shearer brought in as his assistant), an illustration of how hot a seat the Newcastle managerial job will always be.

This time the rehab went much more smoothly in a healing sense, but it wasn't until the second last game of the season that I was able to come on as a sub against Birmingham on April 29th.

While I wasn't entirely match fit, I could still feel discomfort in my foot and my leg muscles were considerably de-trained because my leg had been in a plaster cast for pretty much twelve weeks, at least I was there, showing that I could be out there running around on a pitch.

I was grateful for small mercies. I could play football again.

REBØOT_14

MIXED SIGNALS

Unsurprisingly, the 2006 World Cup in Germany is the only major tournament I played in that I'd be quite happy to erase from my memory.

Obviously I'd been injured for the best part of six months in the run-up and even by the time I'd played in a couple of pre-tournament warm-up games against Hungary and Jamaica, both at Old Trafford, you could still look at my two legs and clearly see a huge difference in muscle tone between my right and my left.

Although I scored in the second game, I would never say that I was anywhere close to my best in either of them. I'd just not had enough game time to get back to peak fitness.

At the tournament proper, nothing much changed. I played a quiet fifty-odd minutes against Paraguay in a game we won 1-0 in Frankfurt. In the second game against Trinidad and

Tobago in Nuremberg, we struggled. Crouchy and Stevie scored late to get us out of trouble. Meanwhile, Wayne Rooney replaced me after fifty-six minutes in a 2-0 win.

In neither of those games did I feel as sharp as I wanted to. Being out for so long, combined with a rushed, incomplete rehab made me feel as if I was incapable of going out and taking any of these games by storm. I was just there, happy to be back, but completely undercooked.

And then we played Sweden in the third group game on June 20th in Cologne, and there my tournament came to a premature end after just four minutes.

There are certain very specific things I remember about the events leading up to that injury. Since the foot surgery, I'd probably passed a ball a thousand times during that one month that I was back playing. The muscle memory required to pass a ball and then plant the foot to push off in any given direction was there. I'd done ladder drills in training for that very purpose.

But for some reason, in that game against Sweden, as soon as I passed that ball inside from out on the touchline, it was as if there was, for a split second, absolutely no signal between my brain and my leg. I literally didn't know where to put it.

In what seemed like slow motion, I clearly remember thinking: *my foot is floating.*

Even today, I have no explanation for this. On reflection, I've often wondered whether, deep in my subconscious mind, I was conflicted about what I was going to do.

Did I change my mind? I'm not aware of doing it.

Regardless, I had no idea where to put my foot and when my body went into one position and while my leg was doing something else, everything just buckled and snapped.

Everyone will always tell you that doing your cruciate is one of the most painful things you can ever do. For me, that wasn't the case at all. There was no drama about it whatsoever – just a firm click in my knee, reminiscent of someone snapping their fingers. There was no pain at all to speak of, but I just knew something hard had snapped.

I thought, *that's bad.*

As soon as the physio came on, I told him, 'Something's gone in my knee.'

I was loaded onto a stretcher, straight into the dressing room. And when the physio lifted my knee he confirmed the news that part of me (as unknowledgeable as I was about the various structures in my knee) already suspected – 'you've done your cruciate ligament.'

A scan would confirm it, of course, but any seasoned physio could tell by the instability what the problem was. Louise and my parents meanwhile had come down from the stands to the dressing room to see me. They perfectly understood the gravity of what had just happened. From memory, I hung around the hotel for two more days before flying home. My World Cup was over. Dark days lay ahead.

When you're representing your country, there's obviously a huge emotional attachment to a major tournament, but there's no doubt that this attachment can lessen when you're not directly involved.

As unselfish a person as I like to think that I am, I genuinely believe that that's an entirely human reaction to a situation of this kind. Once you've gone home, it's just not the same. Yes, you care – but you don't think of it like life or death, as you do when you're on the actual pitch.

In any case, in this kind of scenario where an important

player is badly injured, the club always wants that player back as soon as possible to assess the injury further and put a plan in place which would, if required, include booking dates for surgery.

This is what I did. I travelled to Newcastle, and we looked at all the various specialists available. Getting it right was vitally important for my playing future. For Newcastle, there was a valuable asset to protect also. At no point did I ever consider that, at the age of twenty seven, a cruciate injury would be career ending. As bad as it was, I knew I'd be back.

With the physical side of the recovery in motion, from a mental perspective I reconciled quite quickly with the fact that I was probably going to be out of the game for a minimum of six or eight months. In those terms, with some kind of target on the horizon, the outlook was frustrating for sure, but certainly manageable. As usual, I was able to shit-filter any negative thoughts.

Having looked at all the options, we decided that Dr Richard Steadman, based in Vail, Colorado, was the best person for the job. Anyone you asked around that time would have confirmed that he was the best knee specialist available anywhere – not just for the revolving door of injured skiers who no doubt kept him busy in his home town, but also for fellow footballers that I knew like Patrik Berger, Ronaldo and Jamie Redknapp.

I flew over there to Colorado in late July of 2006, and dived deep into the complex world of cruciate ligament surgery.

Before long, under Dr Steadman's guidance, I came to realise that cruciate repairs are basically akin to rather complex carpentry.

They open you up, look at the bits, assess the damage – and then figure out the best way to put it all back together.

Perhaps I'm over simplifying it a little, but that's basically how it seemed to me.

Cruciate surgery, like most fields of sports medicine, has undergone quite a bit of evolution over the years. In the past, specialists have experimented by replacing knee tendons with various kinds of synthetic alternatives. What they found was that, while these replacements were strong and mimicked real material quite effectively, they also caused other problems down the line.

The more recent approach was to either use part of the patient's hamstring, or the middle third of the patella tendon. Those of a squeamish disposition should look away now when I tell you that this section of patella tendon is removed, with a bit of bone on either side, and then used to plug the cruciate ligament damage.

Again, I'm possibly oversimplifying what are probably really complex medical procedures, but this is pretty much how it was described to me at that time.

The upshot of all of this is that, when someone has cruciate surgery, it isn't always just the cruciate ligament that needs rehab afterwards. The 'donor' parts, for want of a better description, also have to recover. After all, if you're taking a third of another knee tendon away, or a big chunk of hamstring – it stands to reason that these both require a recovery programme of their own.

At this point, my history of bad hamstring issues became a governing factor in terms of precise treatment options. The last thing anyone needed to be doing was taking part of a hamstring out of a leg that already had one hamstring gone AWOL somewhere up near my arse cheek.

Consequently, I was expecting to wake up from surgery to

the news that another part of my knee had been used to fix the break. But that's not even what happened …

When I came round after a three hour surgery, I was confronted by Dr Steadman's face looking straight at me.

'Well, Michael,' he said, 'I've got some good news, and some bad news for you.'

In my groggy state I said, 'Eh, right. What's the story then?'

'Well, I haven't actually repaired your cruciate ligament,' he replied.

When he opened my knee up, he'd found that there was damage to my meniscus (the surface of the knee cartilage, basically) that wasn't previously visible on the scan.

'I had to do that operation first,' Dr Steadman explained. 'And I've also prepared your cruciate for when we do it in three months.'

At this point I thought: *So there's no good news, Doctor? Only shit news …*

Because of the conflicting nature of these two injuries from a rehab point of view, where the meniscus needed to be braced static and the ligament needed movement and range as soon as possible, six months out of the game had just become nine. I had great knees, he told me, with no arthritis or damage – better than most athletes he'd treated.

Maybe this was the good news?

But he went on to say that he was in no doubt that the foot injury, and the subsequent de-training of the muscles on my right leg it had caused, was the reason behind why the cruciate had given way. It was a definite chain of events – with the metatarsal break as the catalyst. With that I was stitched up, put in a brace and sent home for three months.

Three months later, I went back to Vail and had the cruciate ligament repair done as scheduled. It was only after that operation that the doctor told me that he initially wanted to use my patella tendon. But then, when he got in there, something made him change his mind in favour using a stronger structure – which turned out to be something quite unexpected.

'The operation went fantastic,' he told me, 'but just to let you know, we ended up using a third-party donor part.'

'Right. That's fine,' I said.

I gave what he said no more thought whatsoever until a few days later when Dr Steadman invited me to his house at the foot of Vail's ski slopes for dinner. Here, he explained to me that the third party part in question was the Achilles tendon that belonged to a person that had died.

'It was a motorcycle accident,' he explained.

Confronted with this kind of news, some people might have been a little unsettled. To me, it was a non-issue. I knew this was how things worked – and I also knew, based on our continuing discussions, that there was a very slight chance that my body could reject the donor tissue while building its own capillary network/cells etc.

Thankfully, this rejection never occurred. In fact, with hindsight, his decision to not weaken another part of my body to fix my knee was a great decision.

Obviously, having been in football all my life, I've met hundreds of people who've had cruciate surgery at one time or another. Very few are total success stories.

Most people get back to somewhere close to where they were prior, but ninety per cent do so having to apply ice after games to quell swelling, or miss one day of training each week, or have to take painkillers all the time or can never again play on an artificial pitch. There's often a price to pay.

In my case, my knee surgery had absolutely no impact on my career thereafter. Yes, I would slow down – but I slowed down not just because of knee surgery, but because I was getting older and had had a whole host of muscle-related injuries.

When I was fully recovered, aside from the scars on my knee, I'd have never even known I had knee surgery. I had no pain, no swelling; I could play ninety minutes on an artificial pitch any day of the week nowadays.

I've got the perfect life from a knee perspective today. There's nothing I can't do. I've got Dr Richard Steadman and a kind, deceased person who was willing to donate his or her parts to medicine to thank for that.

This post-surgery rehab period back at Newcastle during the 2006/2007 season is where the initial rumblings of discontent started surfacing from the fans. This is where events start to get a little unsavoury.

The initial injury that had set the whole sequence of events in motion had been done playing for their club, putting myself in harm's way to try and nick a goal on New Year's Eve. But because the more serious knee injury had happened playing for England, a club versus country debate ignited publicly and I felt that the tone of it drove the beginnings of a wedge between the Newcastle fans and me.

I didn't, and still don't, see any of this as being my fault. I didn't try to break my foot; I didn't intentionally do my cruciate ligament.

But I have no doubt in my mind that, regardless of whose fault it was, my getting injured served to magnify small things that under any other circumstances wouldn't have mattered. By that I'm referring to, among other things, my having a helicopter. I'm sure that if I'd never got injured, nobody would have bothered their arses about it.

But I *did* get injured, and I could sense that the little things were being used against me – probably out of sheer frustration by people who had spent their hard earned money buying tickets to see people like me play.

Anyway, while a protracted row ensued between the club and the FA regarding the scope of insurance for players injured while on international duty, I had no choice but to focus on recovering from knee surgery to get back to playing football for Newcastle United.

Obviously, too, because of my injury at the World Cup, the conversation about having an option to buy me back for an incrementally reduced price (twelve million at that time) as per my contract, was never even had with Liverpool.

There was, after all, no point. I was injured long-term and worthless to them. It went without saying that I'd be staying at Newcastle for another season – even though I would be participating in very little of it. All of the above was fine by me given the circumstances.

As the club's main asset who they'd just paid sixteen million pounds for, naturally it stands to reason that my injury should require fairly intensive monitoring. At that time, under Glenn Roeder's management, Newcastle had two physios working at the club – Paul Ferris and Derek Wright.

Without wanting to sound like an entitled dick, as much as there were another twenty five players at the club who needed care – more than I did because they were actually playing – I nevertheless still needed pretty much twenty four hour monitoring for nine months. No disrespect to either the club or the two physios but it seemed to me that there just weren't enough focused resources to go round.

When I started back on my rehab, with the primary goal being to get as much motion into my knee as was humanly possible, all the instruction I got was a sheet of A4 paper with a few exercises listed on it and a place in a corner to lie and do them in my own time.

Granted, this didn't require much in the way of supervision. But I couldn't help feeling that, because of these circumstances, I was pretty much left to my own devices. Again, in no way is this meant as a criticism against the club because it's just how it was; I'm sure things are better now.

What didn't help much either was that one of my many weaknesses as a human has always been that I'll look for shortcuts wherever possible – including knee surgery rehabilitation. I'd be lying there on my back for an hour, having been told by the physio to do ten sets of eight of a certain type of tiny leg raises. Then someone would come into the room and I'd start talking to them … then the day just slips by … and by the end of it, I've barely done four sets, far less ten.

Basically, I get bored and I really need someone pushing me all the time. That's just how I am. Even nowadays, if somebody said to me: 'You need to go and lose weight …' I just can't do it – particularly if there's no good reason. I need to be motivated. And to be motivated there has to be an incentive – a tangible end result.

Fortunately, I acknowledged this flaw in my character at an early stage. All of us have flaws, but many of us never admit

Backing the bid: Taking time out in 2005 to support London's quest to host the Olympic Games

Fitness race: Back in England training with Wayne Rooney, Jamie Carragher and Frank Lampard. I was desperate to be available for the 2006 World Cup

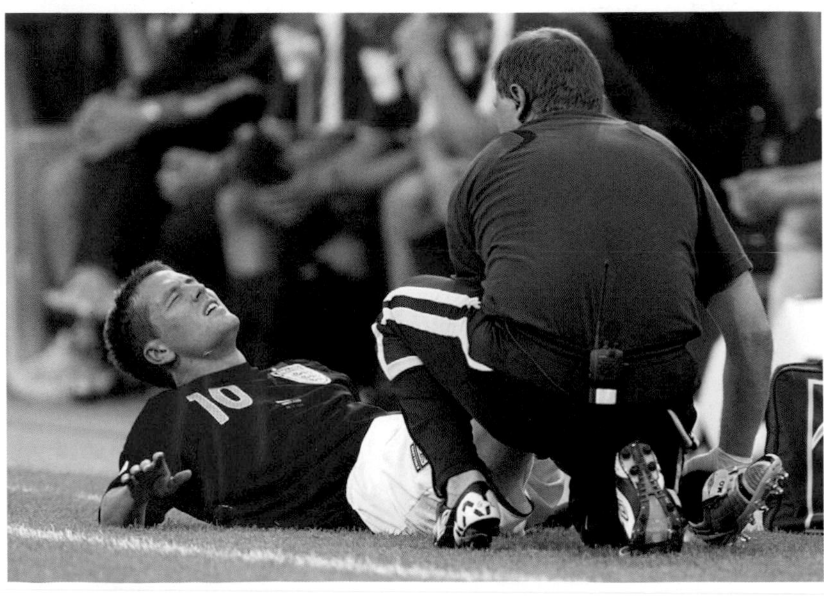

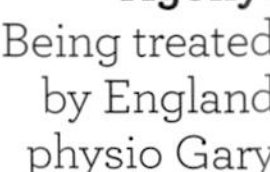

Agony: Being treated by England physio Gary Lewin after tearing my cruciate ligament against Sweden

Frustration: Unavoidable injuries meant I spent long spells on the sidelines at Newcastle

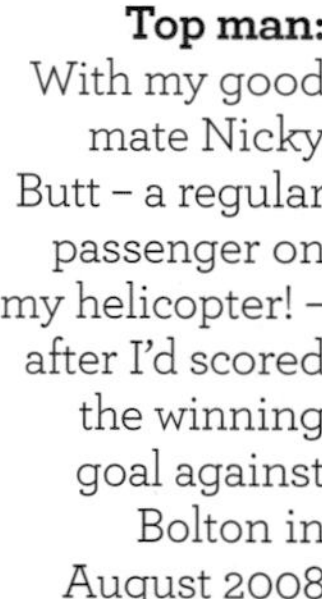

Top man: With my good mate Nicky Butt – a regular passenger on my helicopter! – after I'd scored the winning goal against Bolton in August 2008

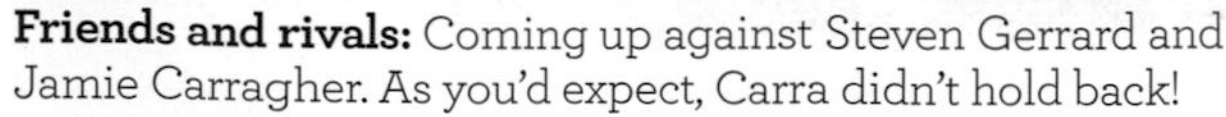

Friends and rivals: Coming up against Steven Gerrard and Jamie Carragher. As you'd expect, Carra didn't hold back!

Fab four: At a kit launch with new boss Fabio Capello. His arrival would signal the beginning of the end for me at England

Signing in: With Sir Alex Ferguson, Gabriel Obertan and Antonio Valencia as I join Manchester United in July 2009

Up and running: Opening my account for United with a goal against Wigan in August 2009

Fine margins: I had a split second to weigh up angles and percentages but I took Ryan Giggs' perfect pass in my stride to slot past Shay Given and give United a famous late derby win in 2009

Champions: With my young family after United's 2010/2011 Premier League triumph

Cheers: I scored the first goal in a 2-1 Carling Cup final win over Aston Villa in February 2010

Right to the wire: Signing for Stoke City happened in a blur. *(Above)* It wasn't always easy to read what Tony Pulis wanted of me

Tall story: With fellow substitute Peter Crouch. There was a good dressing room buzz at Stoke

Lost: Crystal Palace v Stoke City in January 2013 was when I realised it was all over for me as a footballer

Proud day: With jockey Richard Kingscote and Brown Panther after winning the Artemis Goodwood Cup in August 2013. Horse racing is in my blood

Taking the reins: It was my dad *(above)* who first got me into racing. *(Top)* with Prince Charles and *(left)* saddling up

Back on old ground: Playing in a Liverpool Legends charity game against Bayern Munich in March 2018 and scoring again at Anfield. *(Above right)* reunited with Robbie Fowler and Ian Rush

Speed king: Meeting sprint legend Usain Bolt during Soccer Aid and *(above right)* taking on my old teammate Roberto Carlos in the England v World Eleven game at Stamford Bridge

Pundit: With presenter Jake Humprey, Owen Hargreaves and Steve McManaman covering a game for BT Sport

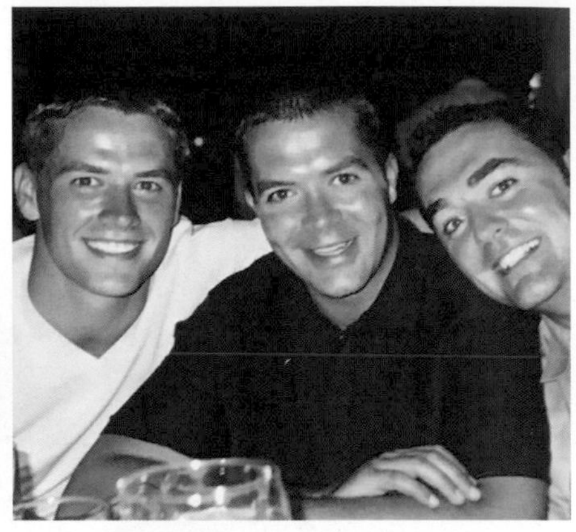

Family time: *(Clockwise from top left)* with Mum, Dad, my brothers and wife Louise

The best team: Enjoying a day out with Louise and the children

them. But I knew I needed leaning on – and I knew had to create those conditions if I was to be motivated to recover. To his eternal credit as a man manager, Glenn Roeder could also see what was happening.

'Are you doing alright, Michael?' he asked me one afternoon.

'If I'm being honest, boss,' I explained, 'I'm just not a good patient.'

'I've got a suggestion that might help,' Glenn told me.

Glenn knew of a physio called John Green from his days at West Ham. When Alan Pardew came in, he sacked a few staff and John Green was one of the people that the club had let go. He then became available as a freelance physio who specialised in knee injury rehab.

'You're the club's biggest asset,' Glenn said, 'you need one-on-one care. You need to be back for your sake and for everyone's sake.' Essentially, Glenn was saying that I needed my own personal physio and, for all the reasons I've mentioned, I agreed with him.

When this was mentioned to the existing club physios, Derek Wright and Paul Ferris – both of whom I really liked and thought I got along well with at that time – I'm not certain that it went down very well. I explained what I needed to get back to full fitness and that it wasn't a reflection of their ability whatsoever. They, and everyone else at the club, also knew that I was perfectly willing to pay for this care myself.

Nowadays, this kind of thing happens at every club in the land. For example, I'm told that if someone under Pep Guardiola's management gets injured and looks like they'll require an operation, the first thing he does is fly them to Spain. That's where he knows they'll get the best treatment. Spain is where he trusts.

But how does that make the physio at the club feel? I'd hazard a guess that they'll feel undervalued – and I knew that I was about to do that to two very able guys whose ability I respected.

As a result, I was at pains to say: 'Guys, it's nothing to do with you or your ability.' And it helped that I had Glenn's backing to get it past the board, even though there might have been a concern about what kind of precedent this was setting by making an exception on my behalf.

On reflection, people might have thought: 'If Michael Owen has his own physio, won't everyone else want one too?' I guess the club wanted to avoid a situation whereby everyone disappeared elsewhere or sought out their own treatment.

As it stood, whenever foreign players got injured, often they'd want to go back to their own country to be assessed. The cynical among us might think that injury was sometimes welcomed if it meant going back home for a holiday. As I recall, both Emre and Babayaro had injuries and went home to their respective countries during my time at Newcastle.

Anyway, Glenn was happy and I was motivated by the fact that I'd have someone dedicated to leaning over my shoulder, counting every last rep.

Although John Green was from London, he travelled up from Newcastle from around Christmas in 2006 for four solid months. John and I worked morning, noon and night. On occasion, he would come and stay at my house and he'd watch everything that I ate. For those few months, John and I lived like monks.

During this time, I became an absolute physical beast. I'm not one for taking my top off, but if I had done during these few months you'd have been impressed – I was totally ripped.

At four o'clock each day, as he was leaving work to go home, Glenn Roeder would often come out to watch us. There we'd always be, out on the pitches, grafting. No matter what the weather was: snow, rain or freezing cold, I was out there – and so was Glenn.

Seeing him there, taking an interest in me, gave me even more motivation. I felt like I could have set marathon records or hundred metre records. I was in absolutely the best shape of my life; I felt so strong – both in terms of my upper body and my legs.

During this rehab period, John and I took the weekly trip down to a facility, a Total Fitness, in Manchester that had a water treadmill – a piece of equipment that was important for knee rehab in that you could exercise without having to bear weight.

Because he'd been injured at Newcastle, Kieron Dyer had seemingly been there at some point prior. I think he might have even been there with us on some days.

Rightly or wrongly, from the beginning of his career, the press seemed to paint Kieron with this image of being a bit of a boy who liked to go out in town to chase girls around. There was a group of them at the club at that time and I guess the press loved it, following hot on the heels of the Spice Boy era at Liverpool.

Whether he did or not, I have no idea. And even if he did, that was probably more to do with him being nineteen or twenty at the time than because he was a footballer. Kieron was a good guy and a talented player but being a footballer isn't always the fairest of environments to grow up in.

Yet, the press just loved to label him as another entitled footballer-type – flashing his money around and generally taking the piss. As much as I knew and liked Kieron from England, I learned another side of him in this Total Fitness centre in Manchester.

As I was doing some exercises in the gym, this fella approached me.

'Can I just tell you one thing?' he began, 'Kieron was here one day; you were over in that pool.'

'Ok,' I said, waiting for what was coming next.

'My disabled son was getting lowered into the swimming pool and Kieron saw us. He came over and talked to us. He was genuinely interested in us and how we coped with my son's condition.

'Then, the next day, he came in with a chequebook in his hand and wrote us out a cheque for twenty grand. "I want you to take your son to Disneyland," he then said. "But I don't want you to tell anyone about it".'

At that moment, two thoughts occurred to me. Firstly that Kieron never once told me about this. I consider this to be a great quality. People shouldn't have to brag about charitable work or going the extra mile for somebody.

Secondly, for everyone out there who thinks footballers are just wealthy, brash, entitled brats – what Kieron had done just serves to illustrate just how misrepresented footballers often are. Don't believe everything you read in the press.

All the public ever sees is when footballers turn up at hospitals at Christmas to shake hands with sick children and be photographed doing it.

There's nothing wrong with this kind of charity appearance, far from it – but I know for a fact that it's a tiny part of what many footballers do for charity, all year round, with no fanfare or press coverage.

I could name many teammates of mine – Steven Gerrard and Carra to start with – who give a hell of a lot of themselves for charitable causes. I do it and have done it many times myself. The Kieron Dyer story really reinforced this for me. I'll never forget that guy telling me this story with tears in his eyes.

I thought, *if only people knew …*

The best news of all was that, throughout all of this intensive rehab, I never experienced any pain or any swelling whatsoever. Because of a combination of the quality of my surgery in Colorado and the expertise of John Green's rehab programme, I was able to do the volume of important exercises – squats in particular – that are vital for good knee rehabilitation.

John was truly an expert and he was exactly what I needed at that time. Not just that, Glenn Roeder was a good enough man manager to understand how my psyche worked.

It should be said that I've always considered Glenn to be a really good guy. It's a shame he was always on borrowed time at Newcastle despite having won the Intertoto Cup that year – the only Newcastle manager to win a significant piece of silverware since 1969.

By the time I was back from rehab, which would have been early April of 2007, I was raring to go.

Meanwhile, as a result of conversations he'd already had with John, Glenn knew what he could expect when the new and improved Michael Owen showed up. I'm sure John must have said to him: 'When this guy comes back, don't even think about not starting him. He doesn't need to sit on the bench. He's *ready.*'

A warm-up game was organised specifically for me – a friendly behind closed doors against Gretna. I felt great, scored a nice goal and set up another for fellow striker Shola Ameobi. I came off after a solid hour thinking, *that was bob-on.*

As far as I was concerned, I was ready to start for the first team. I was in the zone; I was wired for playing games before the end of the season.

Not so fast though …

Prior to an away game against Reading on April 30th, the third last of that season, the Sky cameras were due to be at St. James' Park. This wasn't anything unusual; they came every Friday, interviewed the manager and showed five minutes or so of training on TV.

By this point, as far as I was concerned, I was training with the understanding that I would be starting against Reading. Having got so fit, I was thinking, *no way will I not be playing.*

But when Freddy Shepherd got wind of the fact that Sky were coming, and that they would be filming me in training for all to see, he must have panicked. The whole news juggernaut of my return to action would have started the moment those pictures were beamed to the world.

This in turn brings me to one of the most burning and contentious issues of my whole time at Newcastle: the insurance policy that the club had taken out on my injury.

During my recovery from knee surgery, I heard a bit of dissent from fans complaining about how I was getting paid a fortune and, by extension, how they were paying for me to sit around being injured. Had that been the case, I would have understood their position to some degree. Many Newcastle fans are working class people who make huge sacrifices to buy season tickets. I get it.

In no way would I ever want to ram my wages down their throats. That has never been my style. I never had anything but respect for Newcastle fans – even though I heard rumblings that some felt I should have kept in touch more during my recovery via a column in the paper. The truth is that the club never pushed for this and my focus was always just to get back playing, rather than talk about getting back.

Although my return to playing was a day that was always going to come, Freddy Shepherd wasn't keen for it to be in April of 2007. The reason for this is that the moment I played, the insurance money paying my wages stopped.

Conversely, if I *didn't* play, Freddy Shepherd would have another summer of this insurance cover which, when you added it up, was a hell of a lot of money.

Given that the club had organised a warm-up game for me and had me in training with a view to playing against Reading, it seems to me that Glenn initially had no knowledge of Freddy Shepherd's desire to sideline me to save money. I'm sure Glenn was just happy to have me available at all.

Five minutes before I'm about to go out and train in front of the Sky cameras, Glenn called me into his office.

'The chairman said you're not allowed to train today,' he explained.

You can imagine how this felt given everything I'd been through. At the beginning, I'd come to terms with how long I'd be out. Having mentally noted how long it would be, and looked at the games I'd miss, I accepted it and just got on with it. I had a target.

Every day was one day closer.

But once you're a few days from that date you've had in your mind and in your diary for months, you start getting excited, and impatient with people.

Everyone would be saying: 'You should be happy now, you're nearly fit!' I was the opposite. I was getting my nasty head on again because I could taste that feeling of what it's like to cross the white line and to fight again.

And then for someone to tell me that I couldn't train on this day – I just lost my cool.

I started thinking, *if I don't train today, does that mean I'm not playing?*

I wasn't having any of it.

'I'm training,' I told Glenn, 'he isn't stopping me training.'

'He's *telling* me …' Glenn said.

I could tell that his hands were tied.

'Put him on the phone now.'

Glenn called Freddy Shepherd and handed me the phone.

'Hi Chairman, the manager is saying you won't let me train today. Is that right?' I asked – trying to keep my composure.

'Yeah,' he said, going straight onto the front foot, 'because the cameras are there and, if you go and play before the end of the season, we're going to miss out on a fortune.'

'So you're saying I'm not allowed to play at all this season?' I queried – feeling my pulse quicken.

'Yeah, you can't – otherwise we've got a full summer of paying you when we could be getting it from the insurance.'

At this point, as furious as I was, I should say that I understood why Freddy Shepherd was acting like he was. Regardless of what your views are about the concept of insurance in general, these situations probably happen all the time.

But I didn't think it was morally or legally right – and that's not just me being selfish because I wanted to resume playing. 'Well, you can fuck right off,' I said. 'I haven't trained this hard for this long to be told this shit.'

All I can remember next was a blur of time while he was shouting down the phone.

'Listen,' he yelled at me, 'you've earned a shit load of money since you've been at this bloody club. All I'm asking you to do is fucking go and hide in the toilets for five minutes for one day.'

He was clearly frustrated and under pressure. But his logic didn't even stack up. From what he was saying, it wouldn't have just been one day. It would have been one day – plus every other day including three league games until the end of the 2006/07 season.

At some stage, there was an unspoken agreement reached that I wouldn't go out and train while the Sky cameras were there but as soon as they went, I'd train as normal.

But from that point, knowing that it would have been terrible PR for the club if I was to come out publicly and say: 'The chairman won't let me play,' Freddy Shepherd's hands were then tied too.

For the record, I didn't hide in the toilets as he suggested.

And the history books will tell you that I did play against Reading. They may not mention that I scored a goal that was disallowed in a 1-0 defeat.

Regardless, I felt so incredibly powerful. Because I'd never really been too reliant on being overtly physical when using my upper body, now it felt like people were bouncing off me. All of a sudden I enjoyed shoulder-charging people!

I had returned better than ever – and because I had, Newcastle would have had to pay my wages during the coming summer. All of this, in my eyes, is exactly as it should have been. Whether it had been the first game of the season or the last, the moment I played, the insurance payments should have stopped. And, I assume, they did.

The fans, of course, never knew anything about any of these behind-the-scenes goings-on. Nobody did. As much as I knew, on a basic level at least, what the machinations of the insurance policy taken out on me were, I didn't think it was appropriate from a professional standpoint at that time in my career for me to say anything about it. Instead, I had to endure a fair amount of criticism from Newcastle fans – mostly because they weren't privy to all the details of my situation.

And then the roof caved in again …

The last game of the season in 2007 at Watford brought with it more bad luck that in no way helped my relationship with the support.

As I said, when I was on the road to recovery, I started getting a sense of that slight dissatisfaction the fans felt towards me. To that end, I was very much thinking, *I need to hit the ground running here …*

I knew how good a relationship I'd had with the fans in that first season and I desperately didn't want them to forget the significant part I'd played in those good times when we were playing well and I was banging in the goals. When I got a standing ovation on my comeback against Reading, everything seemed okay, albeit with some reservations from the fans' perspective.

Even still, I didn't feel like I had to justify anything to anybody. I knew that when I played, I played well. And in my constantly shit-filtering mind I'd already spun it round anyway into thinking, *sorry I've been injured and you haven't seen me for a while. But don't worry – the club hasn't had to pay my wages while I've been out anyway.*

However, things changed on May 13th, 2007, during the last league game away to Watford.

A few minutes into the game, I was running at full speed and then turned as if to dart in the opposite direction – failing to see that one of my teammates, Matty Pattison, was right in front of me. His shoulder collided squarely with my jaw. I was knocked unconscious there on the pitch.

There are a few things that you'd expect to see when you regain consciousness in the dressing room at Vicarage Road. Let's just say that Steve McClaren, the then England manager's face at close quarters, isn't one of them. He'd come to the game to watch me, then came down to the dressing room and apparently he'd been talking to me as I lay there in a daze.

'Are you alright, Michael?" I vaguely recall him saying.

'Alright Steve?' I said. 'How's my luck, eh?' It was such a strange situation – but in the scheme of things I didn't think the injury was significant at all.

When I got home that night, I switched on Match Of The Day to watch the game back. I watched myself getting knocked out, but in the background I could hear Newcastle fans, my fans, singing 'what a waste of money!' as I'm being stretchered off.

I can't deny that their actions that day changed things for me. I hate generalising about football players, managers or fans, but their reaction to what was just a freak accident told me that the Newcastle fans just didn't get it at all.

From that moment onwards, my stubbornness kicked in. No longer was I even going to attempt to ingratiate myself with the fans. Instead, I flipped it in a slightly more resentful way thinking, *I don't need to justify myself to fucking Newcastle fans.*

And I have a long memory.

As much as there were some good times to follow at St. James' Park, my relationship with the fans was irreparably impaired that day at Vicarage Road.

The love affair, if you could call it that, was almost over.

REBØOT_15

RESPECT

Glenn Roeder left Newcastle just before the end of the 2006/07 season. At the time it was presented publicly as one of those 'by mutual consent' arrangements and it came after he'd been summoned to an emergency meeting with Shepherd and the board.

I felt he'd been a little hard done by if I'm honest. Given the level of injuries there had been to not just me, but also to a variety of other major players during his tenure, some would argue that Glenn Roeder was not just unlucky but also under-appreciated at St. James' Park.

On reflection, when you consider what was about to transpire at boardroom level, it might just be that Roeder was the unfortunate fall guy who was sacrificed to appease the fans' general dissatisfaction with the Shepherd regime.

Sam Allardyce was brought in as manager in June 2007 and I have to say that – while I didn't have anything against him as a person – when I said that Graeme Souness was my kind of manager, let's just say that Sam Allardyce wasn't. As soon as he came in and I watched a training session, I just knew.

Now, I know he and a few others might point to his time at Bolton and how he got them into Europe for that 2005/2006 season. That was without doubt an impressive achievement. But nobody could deny that he had some amazing players to get him there: Hierro, Ivan Campo and Youri Djorkaeff – to name just a few that spring to mind.

Allardyce is one of these people who, despite being an older guy who's probably seen a lot, would rather have you believe that he's a modern thinker, outside the box and that he goes with the times.

On some level he does go with the times but perhaps only in the sense that he brings in as many people as he can alongside him within his budget at a club – physios here, sports scientists there, masseurs, yoga practitioners etc. He enlisted as much assistance as he could get.

Training under Allardyce was pretty mundane too to be honest – lots of eleven against eleven and so-called 'patterns of play' exercises. In doing this, basically he would always be a big advocate of sticking the ball over the full back, chasing it down and winning a throw-in. Losing the ball in the middle of the park would have been his worst nightmare.

Consequently, you could forget about any nice, passing movements. These were something he'd just about tolerate. They certainly weren't his cup of tea. Cynical, route-one football was.

What irritated me personally most about his tactics was his adherence to the concept of P.O.M.O or, in full form, *Position Of Maximum Opportunity.* When I first heard about it, I thought, *what the hell even is P.O.M.O?*

I wouldn't be long in finding out. We'd be playing eleven against eleven and then, whenever the ball went wide he'd just stop the play. The bloody clipboard would come out.

We'd just stand still.

He'd then reel off various stats and percentages before telling the strikers exactly where in the penalty box represented the best percentage opportunity to score.

It was all too numbers based for my liking. Goalscoring had never been about that for me. I preferred a more instinctive approach. And I didn't like being told: 'Stand there ...'

From that perspective I didn't really have a huge amount of respect for him as a manager. I never got the impression that the fans took to him either.

I never got a sense that he rated me much either, not that I was bothered. I don't think he ever came and spoke to me individually at any time. And that's no surprise. After all, when you looked at his track record, it was pretty clear that I wasn't the kind of player he'd have chosen to buy in a million years. His purchases were all of a certain type – but not *my* type.

Conversely, his away trips weren't my type. I was never a fan of how he interacted with the team. Whenever we went to London, we'd usually go down on the train the day before and arrive at the team hotel around four or five o'clock.

At around seven, we'd all come down to the dining room for a meal and there'd be Allardyce and all his backroom staff, dolled up in their finery, ready to head out to a fancy restaurant for dinner.

This, for me at least, felt a little strange. At every other club I'd been at, everyone always ate together. To do so boosted morale. I had nothing against Allardyce's approach if he felt that it worked but his culture just wasn't for me.

The 2007/2008 season not only brought in Sam Allardyce as manager, but it also heralded a significant shift in both the club's structure and my life.

On an ownership front, Freddy Shepherd was on his way out of St. James' Park having negotiated some sort of a deal to sell his remaining shares to London-based business tycoon, Mike Ashley – in some people's eyes a controversial character, but one with whom I had almost zero direct contact during my time at the club.

I should say that, as much as Freddy Shepherd and I had had notable moments of disagreement, I didn't hold any personal grudges against him. In general he was pretty open and forthright as chairmen go.

On some level, I even admired him for being such a huge fan, and on another I actually pitied him for the situation he often found himself in with the fans.

At the end of that 2006/2007 campaign, when the annual, contract-based option of my returning to Liverpool had come around (I was available for eight million pounds at that point), I remember Freddy making some kind of comment in the press to the effect of: 'I'll carry Michael Owen to Liverpool myself.'

It was a nice soundbite I suppose, but it didn't really bother me for long. After the first five minutes of red mist, when I wanted to get into a mud-slinging match and shoot him down, instead I just laughed to myself and thought, *nice one, Freddy. You have your moment in the limelight at my expense ...*

On reflection, I didn't feel that, just because the chairman had said something unpleasant about me, I should start hating everything about every aspect of the club from that day forward.

After all, while I was popular and scoring goals Freddy had never said a word. But as soon as fans start turning on a chairman, it actually helps their popularity if they say something over the top – as he had about me.

The truth was, I knew why Freddy said what he said – and in that sense people need to take a lot of what certain people say in football with a pinch of salt. Pure and simple, it was nothing against me. Freddy was just trying to appease the fans. As you can imagine, that statement would have had the desired rabble-rousing effect with the fans in the short term – 'Oh yeah, you really showed him – well done, Freddy!'

There was nothing to be gained from my engaging. Newspaper headlines soon blow over and become the next day's fish and chip wrapping paper as we all know. Sometimes the best policy is to keep your dignity and say nothing.

The thing is, this kind of scenario isn't uncommon at a club like Newcastle United, with the demographic of the salt of the earth fanbase being as it is.

Freddy, being a huge fan of the club also, was only doing what all the fans constantly do at almost every football club: they believe that their club is ten per cent bigger and that their team is ten per cent better than it actually is. It's just like me with my kids. I think they're wonderful and they're going to be world-beaters at everything they ever do. But to everyone else, they're just normal kids.

This kind of blind delusion is especially true of Newcastle United – which, as I reach for the nearest tin hat, is only a big club in the sense that it has a lot of fans and a big stadium. They're historically not successful off the pitch, in fact quite the opposite mostly. And they've never really won much on it in recent times.

The long and short of it all is that Freddy Shepherd had a big club mentality at a club that wasn't founded on much substance. He was the chairman of a team that, at best, could hope for a top ten finish. More realistically, they'd be trying to avoid relegation more often than not.

■ ■ ■

As I mentioned, Freddy departed, Mike Ashley came on board as the new owner and with him came a new chairman – a guy called Chris Mort, who I was led to believe was a lawyer.

With the new regime came promises of a brighter future at St. James' Park. By all accounts, Mike Ashley was a wealthy man.

On paper it all seemed possible. Amid something of a press fanfare that excited the beleaguered fans, Ashley arrived at Newcastle with hints of big name signings, European football and good times.

As I alluded to, in my personal life, things also took on a slightly different dynamic during the off-season in the summer of 2007 – primarily influenced by the fact that the lease on the house in the country ran out so we needed to find somewhere else to live.

Louise, Gemma and I had enjoyed the country retreat for two years, but the balance of opinion was that somewhere with more people around to talk to would have been beneficial for all of us.

Also, I'd become increasingly frustrated by how long it was taking to drive into Newcastle's training facility.

With Gemma due to start primary school that September and our son James still very young, Louise and I agreed to go through with an idea that we'd discussed at various times during the previous year. She would move back home with the kids so that Gemma could go to school with friends she knew.

As drastic as that might sound, it really made the most sense. Given that there was potential for me to be in Newcastle for only one more year, it made no sense for Gemma to start her schooling anywhere other than at home.

Louise had been a fantastic support to me during that two years-plus at Newcastle and, with helicopter transport still available, she could continue to be a support – albeit primarily based at home with the kids.

In parallel, when my mate Scott Parker was sold to West Ham in June of 2007, I agreed to buy his place which was located in the heart of the Darras Hall estate – one of the more exclusive parts of town popular with footballers.

In every sense, the location made much more sense for me. I'd not only be closer to the training ground, but I'd also have a few friendly faces around for some welcome social interaction: Alan Shearer, Steve Harper, Shay Given and Stephen Carr all lived there. There was a petrol station nearby – there was a Chinese restaurant within walking distance. All in all it was a far better situation.

When Louise moved back south, my dad decided to move up to Newcastle to live with me in the house at Darras Hall. What my mother thought of that arrangement, I'm not sure. Maybe she was quite glad to get rid of him for a few days a week because in reality that's all it was!

She'd fly up for home games and he and I would be back home on days off. It was a good, workable arrangement for everybody concerned and his presence, from the perspective of being company for me, was very welcome.

Inevitably, given our shared interests, my dad and I slipped into a comfortable routine more synonymous with a couple of young lads than that of father and son. Because I'm useless at cooking, he'd make meals. On the occasions when he didn't want to, we'd just wander round to the local pub for a bar meal now and again.

In the mornings, when I was training, he'd buy a paper and do the shopping before going to the pub for a couple of pints. Then, as I'd be finishing at the training ground I'd text him and arrange to meet him back at the house to watch that afternoon's racing.

We'd go to a different pub every other day so as not to attract too much attention – dotted around the whole area. My dad loves his pubs and that whole old-school life. Obviously people cottoned on to the fact that we were around, but nobody ever bothered us. We were immersed in the neighbourhood and accepted by the local people. It felt great to be part of it.

In addition to roaming around with Terry Two-Jags, I also saw much more of the lads from the club during those two years. Alan Shearer was also part of a card school that met every couple of weeks.

He'd invite me and a bunch of mates and we'd all go to a local pub, The Diamond Inn in Ponteland, where we'd go upstairs to a private room and play cards for the night. We'd go to the casino now and again and eat at various restaurants in town. Life was fun.

All of this went on for a couple of years until the end of my time in Newcastle. And it flies directly in the face of those who always complained that I was never there, didn't commit, didn't like the people and didn't want to make any effort. The opposite was true. My life in Newcastle was a far cry from many of the fans' perception. They might not have seen me out in the nightclubs on Northumberland Street at kicking-out time on a Friday night, but I was nevertheless in Newcastle and enjoying life.

In hindsight, because we lived like single lads, as much as I wasn't a drinker, I'd be eating pub food some nights in addition to eating at home – where my dad wasn't exactly mindful of the calorie intake. It wasn't his fault and I'd never want to blame him. But I definitely had to be aware of what I was eating and graft a bit harder at training.

All in all we had a right scream for those years and as I look back at those times, I write this with a smile on my face.

■ ■ ■

As much as I didn't really respect Sam Allardyce's methods in 2007/2008, I simply couldn't sleep at night now if I didn't come out and say that, during the eight months of his tenure, I was starting to lose a bit of my respect for myself. It's not an admission I'm proud of.

But it's the truth.

At the time, while a variety of niggling injuries derailed me – groin strain, hernia operation etc. – for the first time, I started considering the possibility that I was no longer one of the top players in the world. In dark moments I'm sure I thought, *what exactly am I still capable of?*

While it wasn't necessarily a conscious decision at the time, the period up until Allardyce left the club in January 2008 was when a certain emphasis changed in respect of my style of play.

From 1997 onwards, I alone had dictated how I played – unless I was requested to do otherwise by a manager, as was the case with Keegan at England, or broader team tactics required something different from me, as was the case at Real Madrid.

If I wanted to play on the shoulder and run in the channels, I did it knowing that I could. If I was told to come short, link play and hold the ball up, I did that too, admittedly reluctantly sometimes, for what was considered to be the good of the team.

From 2007 onwards, however, my body and my mind dictated everything. A seemingly endless stream of injuries – some major, some relatively minor – had brought me to a point where I just wasn't capable of doing what I'd once done. I could still run, but I was so much slower than I'd been in previous years. If the ball went into the channels, I'd have question marks in my head whenever I was required to sprint. Having arrived from Real Madrid and felt like I was miles better than the players around me, now I felt like I was just another player.

This realisation, especially given the relentless nature of my mind-set over the years, was such an upsetting one. I wasn't quite thinking, *Michael, you truly are crap now* – that day would come.

But I was certainly feeling that I was an increasingly pale shadow of the player I'd once been. Even worse, I can't remember making much effort to arrest this mental slide because I knew that, physically, that aspect of my game drove my mental side anyway. I was impaired. It wasn't that I was ever a bad pro.

But what can you do?

At twenty eight, I was still relatively young. At no point did I consider that my career was over and I didn't want it to be – I had a young family to provide for.

Beyond that, as much as I was never a fan of Sam Allardyce himself, I enjoyed not only the camaraderie of the dressing room, but also the pace and nature of my wider life in the North East. Contrary to what the fans were led to believe, I was happy – albeit with serious concerns about how I was going to navigate my time on the pitch going forward.

■■ ■■■■■

Looking back now, Kevin Keegan's arrival in late January of 2008 gave me a mighty shot in the arm.

At the time though, when his appointment was announced, I thought, *I'm bloody finished here …*

Given how our relationship had played out at England, I saw absolutely no way how he and I could co-exist at Newcastle. I remember sitting at home with my dad, getting ready to leave for a cup game against Stoke when it was announced that Keegan would be watching from the stands.

I took a big gulp. Even when he sat in the stand to watch us win (and me score) in that 4-1 home against Stoke in the FA Cup, I was still a bit apprehensive. The fact that I'd also given him a bit of a kicking in my first book didn't help either.

I suppose when I wrote what I did about his management style with England and how I felt that he'd mistreated me, I wasn't exactly considering that our paths would later cross again – not that that would have changed anything. I hadn't liked his management style in terms of how it impacted me and I had no problems saying so.

But the Kevin Keegan that showed up at Newcastle in 2008 might as well have been a different person. From the very start, Keegan was absolutely terrific in every department of the game that a manager can be: positive, enthusiastic, compassionate, inclusive – he was everything I'd been led to believe he was.

I thought, *Ok, this is a relief. Let's see where this goes …*

And where it went was ultimately a better place. But it took a while for us to gather steam. As much as Keegan injected more life into that dressing room, I never felt that he was necessarily the most innovative of tacticians. His first eight games in charge were a bit concerning – in no way aided by a couple of 4-1 and 5-1 hammerings at the hands of Villa and Manchester United respectively.

Awful results aside, this period was a significant one as far as the backroom staff were concerned. Given that Kevin Keegan was still new to the job, there was inevitably a period of transition. At some point during the week of the Villa game, Keegan spotted that one of the backroom staff was virtually falling over while showing us what to do. Keegan was not impressed and changes were swiftly made.

At Newcastle, as people left, other people arrived. That was the way. What we didn't know the details of at the time was that along with Keegan's appointment had come a commitment to a new, upper-management structure above him that comprised Dennis Wise being brought in as Director of Football, Jeff Vetere as Technical Co-ordinator and Tony Jimenez as Vice-President of Player Recruitment.

In 2008, I knew little about how all of this worked in terms of what their exact roles were and I should say at this point that I had very little direct contact with Ashley, his managing director Derek Llambias – or any of the others already named during my remaining time at the club. From my perspective as a player, none of these relationships really mattered.

While these intra-board and management dynamics were settling down off the pitch, it took until March for Keegan to impress his positive imprint onto the on-field happenings and thank goodness he did because with no cup involvement and the possibility of a relegation dogfight looming, you could sense that the St. James' Park faithful were becoming unsettled.

As early in the day as it was, I'd sensed there were serious doubts about the validity of the messiah's second coming.

Strangely, it was an innocuous 1-1 draw away to Birmingham City on March 17th where the tide turned for the better.

I scored to equalise in the second half and thereafter, with Mark Viduka, Obafemi Martins and I available up front, we went on a short but telling run that began with a 4-1 win at White Hart Lane on March 30th and ended with a 2-0 loss to Chelsea in the first week of May. I scored three more including a double in the Tyne and Wear derby at St. James' Park.

As this run of good results went on, you could feel the atmosphere at the club change. At times the place was bouncing. I felt like I was getting just a tiny glimpse of what it would have been like with Keegan at the helm, all those years ago. We were all excited to go into training every day.

Along the way too, it was as if Keegan had completely forgotten that we'd previously met. At no time did he ever raise what I'd written in my book. At England, he had no idea how to man-manage me. At Newcastle, he got everything right. As if to confirm that, he even made me captain.

He was good fun, too. While it was always clear that he

was the manager, he definitely made an effort to join in with dressing room antics and to be one of the lads wherever he could and usually in tandem with his hilarious coaching sidekick Terry McDermott. As such, there is one story that epitomises our time with Keegan at Newcastle. I still chuckle about it whenever I see him or hear his name mentioned.

Nicky Butt and I had become very good mates at Newcastle. As well as being a regular passenger on my helicopter, Nicky was absolutely brilliant on the park.

He had many, many qualities did Nicky Butt, but the one I admired most in him was his constant willingness to sacrifice himself for the team. If you were ever down that cul-de-sac I've described before and were desperately looking for someone to show for you, Nicky would always, always bust a gut to be there – even if, by doing so, he'd be putting himself in a position whereby he'd be open to being the fall guy.

Being in deep shit on the pitch never bothered Nicky. He'd have done anything for his mates. Time and again he'd do these unselfish things while at the same time exhibiting the kind of unflashy qualities that fans might not always recognise but we, the players, value most in our teammates. From start to finish, Butty was an absolutely top man. And if anyone ever considered me in the same way as a person and a footballer as I viewed Nicky Butt, then I'd be a very proud man.

Anyway, Keegan and McDermott knew that Nicky and I were good mates. So, one day, as we were finishing training, Keegan challenged us to a head-tennis competition

'Me and Terry against you two,' he said, 'winners get bragging rights.' Me and Butty just laughed out loud.

'With all due respect, gaffer,' I said, 'Terry can hardly bloody walk. He's nearly a hundred years old!'

'We'll batter you,' Keegan replied.

Nicky and I retired to discuss this challenge in more detail. We weighed it all up.

'Look,' I began, 'the gaffer, as amazing as he was back in the day, he's about a hundred years old too.'

'You're right,' Nicky agreed. 'We're not playing them unless it's for a hundred quid, either.'

The next day, as the gaffer badgered us constantly to commit, we presented our proposal for a money match.

'We're not wasting our time against you two unless there's money at stake,' we told him, 'so make it worth it, put a crowd in there …'

'We'll batter you,' Keegan repeated.

They weren't backing down one inch. Keegan just stood there smirking – awaiting our imminent acceptance of his challenge. This unwavering confidence unsettled us – I can't deny that. It felt like a wind-up. We retreated to a quiet corner to confer again.

'Are we missing something here, mate?' I asked.

'Listen,' Butty said, 'it's physically impossible that they can ever beat us,' he went on.

'They can't, can they?' I agreed. 'With their age, and their mobility, it defies all logic. Terry McDermott will need a bloody scooter to get around the court.'

Having agreed that they were just deluded, we shook hands on Keegan's deal.

'Right, you're on. A hundred quid each,' we said.

When D-Day arrived, with a crowd of the lads assembled around the indoor artificial pitch, let's just say that I have never been so humiliated in my entire life.

The gaffer operated at the back of the court, and covered

ground with so little effort that it was a joke. He got everything back. Not only that, every ball he did get back – had Terry McDermott not also touched it – just barely hit the top of the net and dribbled over.

Terry operated exclusively at the net, sometimes pretending to head it before ducking, or at other times he'd just let it brush his head. His other trick was to look in one direction while heading it in another off the back of his head.

Whatever they did, the ball usually dropped where we couldn't return it. Keegan's precision was staggering; McDermott never moved from one spot. They didn't just do us – they absolutely destroyed us. I have never in my life been given such a footballing lesson. And bearing in mind that it was up to twenty one – it's not that there was any fluke about it.

When Butty and I came in the next day, let's just say that we kept our heads down. We didn't even want to be in the gaffer's company because they were taking the piss so much – in a really friendly way. Whenever we walked into the canteen, these two would start shouting their mouths off in front of everybody, every day.

'Have you got our hundred quid each?' Keegan would ask every time.

'We've got to pay them ...' Butty said to me.

We agreed we should pay them, but we also agreed that we'd somehow come up with a counter wind-up.

My first thought was: *This is a mission for Terry Two-Jags.*

'Dad, if I give you two-hundred quid,' I asked him 'could you go round a few banks and change it all into one pence pieces?'

'Leave it with me,' came the reply.

'Yeah, we'll pay you tomorrow,' we told Keegan and McDermott.

The next day, we all went out training. When we finished, while Keegan was still out there doing a bit of finishing practice with a few people, Butty and I sneaked off and met my dad in the car park.

Have you ever actually felt how heavy two hundred quid worth of one-pence pieces is? I kid you not, Butty and I had to make several journeys in and out to Keegan's office while someone kept lookout. It was bloody heavy.

When we got in there, we cleared his desk and emptied all these bank packs onto it. When we'd finished, there was a two-foot tall mound of pennies!

We scarpered, and hid in one of the dressing rooms down the corridor so that we could watch him go in. Shortly, he appeared. As he opened the door, he looked inside and immediately cottoned on to what we had done.

We saw him turn round, laughing his head off to himself as he spun around to come and find us. Meanwhile, we burst out of the dressing room. It was so funny – then we got all the lads to come and have a look at our handiwork.

■ ■ ■ ■

For team spirit, Keegan was different class while he was at Newcastle. Best of all, having made me captain, I actually felt that Keegan had helped me fall in love with football again.

When the season ended, we were in twelfth place. Nothing too exciting – but an improvement of one position from the previous year nevertheless. For a while there in January and February, that had looked unlikely.

With time at the end of the season to reflect on what Keegan had brought to our dressing room compared to how he'd been at England, I came to a simple conclusion that Kevin Keegan was probably just more suited to club football. Having read what he said in his own book, I doubt that I'm far off the mark.

To me, it always appeared as if Keegan thrived on being in the trenches, with the players, with the press and with the board, I'm sure, as well. In order to be there, he had to have the kind of breathless, day-to-day involvement that any club football involves. Then, when you add in the extra dose of daily drama that managing Newcastle specifically entails, it was obviously right up his street. Newcastle is a pressure-cooker like few others. He'd already demonstrated his appetite for it during his first stint in the '90s.

At England, there was never enough energy to feed Kevin Keegan when he only saw the players one time a month. It seemed as if he was running with the choke out all the time with no daily battles to fight – other than with his own frustrations about being inactive. England just didn't suit him. Club football clearly did.

That we had a really good bunch of players at Newcastle did Keegan's chances no harm either. Given that he also liked attacking players, with three strikers with differing strengths available, he had those options aplenty.

As I mentioned earlier, I'd had to change my game to be effective. No longer was I blitzing defenders for pace. The questions I used to dismiss like: 'Who's the quicker centre-half, here?' became relevant – simply because I knew I couldn't run past them all.

Recognising this, and given how hard it was to drop one of us, Keegan sometimes withdrew me into a role behind the strikers as a kind of advanced, attacking midfielder. He got no complaints from me either – I played some of the best football of my career during those few months with Keegan. I'm sure we both saw the irony in this given the issue between us about my role at Euro 2000.

Bearing in mind that I was no longer able to sprint at full speed and run in channels and in behind, the withdrawn role Keegan created for me *did* play to my strengths.

Now, I was very happy to change my game.

And towards the end of that 2007/2008 season he was saying that he wanted to sign me up on a new long-term contract.

'You've got a great football brain,' he'd say, 'I could see you dropping even deeper …'

This made me feel great. Keegan thought that I could ultimately morph into a sitting midfielder and, as bizarre as it sounds, I didn't disagree with him. Just because nobody had ever seen me in this kind of role, didn't mean I wasn't capable of playing in it. After all, at that time, because I was limited by my body, all I was able to do was get in the box and score.

Someone else could do that, I thought, and it made sense that I could then demonstrate other attributes that I'd never previously had to deploy: range of passing, vision, and tackling etc. As Keegan's enthusiasm sank in, I started thinking, *maybe he's right, you know?*

Confronted with the possibility that I could undergo something of a career rebirth under Keegan at Newcastle, I left for the summer break in 2008 with renewed optimism.

When we came back in for pre-season, there was a sense that dark clouds were already hanging over Kevin's tenure. We'll never know what really happened but clearly issues related to transfer policy had been brewing since the end of the previous season. And with this group of senior individuals overseeing matters above Keegan's head, it wasn't hard to figure out that there was some degree of disconnect between Keegan and the people upstairs.

Contrary to what fans probably think, as players, we're only privy to so much. As I said, I doubt I had more than one conversation with Mike Ashley and I don't think I had as many as that with Dennis Wise. All we had to go on was who walked in the door for pre-season that we hadn't seen before and, on the flipside, which guys didn't walk in who used to be there the previous season.

As it happened, there was a lot of coming and going. James Milner left to go to Aston Villa before the deadline. That raised a few eyebrows given how good he'd been for us, and how he could play anywhere on the pitch, and was two-footed.

A procession of people arrived: Jonás Gutiérrez was one. Sébastien Bassong was another. Then there was Fabricio Coloccini, Danny Guthrie and, finally, Xisco.

It's almost a side note to mention that, as with previous years and as per my contract, I was again available to Liverpool at whatever the incrementally reduced rate was at the time.

Keegan says in his book that I was offered to Liverpool behind his back. If that happened, nobody ever told me about it. Whether he knew the details or not, the exit clause was always in the contract. I'm assuming that he'd have had access to that info. What's more likely, given what's been made public since, is actually a sadder situation: that maybe pretty much everything in his few months at Newcastle was done behind Keegan's back. If that's the case, it's very poor.

From what I understand though, Tony Stephens did indeed put in a call to Liverpool before the transfer window closed.

The answer came back along the lines of *thanks but no thanks*. And it made sense.

Rafa Benitez, as big a fan of mine as he might have been, had Fernando Torres on the books at the time. He'd been a revelation and had just scored thirty three goals in the season prior. I can only assume that Rafa didn't need me. And so, for the third year running, attempts to return to Liverpool came to nought.

In any case, with the thought of good times ahead with Keegan still fresh in my mind, I was happy to stay at Newcastle for what would be the last year of my contract. All things being equal, I was fine with it. Whatever happened after that, I was prepared to wait and see.

As if to confirm that I was making the right decision, I scored in the second league game of the season in a 1-0 win against Bolton at St. James' Park.

Then, out of the blue, Kevin was out the door. The press had an absolute field day with it all – 'Keegan quits again!'

We, the players, on the other hand, were told very little about the circumstances. Instead, Chris Hughton – a really good guy who'd been serving as Keegan's assistant – took over on a caretaker basis after just three league games.

For a while, there was much speculation about who might be taking over. As usual, several names were bandied around. Meanwhile, we were knocked out of the Carling Cup and lost three successive league games. The bleeding had to stop – a steady, experienced hand was needed to haul us off the foot of the table.

'Right guys, obviously it's been a long search,' Hughton began, at a hastily convened team meeting, 'but I've just heard that the new interim manager will be Joe Kinnear.'

Half of us hadn't heard of him – those Crazy Gang years at Wimbledon were long in the past. Among those who had, there was a collective groan. Some of the lads even laughed. It seemed like a bizarre choice. Kinnear wasn't even a coach. Beyond that, he'd been out of the game at the top level, as far as I knew, since the late '90s.

From the beginning, the Kinnear era at Newcastle was bizarre. As nice a guy as he was, I was never sure how relevant any of his football thinking was. Beyond that, it seemed all he ever wanted to do was fight people – specifically the press.

To everyone's surprise, Kinnear's time at the club wasn't a total disaster. He did steady the ship a bit. By Christmas, courtesy of a patchy run of wins, draws and a few losses, we were at least out of the bottom three. I'm told that the board were even considering offering Kinnear a longer-term contract.

Goalkeeper Shay Given and Charles N'Zogbia departed in the January transfer window. Neither of those losses helped us much, or pleased the fans. Peter Løvenkrands, Kevin Nolan and Ryan Taylor came the other way – and there was the added bonus that Joey Barton was available to play having been recently released from jail.

Joey, incidentally, was a guy for whom I always had a lot of time. Unlike a lot of players I've seen who showboat, kiss the badge and are all over social media giving it large in an attempt to ingratiate themselves with fans, Joey didn't care what anyone ever thought of him.

Yes he was a bit mad, and of course when things didn't go his way at training he'd want to fight the world. But I'd take that kind of player any day of the week over the other type I've described. Joey tolerated no con artists or fools. And he'd be there for you if needed.

By January and February we were barely hanging on. Then, Joe Kinnear sadly had to be admitted to hospital having suffered, we were told, heart problems. Chris Hughton, again, stepped in as caretaker boss while a relegation struggle loomed large.

■■ ■■■ ■

Meanwhile, the last throes of my England international career played out in a disjointed and ultimately empty fashion.

Having missed the majority of the qualifying campaign for Euro 2008 because of my rehab, there was a part of me that wondered whether I'd actually play in another major tournament.

My intuition was right. I *would never* play in another major tournament; I'd barely play any more games at all.

After Steve McClaren took over from Sven in the aftermath of the 2006 World Cup, the team went through a bit of a downturn. Some players were getting older; England were in transition.

Regardless, I felt I still had something to offer at international level in 2007. I broke Gary Lineker's competitive goalscoring record for England against Estonia in June and then, a few months later, scored twice in a 3-0 win over Russia at Wembley. A month after that, we travelled to Moscow for the return leg. What a trip that turned out to be – and not just because we'd lose 2-1, severely damaging our chances of Euro 2008 qualification in the process.

As we were coming in to land in Russia, it started snowing.

By the time we touched down on the runway itself, it was absolutely hammering it down. As we pulled off the runway, heading towards our stand, it had gone from being three inches on the ground to about eight, in what seemed like the blink of an eye. We then found ourselves in a queue behind ten or fifteen aircraft, all of them waiting to park up.

Ten minutes passed.

Half an hour passed.

Meanwhile, the snow is still piling down.

'We're not sure what's going to happen,' the pilot said over the intercom, 'there's no movement ahead. You're going to have to prepare yourself for the worst.'

The guy was suggesting that we might be there for hours and might possibly have to sleep on the plane. I was thinking, *this is unbelievable. What's going to happen here?*

'I'll phone Roman Abramovich,' John Terry suddenly said from the row behind me.

John got his phone out, and phoned Roman. 'Roman, we're stuck in a plane queue, at the airport', he began, 'they're saying we could be ages. Any chance of sorting it?'

I kid you not – within three minutes of John ending the call – the plane engines started and we began to move. Before long, we were overtaking all the other planes in the line on our inside, straight onto the stand. We were then out of the airport and straight to the team hotel. It was all so bizarre – but highly indicative of the power that Roman had!

Nevertheless, the defeat in Russia left us in a precarious position in Group E and when we lost 3-2 to Croatia and as a result failed to qualify for Euro 2008, Steve McClaren was sacked amid plenty of headlines about the famous umbrella incident at Wembley. Although I didn't actually play that night against Croatia, it felt as if my international career was now hanging in the balance.

By the way I was one of the few who felt sorry for Steve. He's a good man – I really liked him. Without a shadow of a doubt he was an amazing coach – among the very best I ever played under. Tactically speaking he was just brilliant, even though he too played 4-4-2.

In his defence, that was probably because he'd coached under Fergie who himself played a brand of 4-4-2 when Manchester United were playing at home against the lesser teams when formation didn't matter so much. However, if Real Madrid came to town, you wouldn't see them setting up like that.

Steve could study the opposition and set up to counteract their strengths as well as anybody. Then he could relate this information directly to our training sessions – he really knew his onions, Steve did. He was just a victim of circumstances, I always thought.

And then England hired Fabio Capello.

Initially I had no strong opinion on Fabio when he first arrived. Obviously, on a purely footballing level, he had a decent enough record in Italian football. Beyond that, I knew very little about him.

When he assembled his first squad session, the first thing we noticed was that he was very strict when it came to food: no butter, no sauce etc. We'd seen that before.

The second thing that struck us was that he literally couldn't speak a word of English.

In the meetings he talked exclusively in Italian to his interpreter and my feeling was that by doing this, his messages lost any value they might have had. How do you motivate someone when you can't even communicate in the same language? Everyone was just staring at each other. I was thinking, *how is this guy going to tell us anything?*

Looking back now, I have no idea what made the FA appoint somebody who couldn't speak the English language. It defies belief. But there was a broader fixation on foreign managers at that time. Sven, after all, had done a decent job in most people's eyes. I can only assume that the FA thought that Fabio might offer something similar.

The first squad he picked me in was for a friendly against Switzerland at Wembley in February 2008. He left me on the bench in a sketchy 2-1 win. The second squad was for a friendly against France a month later and he left me on the bench again. Having started for England for several years, this set the alarm bells ringing. As I sat there I thought, *oh no, this is not good.*

With ten or fifteen minutes left in a game we lost 1-0 he sent me on. My abiding memory of that night was my appearance in front of the line of press afterwards. By this time, Fabio's reluctance to start me was a bit of a hot story. The press were all over it – asking me if he'd explained his decision and, if so, what had he said. They could tell I wasn't happy. That was my intention.

'What position did he tell you to play in when you came on?' one of them asked me.

'I dunno,' I replied.

'What? No direction or anything?' he continued.

'No. I just went on there,' I confirmed.

I was making a point – and I'm certain the press got the message.

My implication was that the reason he hadn't given me any direction was quite clear: he couldn't – because he didn't speak

English. I was in a seriously dark mood and I wanted the press to pick up on it. It worked.

The next day's back pages were full of 'Michael Owen not told where to play' headlines. As brief as my press appearance had been, the press wrote the story based on my reaction, in the absence of any specific quotes by me to back it up.

Obviously, you don't need to be a genius to work out that these headlines were pretty damning towards a manager who'd only been in the job for two games. And it's probably no coincidence that Fabio Capello never picked me again. Whether he just didn't rate me or hadn't liked the implication of the headlines, we'll never know.

All I know is that he never once came up to St. James' Park to watch me thereafter. Indeed, to my knowledge, he watched me just once in his life – away at the Emirates – where I was only ever going to touch the ball twice if I was lucky. We duly got stuffed 3-0 while he sat there. He'd have been able to draw no conclusions from that.

It just felt like, having come in as a new manager, Fabio felt that he had to change *something*. And that something turned out to be Michael Owen. To me it felt like a statement.

Thereafter, I obviously continued to follow England on television. I'd watch his press conferences and hear journalists saying 'Fabio, you've left Michael Owen out again. Do you honestly think he's not one of the best three strikers we have?' The press, for once, were on my side. It was ridiculous – I was only twenty nine and had eighty nine caps. Obviously, he never answered them.

It might not surprise you therefore if I told you that, when I now look back on Fabio Capello's tenure, I do so with a lot of resentment.

Not only did he cut short a hard-earned international career with absolutely no explanation whatsoever, but he also went on to be one of the least effective England managers ever. Had he been really successful, at least I could have thought, *Ok, as much as I didn't like that he did things his own way, at least it was for the good of English football as a whole.*

But that wasn't even the case. He was absolutely crap. The World Cup in South Africa in 2010 was a debacle from start to finish. Instead of coming on board, proving the FA right, and actually winning something, he regressed English football instead.

Not just that, he got paid an absolute fortune and couldn't even be bothered to get fluent in the language.

For me, all of that's unforgivable – not just because I was sacrificed along the way. In my opinion, Fabio Capello caused catastrophic damage to both my career and English football in general and got paid handsomely to do so.

Then, he rode off into the sunset and into another job with Russia having suffered no repercussions whatsoever for doing an unbelievably bad job. He was accountable to nobody. What person in any other walk of life would get away with that?

All in all, it was a disgrace – and I really hope the FA learned a lesson with the Fabio fiasco. It seems as if they have.

At this point it would be remiss of me not to say that, in general, and this isn't meant to sound discriminatory or racist, but I've always felt that an England team should have an English manager. If it's not because we're all English and passionate about representing our country, why the hell else are we there?

Furthermore, and it always has been my opinion that, in international football, the players, manager, physio etc. should all be from the country they represent. That's what *international* football should be about.

As much as Sven was a really good guy and did, in some people's opinion, a decent job, the fact that he was a Swede is inescapable. I just don't see how any manager can motivate a bunch of lads with whom he doesn't share nationality. As a proud Englishman, I'd take an English Gareth Southgate-type manager every day of the week over a Capello or a Sven. That's just my opinion – probably best to leave it at that ...

When I look back on my England career as a whole while I sit here writing this book, there's one feeling that I just can't escape: we should have won a major tournament. It was *there* for us.

When you think about it, there was an era between say, 1998 and 2006 where we arguably had some of the best players in the world in certain positions.

Centre halves? Tons of them: Sol Campbell, Ledley King, Rio Ferdinand, Tony Adams, Jonathan Woodgate, John Terry, Carra – the list goes on. Full backs? Gary Neville and Ashley Cole were as good as anyone in the world. Midfield? An absolute embarrassment of talent: Beckham, Scholes, Lampard, Gerrard, on and on you could go.

All over the park, for several generations, we had the players capable of winning a World Cup or a European Championship. Yet, we never did. Do you want to know the reason? I'll give it to you in numerical form: 4-4-2.

When you think about England's more successful managers in recent years: Venables, Hoddle and Gareth Southgate, what do they all have in common? They all favour a variation of 3-5-2 (or at the very least 3-5-1-1).

To me it's absolutely no coincidence that, when we played that system, England came closest to winning something. Sven in 2002 would be the only possible exception. We had a real chance there in spite of his tactical shortcomings, but again we didn't take it

During those key years, 4-4-2 never played to our strengths. If anything, it blunted the abundance of talent we had because it meant that we had to either leave good players out or play them out of position to fit within a system. It was so frustrating – and as a player you could never say anything at the time.

The most irritating one was the 'Steven Gerrard and Frank Lampard can't play in the same team' debate. In a sense, the people that said that were absolutely right, but not for the reason you think.

Steven and Frank were simply too damn good for either of them to be given a sitting role in a four-man midfield. It's just not a role for two of the best players to have ever pulled on an England shirt.

Lampard had players like Essien and Makélélé sitting behind him at Chelsea. Steven had someone like Didi Hamann. They were both seen at their best for their clubs, bombing forward, roaming, turning up at the edge of the box and scoring goals.

That rarely happened for England – and that was because they were being played in a system that didn't suit them. We should have changed system to accommodate them and let them run free as they did at their clubs with an Owen Hargreaves-type of player sitting.

You only had to look around other teams to realise that 4-4-2 wasn't the formation to play. Teams like Spain started packing the midfield. And in doing so you'd never get the ball off them. Other sides did the same – until it got to the point where if you didn't have some variation of five across the middle, you'd lose the midfield. And in modern football, you just can't afford to lose the midfield.

Yet, we often stuck with 4-4-2 despite the obvious warning signs that the game was evolving. We had a guy like Paul Scholes, who started off for his club as an attacking midfielder, before becoming a quarterback type – orchestrating play. Despite that, we played him left wing half of the time!

We played loads of guys in positions that just didn't suit them. And because we did, not only did we never win a major tournament, we also wasted the immense talent of one of the greatest generations of players English football has ever had.

Looking back at my career, I honestly have never had any regrets. Of course it would be nice to have won the league or Champions League with Liverpool, or the league with Madrid or a World Cup with England, but I honestly never dwell on any of it.

It wasn't like any of these things were written in the stars anyway. What I won was what I won. The career I had was the career I deserved to have. I rarely think *what if?* I prefer to look forward.

Having said that, if you *forced* me to pick something that would have made me feel most fulfilled, then it would definitely be to have won something with England. I look at players like Geoff Hurst and Bobby Moore and can't help feeling that it would have been great for our generation to have been held in such high regard.

Having said all this, I am immensely proud of my England international career – and that pride extends to all the age groups that I represented over the years from the age of fourteen upwards.

Although I've lived just across the Welsh border for my entire life, I consider myself to be as proud an Englishman as anyone could possibly be. I'd like to think that throughout my twenty-year long career – the eighty nine caps and the forty goals – I always gave my all and did the jersey proud.

REBØOT_16

HEROES

To put it simply, there has been a lot of lies, bullshit and general mis-information surrounding the end of my time at Newcastle. Much has been said and written about those last few weeks, and most of it has painted a picture of me as a selfish mercenary – the villain of the piece.

Paul Ferris even decided to throw me under the bus when he wrote his book. At the time, again, I made no comment. The reason I didn't was because I knew my time would come. This is my time.

As I've been at pains to mention throughout this book, as far as I'm concerned, my relationship with Alan Shearer throughout my time at Newcastle was great. I'd lived with him in the early days and we saw each other socially when we both lived at Darras Hall.

In my eyes, he was not only a strike partner on the pitch from a playing perspective; he was also a good mate. At no time did I get the impression that he saw things any differently.

When Joe Kinnear required more time to recover from his health issues, Newcastle were in dire straits in league terms. In short, we were going down – so the club, faced with a desperate situation in Mike Ashley's first season, brought in Shearer as temporary manager, presumably hoping that his legendary status at the club would galvanise the players and the fans – and get us out of trouble.

To understand Alan Shearer, you have to also understand not just his personality, but also his status in his hometown. In Newcastle, as much as Kevin Keegan was seen as the messiah, Shearer was seen as God himself.

As a player, few guys epitomised the Geordie spirit more than Alan did. By rejecting a move to Manchester United from Blackburn in the late '90s in favour of returning to his hometown, he'd demonstrated his loyalty in the eyes of the fans. In those same eyes, therefore, Shearer could never, ever, do wrong.

As much as I liked him, it was always obvious to me that Shearer was a domineering character. He was exactly the same way as a player – and that was one of the many attributes that made him truly great. Alan Shearer was probably the only player I encountered in my career who I considered my equal in terms of unwavering will and self-confidence.

On or off the pitch, it was his way or no way – and because of that, people around him soon realised that the only way to survive was to be on his side. And if achieving that meant having to crawl up his backside to get on his good side, that's what some of them did.

To that end, by the time those last few weeks of the 2008/2009 season came around, as the club stared into an abyss called the Championship, Alan Shearer had surrounded himself with hangers-on, tasked to do his bidding for him. None of this, however, guaranteed that he'd be a successful manager when the chips were down.

Prior to all of this and given that I was close to completing the four year contract that I had signed at Newcastle and as such would be free to leave at the end of that season on a Bosman, at some point between December 2008 and February 2009, the club offered me, in theory, a new contract.

I can't remember the precise specifics of this contract in terms of duration. We didn't even get into those details because what they offered me was so insultingly pitiful; we barely got into serious negotiations at all. Without sounding entitled, it was a fraction of what I'd previously been on.

'What do you think?' Tony Stephens asked me.

'They've got to be joking,' I replied.

I understood their position. Had I signed, they would have at least had an asset to trade later. However, given the situation, I had the power for once. Or so I thought.

Instead of committing to anything, Tony and I agreed that I would see out my contract and then figure out my options after the season ended.

The problem was, somebody had leaked what should have been private conversations between the club and my agent to the press. Literally the day after the conversation took place, it was in the newspapers.

Not only was this wrong – and whoever did it should be ashamed of themselves by the way – but it also heaped a lot of pressure on me from a fan perspective. All I ever heard was people saying: 'Any news on your new contract, Michael?'

Here's where it gets messy.

In my eyes, I felt that while the club wanted to make these

noises about offering me a new contract, I don't think they ever actually intended to go through with it.

The evidence was clear.

While they weren't lying in that they could come out and say: 'We've offered Michael Owen a new deal,' they knew very well that I couldn't respond by saying: 'Yeah, but the cheeky bastards only offered me twenty grand a week!' What would the man in the street have said to that? I couldn't win.

All along, to me it seemed like Newcastle knew that they'd offered me something that they knew I'd turn down – and they did it only for leverage, and to look good in the eyes of the fans and the press. At the same time, it made me look bad. Fair play to Ashley and Llambias, I suppose – my reading of the situation was that they hung me out to dry in a tactical sense.

It was just another example of how a club always has the upper hand over a player by saying things like: 'Oh yeah, this player put in a transfer request', or 'this player refused to play' and how the fans will always blindly believe their club.

But I can guarantee you that for every one of those examples, there's a few scenarios where a club treats a player like a second class citizen: makes him come in at eight in the morning and sends him home at ten at night, makes him train with the kids and so on – all of these things designed to make his life hell and drive him out of the club.

None of this news makes it to the press other than the odd time when a player might say something like: 'Oh the manager's not giving me much of a chance. I'm not sure why he bought me.' You're a brave man to start saying that kind of thing anyway – you'll only get treated worse and also face the possibility of being branded a troublemaker. As a player, sometimes you just can't win.

I knew all of this very well because I'd seen it first hand at Newcastle with a guy called Albert Luque. He'd been bought by Souness in 2005 for quite a lot of money on a five year contract – he was a decent enough player.

Pretty soon, though, it became apparent that he was never going to settle – he was visibly homesick. From that point on, he was effectively parked throughout the Allardyce era until he eventually left the club in August of 2007.

During this time when he was parked, Newcastle made his life an absolute misery by doing all the things I mentioned: never playing him, making him train with the kids and touting him around Europe. Allardyce even left him without a squad number, which I thought was an unnecessarily low blow.

Basically, it appeared to me that the club did everything they could to encourage him to leave – so that they wouldn't be lumbered with his wages. But the fans never hear the details of cases like this. And even if they did, they're always too blind to the badge to see what's really going on.

This was the position I was being potentially thrust into. And to make matters worse, I picked up another annoying groin injury when there were just a few games left. Obviously, I had been in the position many times before – and knew very well (a) how it felt and (b) how my body responded to rest from the standpoint of being able to play again.

To rewind a little, when Alan Shearer took over as manager with ten games left, I know for a fact that Mike Ashley had dangled the incentive of a long-term contract in front of him if he was able to keep Newcastle up.

From the start, it seemed doable – the atmosphere in the dressing room was good despite our precarious league position. Shearer would definitely be on the tougher end of the scale when it came to measuring managers but, that aside, everyone was loving his attitude and the fact that he'd brought Iain Dowie in as a coach. The training ground was a happy place under Alan Shearer.

Beyond that, Shearer seemed to see me as somebody who was on a different level than the other lads. Possibly because of our pre-existing friendship, it was obvious to me that he felt he could use me as a means of gauging squad morale – 'what do the lads think of training?' type of thing. Given our relationship, I was more than happy to fulfil that intermediary role for him.

In his first game as manager, we lost 2-0 at Chelsea. Thereafter, we drew with Stoke, lost at Tottenham and drew at home to Portsmouth before a trip to Anfield loomed. In these first four games, I'd started and hadn't been substituted.

Then everything seemed to change.

On the run-up to the Liverpool game at Anfield on May 3rd, Shearer called me into his office. He had an expression on his face that I wasn't familiar with.

'I'm going to start Martins tomorrow. I'll leave you on the bench,' he told me.

Immediately, I had a strange feeling. Any time we'd played golf in the past or been in each other's company, Alan hadn't been in any way shy in telling me that he really didn't rate Obafemi Martins.

'Ok, boss,' I said, 'whatever you think.'

I thought, *this is strange. You've told me you don't rate him yet here you are playing him ahead of me.*

I suppose, with the perspective I have today, I can see why he made that decision. We were going to Anfield – a place where we weren't expecting to get much. If one up front was how we were going to play, I suppose it made sense in that Martins had pace and could run in the channels. Nevertheless, Shearer's decision that day triggered alarm bells ringing for me.

We lost 3-0 – with Joey Barton getting himself sent off with thirteen minutes left. Shearer and Joey had a right set-to after the game – there was a screaming match in the dressing room that everyone could see and hear. Shearer had never liked him – that much was evident to mc.

With just three games left, we needed something good to happen. I felt as if Shearer's God-like status was on the line.

The following week, in front of 50,000-plus nervous fans at St. James' Park, we got something – a 3-1 win against Middlesbrough. Annoyingly, I picked up a groin strain with twenty minutes left and was replaced by Martins.

I didn't play in the penultimate game against Fulham – a depressing 1-0 home defeat that left us needing an unlikely point away at Aston Villa to stay in the league.

During the week building up to the Villa game, I was injured, as I said. Bearing in mind that I knew it was an important game and that I'd probably had in excess of thirty muscle injuries in my career, I was doing everything humanly possible, in conjunction with the physio Derek Wright, to be able to play, albeit with a degree of resigned realism.

I have to be clear, here. Had it just been a normal game, there's no way I would have played. I was at three-quarters pace at the very most, building up to just *try* to train. It wasn't that I was being a wimp and didn't fancy pushing through the pain barrier either.

Muscles that are injured just don't function. I knew my body better than possibly any footballer has ever known his body and, realistically, as much as I desperately wanted to play in this vital game, I was at least a week away from fitness. But we only had three days.

Regardless, on the Friday before the Sunday game, I knew that I had to test my groin somehow. I knew very well that if I wasn't able to run on my own with the physio on the Friday, I certainly wouldn't be able to join the full training session on the Saturday. I'd just be a lost cause.

As I started running, gradually building up to three-quarter pace, I started to feel nervous. Through my vast experience, I knew exactly what it felt like to be on the edge. Regardless, we pushed on through three-quarters and as I did I was thinking, *this is going to ping any second.*

The natural reaction in such a situation isn't to push through and let the muscle tear. Instead, you ease down, which I did, before turning to Derek.

'It feels like if I went to 100 percent, it'll tear,' I said

I had no reason to say anything else. As desperate as I was to play in the game, I was just being open – knowing that Derek would relay everything to Alan Shearer and Paul Ferris, who were with the rest of the team on the adjacent pitch.

'What shall we do?' I asked.

'Ok, we don't want that to happen,' he replied, 'so just take it to where you think the limit is.'

I continued at seventy-five or eighty percent for the rest of the session as we agreed and then we went inside. Yes I'd done ten sets of these runs, but in my heart of hearts I knew I was still a week away from being able to run properly.

'How's it feeling?' Paul Ferris asked me when I went into his office.

At this point I should say that, while I'd always got on with him, I felt like I could never totally trust Ferris.

'If I keep going, I'm going to pull it,' I told him straight out.

'But it's the last game of the season,' he countered, 'Are you not prepared to take the risk?'

In his book, Ferris suggested, why I don't know, that I had replied with something to the effect of not wanting to risk getting injured and therefore jeopardise any future contract with another club.

That is completely different to my recollection of what I said. I wasn't in any way bothered about picking up yet another groin injury. I'd had seventeen of them, probably, what difference would another one have made? I'd have had three months of off-season to get over it.

'Of course I'm willing to risk it,' I replied, 'I'm just concerned about what might happen if I try to sprint.'

Again, I was just being honest. I wanted to play. But at the same time I was only making them aware that, given the injury, there was a possibility that the groin might tear and I might have to be subbed after a few minutes.

I thought I was being fair to the manager of the club; in his book Ferris seemed to imply that I was protecting myself, which is simply not the case. I absolutely would have started if the manager had asked me to.

After this conversation, Ferris obviously reported everything to Shearer – who by this point, in my opinion, had seemed to make himself bigger than the club.

This kind of situation, really, is common to a few football clubs. When a player, or a group of players are there for a long time and become fan favourites, they become increasingly powerful. While they're playing, this power is of benefit to the club and it galvanises the fans. But it can later have a negative effect as seems to be the case with the Class of '92 at

Manchester United, who have sometimes been at loggerheads with the club, and to a lesser extent Steven Gerrard at Liverpool, Lampard and Terry at Chelsea and Alan Shearer at Newcastle.

Instead of being a continuing positive, these club stalwarts can become a burden to a club and a focus for conflict. It happens time and time again. I'm not sure what the solution is or even if there is one at all. Sadly, what often happens, as I'm certain was the case with Steven Gerrard at Liverpool, is that the powerful player is forced out.

In Steven's case, I severely doubt whether he really wanted to go and play in the States in 2015. I've heard that the club wanted him out two years prior to when he actually left.

I'm sure he would rather have wound his career down at Liverpool, played increasingly fewer games until he reached a point where he could be integrated into the coaching staff. This only happened later in his case. But instead, because he'd become so symbolic and so powerful, I believe he was forced out in the short term. Steven was bigger than the club.

So, back in 2009, when Shearer was brought in as temporary manager, he was in this position of untouchable power within Newcastle United that I've just described.

On the Saturday, the day before the game, Alan pulled me in. Immediately, as I looked at him across the desk, I could see that something was off. I knew him well. But this wasn't the Alan I knew. As I sat there, I thought, *someone's got to you* …

'How are you feeling then?' he asked. 'What are we going to do?'

'I tried yesterday, and while I'm still in one piece, I still felt that if I'd pushed any further, the muscle would have pinged.'

'And?' he said.

'On that basis, I guess I'm not much use to you,' I continued, 'but, of course, if you want to start me, or put me on the bench, I'm fine either way. I'm just being honest about where things are at.'

And I *was* being honest. I had previous form to prove it – having played in a World Cup quarter-final with a hamstring tear five inches long. I was at sixty per cent if I was lucky that day and I never thought about anything beyond that game.

Some might say I was selfish to have played at all in that state but I never saw it that way. All I wanted to do was win the game. This was an almost identical situation, so why would I behave any differently?

Shearer didn't buy anything that I was telling him. I don't think he was questioning that I was injured – that was irrefutable. Instead, he was doing something much more unsavoury: I felt he was questioning my appetite for the cause. That was a pretty serious accusation.

No matter how many times I told him that I was happy to play, the information just wasn't getting through – even though he must surely have seen that it just didn't fit my agenda to lie.

The fact is that, throughout my career, I had always thrived on being a big game player who could deliver on the biggest occasions.

This final game of the season, where Newcastle's top-flight status was on the line, was just the kind of pressure I relished. But to give myself a chance of delivering, I needed to be fit to play.

'Play me!' I said, getting really exasperated. 'Or put me on the bench. I'll do whatever you want, mate. Just know that I'm fearful of sprinting.'

What Shearer said next was … nothing.

Instead, I talked for him.

'If you want my honest opinion here,' I said, 'start me on the bench. And if we need a goal with ten minutes to go, bring me on.'

Even a neutral could see that this made most sense. If we were winning 3-0 – no need to bring me on. Equally, if we were losing 3-0 – it wouldn't matter either.

But if we desperately needed a goal, I felt I was capable of coming on and hanging around the box in the hope of a chance dropping to me. Even though I knew I might struggle to sprint, I never doubted my ability to bury a chance when it mattered most.

As I left his office that day, he made an insinuation that led me to believe that he thought I had half an eye on my next contract. I'm not stupid – we both knew I was out of contract in a few weeks.

'It doesn't matter anyway,' he said, 'because you'll have the summer to get fit again.'

'Of course I don't want a horrific injury, who does?' I countered, 'but I'm prepared to risk it. I've done it before and I'll do it again.'

As it transpired, even though he didn't say anything further at the time and we didn't part on unpleasant terms at all, he did exactly what I suggested.

I sat on the bench at Villa Park that day and came off the bench with twenty five minutes left at which point we needed just one goal to secure continued Premier League status – after a freak Damien Duff own goal in the first half had given Villa the lead. No chances fell my way. We lost 1-0 and with that we were relegated to the Championship for the first time in sixteen years.

Nothing much was said in the dressing room afterwards,

least of all by Shearer himself. We were all gutted. At no point did he point the finger at me and say: 'You weren't there for the cause' which was definitely his style when he felt a player hadn't pulled their weight. The Joey Barton incident at Anfield was evidence that he would always get things off his chest.

We didn't even part with an argument. All he said was that we all needed to report back to the club, clear out our lockers before leaving for the summer. Given that my contract didn't expire for a few more days, I reported exactly as he requested. The only difference is, once I'd cleared out my locker, I left Newcastle United for good.

It wasn't until three months later, via Tony Stephens' assistant, I discovered that Alan Shearer was apparently seething with me. Not only that, it transpired that he was telling anyone who'd listen what he thought of me. If that's the way it was, put simply, I felt I was being a made a scapegoat.

When you analyse it, it all makes sense. Shearer's record as manager in the last eight games of that 2008/2009 season was dire: lost 5, drew 2, won 1. These are hardly God-like stats.

The truth is, the damage was done long before we went to Villa Park needing to draw. Villa Park was one of the games we were *least* likely to get something – they'd finish fifth that year.

Sadly, this feud has continued to the present day. The more I think about it, the more I understand why Alan behaves the way he does and continues to spread negativity about me whenever he can. He was brought in at St. James' Park as the saviour, the local boy. It could have been a great story. But he failed. Newcastle United were relegated.

Perhaps rather than examine his own shortcomings, it felt easier to blame Michael Owen. After all, given how far apart we live, we'd be unlikely to ever run into each other in person. This delusion is perhaps what gets him through the night. As humans, that's what we do.

And from that perspective I feel a little sorry for him. I'm gutted for him that it never worked out at Newcastle, but I'm so innocent relative to what he thinks. Whatever anybody says to the contrary, it seems that the idea of my guilt is ingrained in his mind.

At one point, knowing that we'd be in the same place at the same time for some TV work, he and I tentatively discussed talking face to face. When the time came, for whatever reason, the opportunity passed.

And on it goes.

During 2018, I was asked by my employer, BT Sport, to come on their Premier League Tonight show to talk about some of the issues in my career – specifically how injuries slowed me over the years. For me it was cathartic to lay it all out there. As far as I know, people in general liked the interview – specifically in regard to how forthright I'd been about some of my trials and tribulations.

I left the studio thinking, *I'm so glad I did that …*

In the days following the show, I received many messages of support from people who appreciated my honesty.

A day or two after that, Shearer started sniping on Twitter.

During the interview, I'd made a general comment about the latter part of my career – how, because of endless injuries and as a result how I'd changed the way played, I enjoyed my football less. At times I even hated it.

Obviously, as someone who'd once been able to run very fast, when I was reduced to a pale imitation of my former self, it made total sense that I didn't enjoy playing as much. I said it, and I stand by it. Shearer pounced on it saying, basically, how unimpressed Newcastle fans would be to hear that I didn't enjoy playing there. He put it out there to his followers probably knowing exactly what would happen: Twitter would explode. And it did.

It was such a petty, cheap shot and one that didn't make any sense anyway. What I'd said wasn't a reflection on any of the three clubs I played for at the end of my career. It was merely a reflection of how I felt about myself in the relation to what I once was.

A text conversation followed. I suggested that what he'd said was uncalled for. He replied saying that he had offered no opinion. Back and forth it went – with me trying to explain myself logically, and him stone-walling me with deflections and pedantic, picky responses (I've still got the texts).

It went, as I suspected, precisely nowhere. Alan Shearer and I still haven't talked this out face to face and that's a shame because, as I've said many, many times, we were very good friends.

REBØOT_17

THE BADGE

Typically, I got all kinds of flak for having a brochure produced by Wasserman Media that was made available to clubs that might potentially be interested in signing me. This happened, from memory, sometime in July of 2009, although I knew nothing about the brochure until details appeared in the press.

In all honesty, as much as I was out of contract and, as such, Tony was merely advertising my profile, just like someone would if they were serious about selling a house, or a car, or anything with value – I thought it was a mistake to do what Tony did, knowing what the press were like in those days. Obviously somebody was going to get hold of the brochure and I could only end up looking bad as a result.

In normal situations, when clubs know that a player is going to be available on a Bosman, they'll call the player's agent in advance to register a bit of interest. The problem was, no calls came for me while that last season wound down at Newcastle.

At this point we didn't panic as there was still time, people were going away on holiday and so on. Given that it was common knowledge that I was available, we thought we'd just let it run.

When the time came when most clubs were getting ready to meet up for the new season, we still hadn't heard anything. At this point I was thinking, *oh my God, my career could be over here ...*

Don't get me wrong, I knew I was a tough sell. But as much as I could see why there might have been limited interest given that I was a fraction of the attraction I had been five years earlier, I nevertheless felt strangely unwanted.

The first port of call had obviously been Liverpool.

They didn't want me.

Eventually, Hull City came in. They'd just avoided relegation by one point, ironically at Newcastle's expense.

I considered it briefly and thought, *no, I just can't do that.*

Towards the end at Newcastle I'd realised a couple of things. First, I had no appetite for playing in the Championship.

Secondly, it had become apparent that the Mike Ashley era wasn't going to be one where large sums were going to be spent on players. The days of the Ginola, Asprilla and Les Ferdinand type glamour signings seemed to be over.

On that basis, there had to be a concern as to whether they'd be able to get back up again should they be relegated. To me, it seemed that by signing for Hull City I might be walking into a similar situation. (As it turned out, I was right. Hull would be relegated in 2009/2010).

Then I thought, *Ok, but what am I going to do?*

I had no answers. As much as Tony was meeting people and having talks, it was all getting a bit fraught.

Faced with no alternatives, I was resigned to the fact that I would possibly have to keep training on my own while simultaneously hoping someone else might come in.

Then Tony got a sniff of Everton's interest.

My immediate thought when he called me was, *oh, God – this could be a tricky situation …*

At this stage, it's important to say that I have views on club loyalty that are probably different from many players.

When I was a kid, given that we lived outside Liverpool, I was exposed to a broad demographic of people who supported a variety of teams. There were Liverpool supporters, Everton supporters and there were Manchester United and City supporters – probably in equal measure.

But because my dad had played for Everton and my brothers more or less told me that they were the team I should support when I was five, that was the club I supported when I was a kid.

When I signed for Liverpool at youth level, you could say that, when the game became my career and a means to support my family and myself, I ceased to be a fan in the true sense.

As much as I was employed by Liverpool and loved every minute of playing week in, week out, for them as well as doing everything I could to help them win, that didn't mean that I didn't look in the paper to see how Everton did, or how Chester did. I was always still interested, but I was approaching it from a different place than a football fan would. There's an important difference.

Throughout my career, I've heard so many conversations from football fans about which player is loyal and which other player isn't. To me, this is complete bollocks and a way of thinking perpetuated by fans that are blind to the badge, as I see it.

The truth is: most players just aren't as loyal as the fans like to think they are. While they're at their current club, they'll say they're loyal – they have to. But if another, bigger club came in for them offering a deal that could improve the lives of them and their family, then you'd see how loyal they really are.

And then there's another type of player – a Paul Scholes or a Ryan Giggs-type to name a couple that spring to mind – guys who stayed at one club for their entire career. When discussing them, football fans just love to say: 'They are so loyal.'

But the reality is, they only stayed at their club because there was no obvious way to improve on their situation. Manchester United were winning everything. Why would they leave? Their loyalty was never tested because there was nothing to test it with. I'd have done the same.

Being a footballer, therefore, isn't really about this mythical concept of loyalty. Working in the media as I do now, I could name you a dozen players who were considered very loyal to a particular club but who now couldn't care less if that team won or lost. It's all for show – but fans just don't want to hear that.

Regardless, when Everton came in for me, as much as I had supported them, I could also envisage all kinds of grief being directed at my family and me by Liverpool fans that would inevitably accuse me of being disloyal by signing for one of their bitterest rivals.

Did we need all that aggravation? Not particularly.

Would I have signed? *Of course* I would have had they been the only option. As I said, it was my career. I had a family to support.

'What do you want to do?' Tony asked.

'I've got to go to Everton. I've got no other option,' I replied.

At this stage, David Moyes wanted to meet me in person.

The problem was, he was on holiday in the US at the time. 'We've got no options here,' Tony said, 'you're going to have to show willing. You need to get on a plane.'

We discussed the alternatives. None appealed.

'We could wait for two weeks,' Tony said, 'but I'm telling you now, if that doesn't work, we've got no club.'

Despite feeling deeply conflicted about the whole idea of going to Everton, I nevertheless flew to America and met David Moyes on the quiet for just one day. We played golf; the meeting went well. Along the way, he laid out the plans he had for me if I signed.

'Now,' he began, 'I don't want you playing the way you played at Newcastle latterly,' he continued, 'I want the old Michael Owen – running in channels, into the penalty area, scoring loads of goals.'

Knowing what I knew about my physical limitations, I thought, *Hmm. I'll agree to this now, of course – and I'll worry about how I'm going to do it later.*

'No problem, boss,' I said.

I flew home a day later, fully expecting to sign for Everton and fully expecting Liverpool fans to totally disown me because of it.

I should say, even before I made my next move to a club, I was never exactly sure what the Liverpool fans thought of me after I left anyway. The only indication I'd ever had came during one of the first games I played back at Anfield as a Newcastle player.

Initially, there was no detectable animosity whatsoever. I might have even got some applause from the home fans when my name was announced. As the game wore on, the Liverpool fans became impatient because it wasn't all going their way.

Then I committed what was just an innocuous foul at the Kop end. A few boos rang out from the Kop.

The next time I touched it ... more boos and derogatory shouts generally. I thought, *aye-aye – this isn't great ...*

Then, every time I touched the ball, I got what seemed like wholesale abuse. How many people it actually was, I'm not sure. I was taken aback and more than a little hurt. After the game I was still upset – even more so when I discovered that my parents were very distressed too. They'd had to sit there while Liverpool fans abused their son.

It felt so strange to be rejected by fans with whom I'd had such a great relationship with and shared so much success and so many great times with. At the time, my shit-filter kicked in and I tried to explain it away in my own head to soften the blow.

I thought, *this is a game they need to win. Maybe they're just frustrated and it's not really about me?*

Whether there's any truth in that theory, we'll never know. Would they have still booed me if they'd been coasting along 5-0 up? Again, who's to say?

But what that day did do was give me an early warning as to how fickle fans could be – even when it comes to a player that they'd once considered to be one of their own. And at that time I wasn't even at a club that could be considered a rival.

On the same subject, while I was writing this book, I was told about an interview that Ian Rush had done on beIN Sports with Richard Keys and Andy Gray. I immediately went on YouTube to find it. I couldn't believe it. He was describing a near identical situation that he, a Liverpool legend to this day, found himself in in 1988.

After a year at Juventus, he wanted to come back to England

to play and seemingly both Alex Ferguson and Colin Harvey, Everton's manager at the time, had been in touch with a view to signing him.

Rushie said he was ready to sign with either Manchester United or Everton. And he'd have done it without even having called Kenny Dalglish. As it turned out, Dalglish called him at the eleventh hour and he returned to Anfield for a second spell.

As far as I know, Liverpool fans have never had any issue with this. Rushie remains untouchable in their eyes – even though he would have willingly signed for one or other of Liverpool's main rivals.

Would he have received the same level of abuse that I have? We'll never know. But our situations were almost identical except that he got the call and I didn't. If anything, my willingness was greater than his in that at least I'd tried! To this day I'm still completely disillusioned by the attitude fans take to my situation.

■ ■ ■

Two days after returning from the meeting with David Moyes, I was just having a quiet day at home when Nicky Butt's name appeared on my phone.

'Be prepared, Sir Alex is going to give you a call,' he said.

'Ok,' I replied.

' Yeah. I think he wants to sign you,' Nicky told me.

I couldn't believe it. I legged it to the lounge and told Louise. My head was spinning at the thought of a chance to be at a club where winning trophies was the norm. Big games, Champions League, 75,000 fans for every game – we were both buzzing.

For the next hour I literally sat in my hall staring at my phone then, all of a sudden, it rang. It was a private number. I don't often answer those but this time was an exception. I let it ring for five or six seconds before answering. It was him. After a few pleasantries, Sir Alex invited me to his house the next day.

I hardly slept. Conscious of making a good first impression, I chose my clothes carefully and drove there early, parked in some supermarket car park half a mile from his house and sat there fifteen minutes before the appointed time. Arriving ten minutes early was the target. I was desperate to impress him in every way. I drove to his house and pressed the buzzer.

Obviously I knew him given our shared interest and connections in horse racing, so we probably spent more time talking about racing than football in that first meeting. Strangely, I don't think he ever directly said that he wanted to sign me. It was just assumed on both sides. I left knowing that I was probably about to become a Manchester United player. Tony Stephens hadn't even spoken to David Gill.

By this time, I had honestly just resigned myself to the fact that Liverpool fans were going to hate me whatever I did. Would they hate me more for going to Manchester United than going to Everton? Toss a coin …

All I could do was make a career decision with only myself and my family in mind. Knowing that I'd done everything possible to engineer a return to Liverpool, it was clear that it was never going to happen.

Faced instead with the possibility of playing at a big club, with great facilities, in the Champions League, with players that I'd known and played with at England, it really wasn't a difficult choice at all to sign for Manchester United. I do not regret it for a second. What's more, my family was delighted for me.

First and foremost, I was a footballer. Football was my means of earning. As such, I had an opportunity to play the game at the highest level late in my career and provide for my family at the same time. I severely doubt that many players – despite what they might say – would have turned it down.

There was, however, a late hitch.

'We have a problem,' Tony Stephens said when he called me. 'I've just met the club. We just can't do it.'

'What?!' I replied.

'We haven't got much bargaining power here or leverage with another club,' he explained, 'they're holding us to ransom.'

'What are they offering?' I asked.

'Twenty grand a week,' he told me.

Obviously I was well aware that I was no longer worth a hundred-plus grand a week. But as much as twenty grand a week is a lot of money by any normal standards, both Tony and I knew that they were low-balling us, just because they could. After all, given that I was on a Bosman and I'd therefore be costing them nothing from a fee perspective, they were clearly trying their hand knowing how desperate I was.

And desperate I bloody well was!

The reality was, I'd have signed for twenty grand a week. I'd have signed for ten grand a week. I'd probably have signed for five grand a week! All of those numbers would obviously have rankled with me later in that I'd have always known that, in a world where wages were only going up, while I certainly wasn't in Wayne Rooney territory, my market value was probably still in the region of fifty grand a week given I was on a Bosman.

'I've still got to sign, Tony,' I said, 'just get whatever you can.'

He still thought they were just chancing their arm, but he arranged another meeting anyway. He called me straight afterwards.

'Ok, well I've agreed something,' he began, 'it's not great, but it's a bit better than it was.'

Manchester United had agreed to raise their offer somewhat. In addition, given the risk they were undoubtedly taking by signing someone with a track record of injury like mine, they incorporated a bonus that would amount to an extra hundred thousand pounds for every so many appearances. It wasn't perfect – but I remain very grateful that they signed me at all.

During our first meeting, Sir Alex had been quite upfront about where I stood. 'Rooney and Berbatov, so …' he said – as if to confirm something I already knew: that I was behind them in the queue.

As far as which squad number I'd be wearing, that was an interesting story also. From memory, Antonio Valencia had initially been earmarked as a potential candidate for the revered number seven jersey – the shirt that had been worn in the past by the likes of Best, Robson, Cantona, Beckham and most recently, Cristiano Ronaldo.

Seemingly reluctant to endure the pressure of such an iconic squad number, Valencia wore it for a period of time before Sir Alex called Michael Carrick and I into his office.

'With this shirt comes a lot of tradition …' Sir Alex began, 'I don't want the person wearing it to feel burdened by its history. I need to know that they understand its significance. Michael, you're my first choice.'

Instantly recognising its significance and wanting to do it justice, I said yes without hesitation. Looking back, there was possibly a part of me that may have been subconsciously putting pressure on myself by accepting such a revered squad number.

I needn't have worried.

When I turned up for pre-season, I was in really good physical and mental shape. We went to Malaysia on a short tour and I sat on the bench for my debut before coming on and scoring the winner against a Malaysian XI in Kuala Lumpur on July 18th. Two days later, I scored again in a rematch against the same side.

When I scored another two against Hangzhou Greentown six days later in an 8-2 win, my confidence was sky-high. Surrounded by great players that were clearly on my wavelength in terms of understanding each other's movement, those early pre-season days felt like yet another career rebirth.

My fellow strikers, Rooney and Berbatov were contrasting personalities. Wayne was like a kid and definitely one of life's good guys. He was always last off the training ground and last to leave in the afternoon because he was fooling around at the lunch table. His absolute love for football was evident in everything he did. I found him to be a lovely lad that you could trust totally.

Looking back, I think he and I had a certain relationship given that he came into the England team when I was the main striker. In fact, I later discovered that, although he was an Everton supporter growing up, he'd pretend to be me when he was playing in his back garden as a kid. 'My favourite player was Michael Owen,' he told me. Apparently both Sergio Aguero and Kevin De Bruyne were big fans of mine when they were kids. It's always so gratifying when you hear that you were the hero of current stars when they were growing up.

Given that I'd seen Wayne since his early days, I always knew that, on the pitch, he was absolutely exceptional. Loads of natural gifts and so much instinctive vision. He was always such a clean striker of a football and he was better in the air than he was probably given credit for. Just like most players, his game changed over the years.

By the time I arrived at Manchester United, Wayne had started playing a bit deeper – first as a number ten, then, when we were short, in midfield. As much as he could perform those roles, I would have loved to have seen him playing as an out and out striker more often.

The problem was, he actually enjoyed being involved in the game more, as he would inevitably be, in these deeper positions. Wayne was very unselfish – which for someone who scores a lot of goals is a rare trait. He would square anything. He loved assisting as much as he did scoring. Without doubt he was one of the truly great English players.

Berbatov was a completely different kind of guy. Among the lads, he very much kept himself to himself. And whenever he did speak it was often a moan of some kind. I always found that quite strange – that someone who was shy or quiet should have no issue having a go at people. He had no problem offering up criticism.

As a player, he was obviously very talented. If there were to be a criticism, given that the Manchester United way of playing was all about speed, it would be his lack of pace. Because nothing happened too quickly with Dimitar, some people felt that his presence slowed the game down. Whether you agree with that or not is a matter of personal preference.

Regardless, he was tall, strong and good in the air – with great touch and excellent vision. He was a top player without doubt – particularly on match days. I'm not sure how much you'd want him on the training ground though. He would never be one for putting in a huge shift!

And then there was Scholesy. What can you say about that man! He is, without a shadow of a doubt, one of the most unique professionals I've ever met.

There was just no nonsense with him. He'd turn up at training, put his gear on, never worry about looking smart or smelling pretty, do his work, blast balls about the place because he was bored before training even started – and then, afterwards, he'd be in the shower and in his car on his way home before anyone else was even off the training ground.

People almost laughed at him because he was so no-frills. Scholesy was the polar opposite to what people thought a footballer would be. As much as he was great company and definitely part of the laughs and jokes within the group, he was always keener to get home. Fame just never got to him.

But, oh my God, while he was there at training, he was a magician. If you were playing five-a-side or possession games, if you had Scholesy on your side, you won. If you weren't on his side, you could forget getting the ball off him. It couldn't be done. You couldn't get close enough to him to get the ball off him.

In these box possession games we played, if you thought, *he'll take a touch here, I'll close him down,* he'd ship it with one touch. Then, when you thought he'd pass it first time, he'd take a touch, turn and be gone. You couldn't get near him. His passing was sublime. He saw pictures that nobody else saw.

On match days he was similarly no-nonsense. He'd usually start by moaning that we'd got to the stadium too early. He hated that. Then, when everyone else was in the dressing room, he wouldn't even be there. It wasn't that he didn't like being in among the group. It was more that he wanted to get on with things.

So, he'd be out in the corridor, often with Rio Ferdinand, doing keepy-ups or kicking the ball against the wall. For Scholesy, kick-off could never come quick enough.

And then, on the pitch, he was a level above whatever he did in training. Although his role changed over the years, again because of injury, Scholesy still retained the ability to dictate to every one of the twenty two players on the field.

I always remember one particular game at Stoke while I was sat on the bench during my first season at Manchester United. Scholesy demonstrated how to single-handedly run a game. It was unbelievable. Everyone tried to press him, but they couldn't get near him; he'd just drop back. Then, as soon as they tried to push on, he'd just take a step forward and move to the other side of them. Meanwhile he was spraying the ball everywhere; it was just artistry. He could dictate games on his own.

If Scholesy had a shortcoming at all it would be his lack of pace and ability to cover ground – particularly in the heat. Granted, given he has asthma; he was already at a disadvantage. But beyond that, when we were in Japan with England in 2002 for example, when it was thirty five degrees, where Lampard and Gerrard would have the range to cover ground in such difficult conditions, Scholesy would struggle. That aside, he was an absolutely world class player that I was proud to say I played alongside for many years.

Anyway …

When we returned from pre-season with Manchester United in 2009, I was absolutely buzzing in myself. I had gained the respect of my teammates and the manager straightaway. Signing me was a risk for them – but within three or four games I felt as if I'd allayed any doubts they may have had. I thought, *they'll be delighted to have me here ...*

I wasn't wrong.

'Listen,' Sir Alex said prior to the first league game against Birmingham City, 'you've almost earned your starting place here. I'm sorry I won't be starting you on this occasion but trust me, you'll be getting loads of chances.'

I really respected Sir Alex for acknowledging the bright start I'd made. And he did put his trust in me soon after when I did start in the second game of the season against Burnley at Turf Moor. When he pulled me off after an hour in a game we lost, I was gutted because I felt like my pre-season work had been undone. The first time I got a chance to shine and we got beat 1-0. I almost felt like I was to blame at the time.

The following week away at Wigan he brought me on for Wayne Rooney and I scored my debut league goal in a 5-0 win.

Having been an unused substitute in back to back wins against Arsenal and Tottenham in the league and an away 1-0 Champions League win against Besiktas in Turkey, the first Manchester derby of the league season loomed.

The Manchester derby of September 20th is another that'll go down in footballing folklore – more for the red side of Manchester than the sky blue of course.

City were undeniably on the rise, but still just the noisy, upstart neighbours. Carlos Tevez had just moved from United to City; there were billboards all around the city that read 'Welcome To Manchester'.

Mark Hughes thought they had the potential to claim

bragging rights in the city. Sir Alex thought otherwise and was at pains to say so in the build-up. There was more bad blood in the game than there had been for a long time. The scene was set for a classic – and for once the action exceeded the hype.

As I sat on the bench watching the action pulsate from end to end in a sold-out Old Trafford, I thought, *this is exactly why I signed…*

As Sir Alex gestured for me to get ready after seventy eight minutes with the score hanging in the balance at 2-2, I thought, *I'm scoring the winner here…*

Reading this, I'm sure you'll either think I'm deluded or just an arrogant so and so. But honestly, across my career, there were so many instances where it felt like my thoughts – my relentlessly positive thoughts – actually influenced what would later happen. On many occasions I'd think, *I'm scoring the winner …*

And sure enough, on many such occasions, I did.

It comes back to that shit-filtering attitude that I've referenced in this book. I just didn't see negatives, only positives. I'm certain that if I never believed I was going to do something then I certainly wouldn't have. And even on the occasions that I didn't score, I'd walk off the pitch thinking, *Ok, well I guess I didn't score the winner.*

Then I'd just let it go and never give it another thought. It's just how I'm wired.

For anyone who wants to understand how football really works, the winning goal I scored that day had everything. My finish was just a small part of it.

The weight and angle of pass communicates everything that's happening on a football pitch. Because nobody can hear anything (unless you're five yards away) players have to rely on what a pass from a teammate is telling them. For example, if a teammate raps a ball hard into me when my back's to goal, I know that he's telling me: 'You've got time to turn quick.'

If he drops one short, he's doing it because someone's right on my back. The pass is *telling* me this, because he can't tell me: 'Man on!'

If he drops the ball to my right, he's telling me: 'There's a man immediately to your left.' He knows that, if he plays the ball either straight to me or my left, it'll get nicked. This is how footballers communicate. The pass explains the wider picture to the receiving player that can't see it.

The build-up to the winner against City exemplified all of this. From what I remember, play had broken down and the ball had been cleared. As I was jogging back out to get back onside, I suddenly noticed that Micah Richards was horrifically out of position. Meanwhile, the right back was far too wide.

Normally, there would be no space to thread a ball in this situation. City had just cleared a ball and had numbers back. However, as play developed and Giggsy took a touch, I could smell an opportunity arising.

Micah Richards was over covering and there was a void in the right back position. I was at pains to show no emotion. Waving my hands too early would have alerted somebody to the danger.

At this point, I could easily have stayed where I was and made Giggsy's pass harder. Of course, he would have played it. There isn't a ball Giggsy can't play. But I had to maximise our chances of scoring. I pulled out as much as I dared, to give him an extra three or four yard channel to pass into. In these split seconds I was weighing up angles and percentages. Pull out too wide and I'd make his pass easy but my finish harder from a tighter angle. Stay narrow and I'd make Giggsy's pass a difficult one.

Calculations made, it was time to angle my body to give Giggsy the sign that I was ready. Even still, he *had* to rap it into me hard. Openings on the edge of the box rarely last more than two seconds. He had to smash it at me as hard as he dared, but not so hard that it made my first touch too difficult.

I put both hands in the air at the last moment, just to make certain that he'd spotted me …

And he just lifted his head and swung that cultured left foot. He literally had ten yards of space to hit it in. It sounds easy, and for Giggsy it *is* easy – but you've still got to do it under pressure. And he did.

As soon as he hit the pass, I knew exactly what the picture was. From there, all I had to do was concentrate on the first touch. I knew that, if I took it too wide, I'd have a one in ten chance of scoring. I had no choice but to receive the ball on the outside of my right foot and kill it dead. From there, it would be, in theory, automatic mode.

All of this sounds easy, but as soon as I saw Giggsy lift his head, every ounce of my body was screaming, *oh my God … goal!*

As much as my eyes lit up and my heart was pounding, I wish I could explain how cold you've got to be in that situation. I've often thought about how I learned to control myself when the footballing equivalent of a million pounds is in front of me and all I need to do is reach out my hand. With hindsight, I think it's a combination of inherent ability and practice.

Obviously I'd seen every conceivable kind of finish over the years. There was no nervousness about the practical act of scoring. But still, in a situation like I was in, 3-3 in a

Manchester derby, you just can't help being overcome by the enormity of the situation.

So, during the one and a half seconds it took for the ball to arrive, I shut everything out apart from total focus on the first touch. Giggsy was gone. As everyone in the stadium's heart rate went up, mine, the goalscorer's heart, went the opposite way. The crowd … didn't exist. Shaun Wright-Phillips, scrambling back to challenge me – forget it. At that moment it was just me left in the Old Trafford penalty area – alone in my head with just that first touch for company.

It all happened in a split second. Again, the target was tiny. The odds were stacked against me, in favour of City keeper Shay Given. The first touch was bob-on. Then I hit it – a straight prod with my right foot because that was all I could do – and, again, that thought, *that's in …*

And then I let the world back in again.

Old Trafford exploded.

The manager and my fellow players besieged me. Rio was the most relieved man in the world because it was his mistake that led to City's third goal. I remember during the celebration near the corner flag some emotional and highly-charged words from him along the lines of 'you just saved my fucking life, mate.'

In the moments and hours after the game, there was a huge feeling of joy and relief. I'd scored an iconic goal in such an important game. I knew right then that it was a moment I'd always be remembered for. I lived for moments like that.

Once the dust had settled, I also hoped that perhaps that goal had broken the ice.

I thought, *maybe the fans will take to me now?*

As much as I always hoped that the majority of Liverpool

fans would understand my career decisions I also genuinely hoped also that the majority of Manchester United fans would take to me after the City game. In my eyes, despite there always being that intransigent minority who'll slag you off just for the sake of it – as far as the majority of numerous, knowledgeable football fans were concerned, I thought that this laid the foundations of a great relationship.

I was of the mind that most people are decent human beings who would understand that I'd simply made a career decision. I'm sure a proportion were more than a bit dubious about a former Liverpool player coming and playing for their team.

Sir Alex and I settled into quite a relaxed relationship over the remainder of my time at Manchester United. As often as I started, an unspoken understanding developed between us whereby we both knew that, by and large, I'd be on the bench – with the similarly unspoken assumption being that, should we need a goal, or were 3-0 up, he'd put me on.

He never specifically said any of this and he never needed to. I think we both understood that this was exactly the role the club had in mind when they bought me. We talked a lot day to day – almost never about football.

He was always approachable and occasionally sought me out. I'd see him sidle up in the morning, Racing Post in hand, and then we'd pass the time of day talking about whatever racing news was current.

It was always very respectful on both sides; I'd like to think that he had a healthy respect not just for the player that I'd been, but also for the man I was.

I never felt anything but fortunate to have spent a small amount of time in the company of a true giant of the game. Sir Alex, from the start, was a top man on a personal level.

As a manager, he was everything I assumed he'd be. He'd rant at half time and point fingers. Very rarely would he come in and offer anyone any sort of praise. Instead of saying: 'You're playing great. Go and do the same again,' there would always be a negative. It wasn't a case of if he'd have a go at a player; it was *how much*.

As ruthless as he could sometimes be, Sir Alex was clever with it. He could judge a player and their character better than anyone I've ever met. When he wanted to get a point across to somebody, he knew that, on occasion, that somebody was too weak to take criticism. Their confidence would ebb away; their game would fall apart if he went directly for them.

Instead, he had an established group of half a dozen lads that he could absolutely bloody scream at – and half the time it wasn't even them he was directing his anger at. With that in mind, the first person that got it, almost every time we walked in at half time, was Wayne Rooney.

Wayne could have scored a hat-trick and made four assists in the first half, but still, if Sir Alex wanted to get a message across to someone who hadn't been moving the ball quickly enough or not passing it, he'd just start screaming at Wayne – 'pass the fucking ball! stop taking so many touches!' And then, for added effect, he'd volley a boot across the room because he was so irate.

Wayne couldn't take this so he'd always have a go back – a lot of the time justifiably because a lot of the time it was nothing to do with him. But the person at whom his anger was really meant for sat quietly in the corner, someone like the enigmatic and often brilliant Nani. And he would still be receiving the message loud and clear – albeit indirectly. Meanwhile, Wayne would go out in the second half and score another hat-trick because the steam was coming out of his ears!

As well as Wayne, Giggsy would get it – so would Patrice Evra, because he knew they could all take it. I never saw him once have a go at Paul Scholes, Edwin van der Sar, Vidic or Rio – not because any of them were soft; he just chose to leave them out of it.

For the record, he never once had a go at me either – but I'm not sure how relevant that is given how often I played. Regardless of who he targeted, Sir Alex was a master at managing people and using intimidation to get the best out of them.

Apparently too, he was ten times worse before I joined. The first time I walked out of the dressing room and said to someone like Giggsy: 'That was some bollocking wasn't it?' He'd say: 'Nah, he's mellowed so much. You should have seen him ten years ago!'

I'd have loved to have witnessed it but would have hated to be on the receiving end. With hindsight, thinking about Sir Alex, it's hard to ignore that the world has changed. Back in the day, extreme bollockings were part and parcel of football. Nowadays, people just don't take that kind of treatment from managers too much. Everybody believes that they should be respected equally.

Some people will say: 'Yeah but it's hard to scream at a guy who you're paying three hundred grand a week.'

I don't subscribe to that. Maybe I'm old fashioned, but I think that respect is something you should have for your manager, regardless of income. If he's asking you to do something, whether it's right or wrong, my view is that a player should always listen.

I always did – that's the way I was brought up. Regardless of whether I was on five hundred quid a week or a hundred and twenty grand, my reaction to my manager was exactly the same. I suspect I'm one of the exceptions, though.

From that perspective, I always think that it would have been interesting to see if Sir Alex could have adapted his ways sufficiently to become a modern manager along the lines of a Klopp or a Guardiola – where the arm around the shoulder is preferred to a climate of fear. Making people feel good about themselves is, after all, the modern way. And I'm not sure Sir Alex could be as good at that as he was ruling with discipline and respect. We'll never know!

As good as my time at Manchester United was, it had to come to an end. My first year had been fantastic and I'd played a lot – with three standout moments: the goal against City, a hat-trick against Wolfsburg in the Champions League and, finally, scoring against Villa in the Carling Cup final prior to tearing my hamstring.

Thereafter, having picked up that injury, it all became a bit sporadic and frustrating. I'd play a few games, maybe score a goal and then I'd strain something – a groin one time, a thigh the next – and then miss five or six games. This pattern continued for the remainder of my time at the club and I can't deny that it became dispiriting.

While the physical side of not being capable was demoralising, I also became aware of a mental aspect to my decline that I just hadn't bargained for.

Everything went in stages over many years. Having started with having to change my game to accommodate my decreasing pace, I then went to a place where, when my mind instinctively told me to run into the channel or over the top, I actively had to pause and tell my body that I was no longer able to do what my mind was asking – 'don't do it Michael, you can't. Just come short.'

That was bad enough. And it got worse. Latterly, instead of making myself available for someone to play a ball for me to run in behind onto, I actually began to put myself in positions on the pitch where nobody in their right mind would even consider passing to me.

I was, essentially, self-sabotaging. And I was doing it so I didn't have to disappoint my teammates or myself. Looking back, it was an agonising mind game that I was playing with myself.

In my last year at Manchester United, it felt like my body was just failing me. I could get fit, but I just couldn't stay fit. I played my last competitive game against Otelul Gelati in November of 2011. I spent the remainder of that year and the beginning of the next trying to claw my way back to fitness.

I never quite made it.

It had to end.

In May of 2012, Sir Alex Ferguson came to talk to me on the bus after an away game.

'It's with a heavy heart that I tell you that we're not going to extend your contract any further,' he explained.

As disappointing as this news was, I can't deny that I'd seen it coming.

They'd already tacked on an additional year to my initial two-year deal. That had been generous enough. I really appreciated the way he explained this difficult situation to me, too. It seemed like there was real remorse in his voice.

As I mentioned, in my initial Manchester United contract there was a nice bonus for every so many appearances I made. From memory, I think the agreement was that I had to have played twenty minutes in a match for that to qualify as an appearance.

I can't recall the precise details but basically I was short of game time by, I believe, one minute. Technically, Manchester United would have been perfectly within their rights to have not paid me a significant bonus.

Instead, David Gill – who anyone will tell you is one of the very best people in the game – phoned Tony Stephens and explained that they were going to pay me anyway as a gesture of good will. But let me be clear: he absolutely didn't need to do it.

People will argue that Manchester United, as wealthy as they are, could easily afford to pay such a relatively small bonus. But for me the gesture spoke volumes about both David Gill and the football club as a whole. It was sheer class.

I left Old Trafford with some great memories and a pleasant taste in my mouth. After all, I received a medal for my role as part of a Premier League-winning squad in 2011 and was involved in a Champions League final that same season. Although I spent the latter evening at Wembley sitting on the bench, these are two achievements that would surely be on any footballer's wish list.

As such, I will always be grateful to Manchester United for the opportunity they gave me.

REBØOT_18

THE FALL

After I left Manchester United in May of 2012, I didn't feel any particular obligation to say anything about my future plans. It was public knowledge that I was a free agent anyway – I'd tweeted an announcement myself to say that I'd be moving on.

Despite believing that I could still play, I was realistic in the sense that I was aware that, whatever my next step was, it was highly likely to be a downward one. To that end, I thought that a mid-table Premier League team was the absolute best I could expect. I made a decision right then that I wasn't prepared to go any further down.

With that acceptance came another dawning. Playing at a lower level, in a team that in all likelihood would not have the ball too often, I suspected that, whatever football I had left in me, I probably wasn't going to enjoy it as much as I had before.

As negative as that might sound, it was true. Inevitably things would be more direct. Inevitably I'd be spending more time chasing shadows when playing against the big boys. Despite these acceptances and misgivings, in my own mind, as much as I knew that injuries might never be far away, I still thought that, in football terms, I was still too young to retire at the age of thirty two.

Quite early on in the process of finding a new club, I got a tip from an agent close to Tony Pulis that Stoke City might be interested.

By this point, I had amicably parted company with my agent Tony Stephens. Part of me thought that I might want to set up a representation agency with Simon Marsh after my career ended so we agreed that we'd use my last transfer deal as something of a practice run. Tony was cool with it. He had already started to wind down with retirement on the horizon and he was only waiting for my career to end in order to bring his own to a close. As such, Simon and I decided to work together on finding me one last club.

On paper, Stoke City matched most of the criteria that I'd had in mind. As much as we wanted to go and talk to them, for one reason or another – whether Pulis was away on holiday or elsewhere – we didn't initially manage to make that conversation happen.

During this delay, I was secretly hoping that a couple of other offers might come in. It's always preferable to have something with which to apply some leverage. But nothing was forthcoming – at least not from a club in the UK.

I did get a couple of enquiries from overseas – one from Vancouver Whitecaps – a Canada-based MLS side – and another from an Australian side, Newcastle Jets. When I considered these two possibilities, neither particularly appealed.

Truthfully, international relocation just didn't tempt me

unless the contracts had been such that I just couldn't have turned them down. And they weren't anywhere close to being on that level, they were just ordinary deals. With four kids and having had experience of playing abroad at Madrid previously, I didn't really want to drag the family away again at such a late point in my career. I politely declined both.

Eventually, however, we sat down with Stoke and they, quite understandably I suppose, were playing massive hardball in terms of money.

Yes, they wanted to sign me, they said, but I got the sense that they wouldn't have been bothered if I hadn't signed. Whether this was a tactic they used for the purposes of the negotiation, I don't know.

But I definitely left there thinking that they weren't going to lose much sleep over it if I didn't accept what they offered. And what they'd offered was a modest basic with a few performance-related incentives here and there on a take it or leave it basis.

Nothing about it set my pulse racing.

'What are we going to do?' Simon Marsh asked me.

'We could wait and see who else comes into the market, I suppose?' I replied.

Part of me considered retiring there and then, I won't lie. Then, when I thought about my parents, and how my football career had been a way of life for them for so many years, I persuaded myself that it just wasn't the right time to hang it all up. Not wanting to disappoint them, I decided to hold out to see what was out there – for what we all knew would be my last hurrah.

Very late in the day, with Stoke City's deal still sitting there on the table, we got a call from Sunderland.

As different as those two teams are today, at the time they were of a similar level: middle to bottom of the table. The problem, however, was that it was just hours before I needed to register on the official database in order to be able to play that season, and Martin O'Neill wasn't contactable because, I was told, he was on a flight.

I had a serious dilemma. Should I hold on to try to get Martin O'Neill on the phone while at the same time jeopardising a move to Stoke City? Or should I just take Stoke City's offer and be done with it?

In the end, I had no choice. As much as Sunderland's chief executive was telling us to hang fire until Martin returned, we couldn't afford to. I could have ended up with nothing.

When I thought about it, I had doubts about Sunderland anyway. Firstly, I'd have to live away from home again whereas with Stoke I could easily stay with the family. Secondly, I'd played for Newcastle. Did I really want all the aggravation that would come with playing for their fiercest rivals?

There honestly wasn't much to choose between these two teams and in the end I just took the deal that was on the table. I just couldn't risk being left without a club.

Simon and I agreed that I should drive down to Stoke at the eleventh hour to sign – while he was in there with the club officials finalising the fine print.

I hadn't even had a medical at this point – not that it mattered too much to Stoke City by then as, given how the deal was being structured, they were in a no-lose situation. If acquiring me didn't work out, they wouldn't lose much. Equally, if I were to rekindle the old flame of greatness, they'd only benefit. Either way, it was a risk worth taking for them based on what they were paying me.

I drove down the M6 and stopped at a junction one short of Stoke City's training ground. It was two hours until my deadline was due to close.

I called Simon. He still hadn't quite finalised everything. The physio and the doctor were seemingly standing by to give me a quick once over – certainly nothing as detailed as scans. It was all getting a bit hairy.

I sat there in the car.

An hour passed.

With forty five minutes left to complete the transfer, the phone rang.

'Right,' Simon said, 'Come down …'

I started the car and began driving. At the time I'd figured that I was perhaps only fifteen minutes away. Given that I'd never been to this particular training ground before, I was solely relying on my car's navigation system to get me to exactly the right place.

As satellite navigation occasionally does, it failed. I missed the turn off on the M6 and then found myself driving *away* from the training ground with no other exit available for what seemed like fifteen miles! Having thought I'd be there in fifteen minutes and would then have half an hour to sign, I was now in a state of blind panic – tearing down the motorway at speeds I'd rather not admit to, to literally arrive one minute before the deadline.

I walked in, signed whatever papers Simon had laid out on the table in a blur of pen and paper. They were then faxed to the authorities. I was now a Stoke City player. There wasn't even any point in doing a medical!

My God, the whole episode was so empty though. In general, when you sign for a new club, you want to feel delirious because it's everything you ever wanted. When I first signed for Liverpool, I literally couldn't write my name quick enough. The same applied at Real Madrid, and, for that matter, Manchester United – particularly given the point in my career when I joined them. These three were all great opportunities for different reasons. As such, signing felt *exciting*.

Again, given that this book is all about honesty, as harsh as it may sometimes be, with no disrespect meant to Newcastle and Stoke as football clubs, I must admit that when I signed contracts with those two, I did so with absolutely no joy whatsoever. In both cases it was just a job, and I signed only because I thought it was the right thing to do at the time.

What else could I do?

From the start, it was really hard to read Tony Pulis in terms of how he wanted to use me. Of some encouragement to me was the fact that, during the negotiations to sign me, they had also signed Charlie Adam, an undeniably gifted footballer, from Liverpool for around four million.

Not only did his signing represent some degree of ambition in a financial sense, but from a footballing perspective it led me to believe that maybe Tony Pulis was of a mind to play more football than he had previously. I thought, *maybe they want to be less direct?*

This theory was further reinforced during my first conversations with Tony in person. Not only were there words, there was also action in the form of signings to back them up. I even felt reassured to be part of a new-look Stoke City that was perhaps committed to a new style of play – all of which would have suited me far more than being part of a team playing one dimensional and direct.

One day we did bleep tests to gauge our fitness. Fortunately

I'd been doing loads of running up and down my driveway at home and I was pretty fit. I got really good results and could tell that Tony Pulis was surprised – to the extent that I think he was considering putting me straight into the first team.

On the Thursday before the next league game against Manchester City – my first at the club – we did a team shape. I was in it. I was thinking, *oh my God, I'm starting here.*

'You're fine to start aren't you?' Tony said, 'you're fit enough, yeah?'

'Yeah, of course,' I replied, 'absolutely fine.'

The next day we did another team shape. This time I wasn't in it. I was scratching my head when he approached me. At this point I could detect hesitancy in his eyes.

'What do you think?' he asked me, 'should we just bring you off the bench?'

To this day I have no idea what changed his mind. It was such a significant moment that would inform the rest of my time at the club. He opted to leave me on the bench against City. Had I started, and done well, who knows? I could well have got in the groove and gone on to play five, ten or even twenty games that season.

But it didn't happen. The team drew the game – always something of a result for a side like Stoke City against one of the big clubs – and hadn't played too badly in the process.

Thereafter, Tony Pulis didn't change the team much. Before I knew it, ten or fifteen games had gone by and I'd barely kicked a ball in earnest. In that situation, at the age I was at, the body starts seizing up a bit.

Looking back on these events, I don't blame Tony and I actually liked him as a fella. It was, after all, his prerogative to pick whatever team he wanted. I thought I'd done well enough in training to warrant more of a chance. However, with retrospect, Tony's training sessions didn't exactly offer a player much in the way of chances to shine.

Pulis was certainly from Allardyce's school of coaching ideology when it came to training sessions. There was a lot of standing around while he talked tactics.

Every time anyone got the ball, Pulis would be telling the lads what to do and where to play it. I felt that his approach created robotic players more than it did free spirits. Furthermore, it seemed to me that the only way to force yourself into the team was by your performance on the pitch.

Beyond this, as much as Tony had been a successful manager and perhaps did want to try and improve the way they played, the harsh reality is that you just can't do it with a couple of players in a squad. To really achieve change, not only does everyone have to be on board with the thinking, but also every player has to be technically capable of putting the plan into practice. One weak link – a right back that can't pass the ball or a centre half who can't control it – and the whole thing just breaks down. Thereafter, the team inevitably reverts to what it knows best. It was nobody's fault – but I think this is what often happens at places like Stoke City.

As time passed, I found myself in a vicious circle of strange bemusement. I wasn't training enough and so, by extension, whenever I did come on as a sub for a few minutes, as I did on just four occasions before Christmas of 2012, I had less and less sharpness.

The strangest thing was – and as much as it was hard to shine in training – I still felt several steps ahead of the players around me in terms of understanding the game.

Some of them might have equally felt the same way about

my being at the club. As we sat in the dressing room after training one day, one of the older lads looked over and said with what felt like a degree of reverence: 'What the hell is Michael Owen even doing in here?' He was joking and being semi-serious at the same time.

Regardless of what anyone thought, as weeks passed, I just sat on the bench while Peter Crouch and Jon Walters started up front. For some reason, Pulis just wouldn't bring me on, even in obvious situations when we were 1-0 down and needing a goal. I kept asking myself the same question over and over again, *how the hell can I not get into this team?*

Dispirited, halfway through the season around Christmas I went to see Chief Executive Tony Scholes after asking Simon to arrange a meeting.

'I think it might be better if I just handed in my notice now,' I told him.

As far as I was concerned, it made more sense. I wasn't getting a game. I didn't want to be just hanging around the club with my pride shot to pieces. Because I always held myself in such high regard, I just couldn't face skulking around the training ground, feeling like a spare part.

I just didn't want to be in a situation whereby I lost all respect for myself. I was already embarrassed as it was and I just thought it would have been better to shake hands and walk away. But the club didn't agree to it at the time.

'Just see it through until the end of the season,' Tony told me.

Reluctantly, I hung on. And ironically, in January 2013, the chance to start finally came – in a third round FA Cup game away at Crystal Palace.

As I've described throughout this book, there have been many, many high points in my footballing career. I've been lucky enough to play for great clubs and score goals in finals and at major tournaments. If these moments combined to be the zenith of my career, Saturday, January 5th at Selhurst Park was single-handedly the absolute nadir.

Let me start by saying that it's one thing when someone else says that you're a shadow of your former self. But it's an entirely worse realisation when you *yourself* realise, beyond doubt, that you're an imitation of what you once were.

That day, it happened.

From the start, it was all so terrible. Nothing about my personal game was good: my touch, my passing, my fitness, my vision – I had nothing. Zero. I seemed like I'd aged five years since the beginning of the season. I felt like I was completely out of touch with football at a decent level.

On a personal level, I felt lost.

From a team perspective, because of the way we played, I was lost too. The Stoke City dynamic was just so different from all of the teams I'd ever played in. I was receiving passes from angles that I'd never experienced in my life. Worst of all, I couldn't physically do anything with these passes when they came my way. Everything crumbled out there, including my self-confidence.

As the game wore on, all I was thinking was, *I don't like this. I can't do this …*

I wanted Selhurst Park's pitch to swallow me up.

From the wilderness of personal mediocrity I found myself adrift in, at various points during that game I paused to consider the players around me – players who, not long previously, I might well have dismissed completely as being far below my level. Now, however, as I looked at these guys around me I thought, *Michael, you just don't belong here.*

And I was right. I didn't belong there. Almost overnight I'd dropped to a level far below Stoke City v Crystal Palace. When I came off after 52 minutes I thought, *that's it. My career is over.* Even though I did play again, and scored my only goal for Stoke, I still knew that my time was up.

At various times since I left Stoke, I've heard rumblings that Tony Pulis felt that my head wasn't fully engaged in football while I was at the club. I also heard that he thought I was more interested in racing. It would be easy for me to get defensive about this suggestion but the reality is that Tony's assessment probably wasn't far wrong.

Certainly, as months passed without game time, my head gradually checked out. Whose fault was that? Well, I don't think anyone was really to blame. Tony wasn't playing me, so I lost interest. Perhaps seeing that I'd lost interest probably made him less inclined to play me. It was a vicious circle; it's really as simple as that. But I certainly don't blame Tony Pulis.

On one hand it was such a sad and depressing end. And the biggest shame of all was that I really liked the lads at Stoke City. Despite feeling as if I didn't contribute much, we always had a great dressing room spirit and had a lot of laughs along the way. Furthermore, I really respected the fans a great deal too.

On the other hand, the manner of my last days at Stoke City was perhaps as clear a signal as I could possibly want in terms of confirming to myself that my playing career was conclusively over.

I left in May of 2013, knowing that, whatever else the future might hold, I wouldn't be signing another professional football contract.

After sixteen years, it was over.

REBØOT_19

STICK

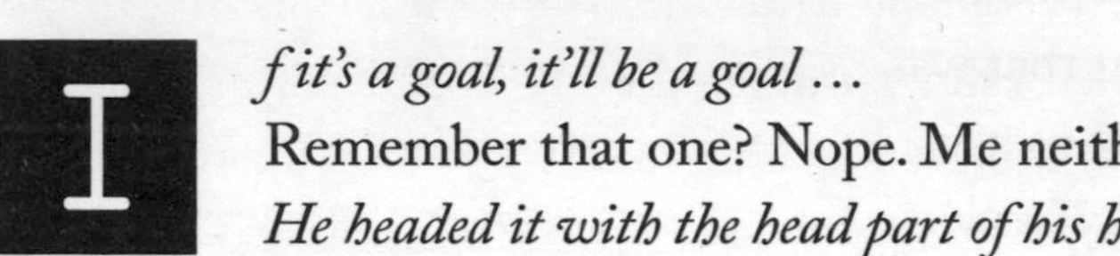

If it's a goal, it'll be a goal …

Remember that one? Nope. Me neither.

He headed it with the head part of his head …

This one? Sorry, I never said it either.

Sometimes even I have to laugh at some of the things that people say that I've said live on air. Someone even told me that there's a whole Twitter parody account of Michael Owen quotes – many of which I'm sure never came out of my mouth. I'll need to check sometime.

While nobody is perfect and I'm sure I have said the odd thing on the spur of the moment that comes out wrong, there's no denying that punditry is an undeniably strange world. It's definitely not as easy as it looks.

The first time I ever appeared as an analyst was towards the end of my playing career. I can't recall where I was playing at the time. I did a couple of Match Of The Days as most players have – dissecting that day's action in an informal fashion. I also did a bit of Sky when asked – most notably with a really awful moustache that I'd grown for Movember. Then, sometime later and completely out of the blue, I was asked to commentate on a Liverpool game, to be aired on Match Of The Day.

I should say at this point that, when I retired from playing, I had no real intention of getting involved in the media side of the game. It wasn't that I didn't want to do it – more that I just hadn't really considered it as a possibility.

However, not long after the Liverpool co-commentary, I was contacted by Grant Best from BT Sport, who wanted to arrange a meeting about the possibility of me working in television on a regular basis.

As soon as he made the suggestion, I became quite intrigued by the whole idea of being in the studio, analysing games. I assumed that that was what they had in mind. As an ex-player who'd played at a variety of clubs at an elite level, I thought that I could give viewers some interesting perspectives. As I warmed to the idea, we arranged a meeting in Manchester.

'I've listened to your co-commentary on that Liverpool game,' Grant began, 'and I thought there were some great aspects to it. With a bit of coaching and help, I think you could do the job really well.'

On one hand I was surprised by his positive feedback and excited by the possibilities. But on the other I was thinking, *I'm not sure if I really want to be driving all over the country, going to football games.*

In my mind, having travelled all over the country for years as a player, I was more thinking of an in-studio role as an analyst. Grant, at this stage, given it was a new channel, was in the process of assembling a group of people to fulfil all of the various roles.

Not long afterwards, he offered me the co-commentator role and, as hesitant as I'd been, I accepted it anyway and would be working alongside Ian Darke and Darren Fletcher for the initial three-year contract.

As much as I enjoyed it, co-commentating on football is a real challenge. Viewers really have no idea how hard it is. You've got a million voices in your ear. It can feel like a no-win situation.

Indeed, at BT, we were actually *encouraged* to make calls without the benefit of replay.

If someone went down, they wanted you to call what you saw and put your neck on the line. But the people in the pub watching didn't know that. They just thought I'd had a nightmare if the replay later revealed that I'd made the wrong call in the spur of the moment. But that's what BT wanted – even if you had to go back later, with the benefit of the replay, and say, 'Actually, I made a mistake there ...'

What helped me greatly in these situations was the fact that I've played the game at the highest level. I know when a player is looking for a foul; I can pre-empt things almost before they happen. My career as a top striker, I thought, allowed me to describe the act of goalscoring from a unique, insider perspective.

As much as everybody inevitably gets things wrong and every commentator makes mistakes in a live situation now and again because they're making calls in the spur of the moment, on balance, I thought I did alright.

On reflection, I definitely *do* think that I made a mistake by taking the co-commentary job when I did. I think I would preferred to have done a few years in front of the camera first – specifically to have the opportunity to build a bit of a visual relationship with the BT viewers. After all, there's no doubt that, once people see you, see your smile and become familiar with your mannerisms, they can at least get a sense of your character. Instead, I went straight *behind* the TV camera, where the only way the viewers could get to know me was via my voice.

On that subject, I'll be the first to admit that I have just an average voice for commentating. Compared to some others, I totally get that mine can be a bit grating.

So, as much as I thought I did a good job of bringing my experience to the commentary booth and called the big moments correctly, I always knew that my voice just wasn't a nice one for viewers to listen to for ninety minutes. I can't change that – that's just the way it is!

Subsequently, as a result of my speaking voice – in combination with the fact that I hadn't been granted that chance to build visual rapport with the viewers – whenever I did pronounce a player's name incorrectly or called a penalty that wasn't, I think I came in for more criticism than I might have otherwise. I'm not sure that I did any worse than anybody else, though.

Despite my voice, I always thought my content was good. I never, like some TV people do, said things for the sake of filling dead air. Nevertheless, after a couple of years, I was keen to discuss the nature of my role with my bosses at BT.

'I'd like to do more studio-based work, if possible,' I said

BT were very receptive to that suggestion, and I've been primarily studio-based ever since. The difference in feedback has been significant, but you still get issues.

Even now, I still feel like I have to overcome the pre-existing impression that I'd created from my co-commentating days.

People just loved taking pot-shots at things I've supposedly said or innocent mistakes I've made at various times – just like anyone else has.

As I've said, people took it further and *invented* things that I had supposedly said. Beside it they'd put quotation marks to make it look legitimate.

The Internet, being as it is, inevitably spins these things relentlessly. And before you know it, there's a whole raft of statements out there on fake Twitter profiles and the like, attributed to me, none of which I actually said! It all becomes a bit frustrating.

What is equally galling is some of the criticism you hear from fans about opinions that you have, or don't have, about teams you once played for. It all goes back to this loyalty subject I mention previously and, honestly, it's so tedious.

The reality is, and this might not be a popular opinion, when I became a professional footballer, I ceased to be a fan.

As much as I always wanted to win – and my desire was as strong as anyone's, trust me – I never went around calling people who wore a different coloured football shirt than mine names like *scum* or *traitor* or *snake.* These are some of the nicer names I've been called.

Equally, when I moved to a new club, as much as I'd done my best for a previous so-called rival club, that didn't mean that I wasn't going to give my all to the new club.

In spite of what some disgruntled fans might think, those people who just can't separate the truth from their own badge-blindness, I've done that at every club I've played for.

By the same token, when I retired from playing football professionally, my views – and the manner in which I approached my past associations – changed also.

To that end, I've never been one of those guys who you'd see hanging around their former club, wearing club gear, doing nothing in particular other than just being seen there. I see guys like that – lads I played with and against – doing that at clubs all over the land.

You wouldn't see a guy like Paul Scholes, Steven Gerrard or Jamie Carragher ever doing that and I wouldn't dream of doing it either. It looks desperate. It makes me cringe.

Yes, a football club was once my place of work. But when I left, that contact was broken. I can't then become a fan – a hanger-on, standing around to remind anyone who might be looking that I once played there. I'm secure enough with my legacy and contributions that I don't need to.

Unless I'm contracted to perform some kind of ambassadorial duty that requires me to be at a club, I'd be mortified to be seen there. I don't know why this is, but I'm actually proud to feel this way.

The same applies to asking favours from former clubs. As much as I played for Manchester United and Real Madrid, I wouldn't dream of phoning them up to look for a couple of match tickets.

I suspect they'd have no problem with it if I did, but I'd never dream of doing it. I'm like my dad Terry in that sense. I respect myself, and the clubs, too much to go cap in hand for anything for free. Again, I'd be embarrassed. Yet, I see ex-pros doing it all the time.

Liverpool is a slightly different situation in that, along with a number of other ex-players, I have an ambassadorial role there. I'm not in there all the time – far from it. But I do my bit.

Not surprisingly, I get a huge amount of abuse from what I suspect is a minority of Liverpool fans who think that, because

I played for a rival club, I shouldn't even be a Liverpool ambassador in the first place!

That, I'm afraid, is fan-centric nonsense. Not just that, when I trawl through my memory banks, recounting all the great moments I enjoyed with the fans and my fellow players, these opinions sting.

My record at Liverpool is a good one. I won trophies there, scored goals, won two Golden Boots there and lifted the Ballon d'Or. I played for the club on two hundred and ninety seven occasions. I went in where it hurts for the club on countless more instances.

How does playing for a rival club negate any of that?

It doesn't. To think that way is just delusional.

And even worse, while fans are happy to question my credentials, you've got guys hanging around Liverpool and every other club, with fancy titles, wearing tracksuits, being ambassadors, who played there for one season, didn't do much for the club and kicked a ball for two minutes while they were at it!

It's all such nonsense – and fans sometimes need to stop and have a long hard think about how some of their opinions are so contradictory. Worth adding too is that these opinions only ever seem to surface on the Internet!

In my daily life, I don't shy away from going anywhere. I go to restaurants, pubs, racecourses, football grounds – I have done so for years and I'll continue to. I can count on one hand the number of times that anyone has come up to me and given me a hard time about whatever football clubs I've played for, or been abusive about so-called loyalty, or challenged my views on this or that. In the real world it doesn't happen. On the Internet however, it's a total free-for-all.

Punditry, inevitably, attracts the same kind of contradictory nonsense – you can't win there either.

For example, early in 2019, I was on the analyst panel for the league game between Manchester United and Liverpool, two of my former clubs, obviously. In the context of Liverpool's title challenge, it was an important game.

During the half time break, with Marcus Rashford seemingly carrying an ankle injury, I made a comment to the effect that, given that United had no more substitutes available, a manager in that situation might well tell his players to test that player's ankle to establish what his appetite for continuing was.

Having played football since I was a young kid, and having sat in dressing rooms all over the world under a variety of different managers, I knew very well that this was exactly the conversation that would be had in every dressing room in the land.

Nobody was suggesting that anybody should inflict a serious injury on Marcus Rashford, or injure him further intentionally. As an ex-player, I was merely offering the kind of insight that BT Sport pay me to give – and that casual fans just *can't* know. And I was doing it because I'd seen it myself many, many times.

Before the second half had even started, the Internet went into total meltdown. People were abusing me left, right and centre – accusing me of encouraging the deliberate injury of a Manchester United player. It was blown massively out of proportion.

Yet, even today I maintain that, as I said on Twitter afterwards, I was merely telling the viewers information that, among those that play the game, is well known. Fans might not like it – but it's part of the game.

And so it continues – to the extent that whenever you're on

television giving an opinion as a professional analyst, as you're being paid to do and, as the words exit your mouth, you know that there's every chance that a Twitter meltdown is occurring at the same time because somebody, somewhere is disgruntled with what you've just said! I've often felt like getting my phone out, opening Twitter and watching it happen in real time – that's how quickly my words seem to be pounced upon and transmitted to the world.

You can't win – and that includes when you say nothing at all, as I'd soon find out.

Not long after the Rashford incident, I found myself in the studio again, this time for Manchester United's Champions League last sixteen tie against Paris Saint-Germain. It was a dramatic night. Anyone who enjoys the game loves such nights – where a last-gasp goal sends an English team through. This time, Marcus Rashford scored a stoppage time penalty.

I have to say that, in general, I don't do a lot of jumping around in the studio. As far as I'm concerned, that's not really what I'm there for – or what I'm being paid for. As I've said, I'm not a fan; I'm a paid, professional analyst – a grown man with four kids at that!

So, when Rashford's penalty went in and everyone else in the studio started jumping around like madmen; I just sat there.

Again, from the reaction on social media, you'd have thought I'd murdered somebody. All kinds of accusations flew around: how I wasn't loyal, how I was betraying Manchester United fans, how I was appeasing Liverpool fans, how I had no passion etc. The level of overreaction was farcical – and all too predictable with it.

Don't get me wrong, I have no issue with what other analysts do – that's their business and it doesn't affect me either way.

These lads are my friends and colleagues. What they do on air and off it are sometimes two different things. But for people to abuse me for not being demonstrative on television when a goal is scored – just doesn't seem reasonable.

That unfortunately, is what you're up against when fans decide that they've got enough information to judge you on and are unwilling to sit down and calmly analyse the contradictions that they're perpetuating, all because of the colour of a football shirt.

Having said all that, none of the above detracts in any way from my enjoyment of covering football for BT Sport – and any other network I've ever worked for. Regardless of the drama that plays out on social media, mostly driven by a minority of idiots, you'll see me on a TV screen pretty soon, I'm sure!

As far as other post-career pursuits, people have often asked me if I had any interest in management or coaching. When I first retired from playing, I thought about management. From a man-management point of view I thought I'd be good at it.

Beyond that, because I'd been involved in various business ventures over the years, I also felt that I had the kind of cool head under pressure that you need in football management.

The main issue for me was commitment. Did I really want to be tied down? The answer was that I didn't. As much as a few of us had started on coaching badges when I was playing at Manchester United and all of us had great intentions, for me it just didn't appeal enough.

At various times in recent years, people have come to me about the concept of my being involved with my local team, Chester, in some capacity. Obviously, for all kinds of reasons not least that my dad played for them, I love that football club. It just never changes. They've had the same tea lady there for thirty years.

For a football romantic like me, that's part of the old-school attraction – and also one of the reasons why I might be hesitant to get involved in a theoretical scenario where a new investor might come in. Yes, they might improve the facilities or even acquire another ground, but at the same time they might also have to strip away some of these features that makes a club like Chester what it is. To me, that's a conflict.

Is an involvement in Chester something for the future?

Let's wait and see.

My side interest – and it's become much more than that nowadays – was always horse racing.

Interestingly – and again it's a view based entirely on myth – a minority of people have always bashed my involvement in horse racing and said that, particularly in the Newcastle days, I was more interested in racing than playing football because by that time I owned my own stables.

Absolute bollocks. Again, it's an example of how you can never win in the eyes of football fans. You create something for your post-career, put a business in place to support you and your family. To me it made sense and was a positive for my life in general. Yet I got criticised for taking my eye off the ball.

The biggest laugh of all is, if I hadn't done it, fans would have given me that whole 'footballers are thick and don't know how to look after their money' type stuff! As I said, it's a no-win situation.

What most people don't realise is that racing has been part of my life since I was about five years old. It wasn't some new fad I got into when I made some money and thought, *what shall I do now? I know, I'll buy a few horses …*

Some footballers have done that, but that's not how it began.

Whenever my dad took me to play football at the local park, we'd always pull over outside a bakery. He'd hand me some money and say: 'Off you go and get yourself a cream cake.'

As I did, he'd go into the bookies next door and put a few bets on. That afternoon, he and I would sit and watch the racing, hoping that one of his bets would come in. This went on for years. We still do it now. But the point is: this was how my interest in racing began – certainly from a betting point of view.

When I turned eighteen, I remember being with David Platt at some point – with whom I shared an agent.

'Why don't you own one?' he said.

Up until that day, I had never even considered owning a racehorse. I had always assumed that that was something other people did. I had no idea that there was an entry point that someone like me could access. I don't really know what I thought.

David's suggestion made me think, *actually, I've got enough money to buy one. Maybe I could get involved?*

David introduced me to the trainer John Gosden in Newmarket – nowadays he'd be considered one of the top trainers in the world. John showed me two horses, a colt and a filly. 'Take your pick,' John said.

Typical of me, wanting to hedge my bets in case one was better than the other, I ended up buying them both. That's how it all began. Thereafter, I owned many more horses with

John, right up to the point when I decided to start Manor House Stables years later. I also took John's assistant, Nicky Vaughan, to help me start up.

Shortly before I'd bought horses with John, Tony Stephens told me that Coolmore – the powerhouse Irish breeding operation – had sent him a proposal. From memory, this would have been sometime in 1999 or 2000.

As far as we understood, they basically wanted to give me a racehorse, to run in my colours, under my ownership name – obviously on the understanding that it would also benefit them from the point of view of publicity.

'There's been this offer,' Tony explained, 'but I recommend that you say no to it.'

'Why?' I asked.

'It don't really think it fits in with your image at this stage of your life,' he told me.

Tony felt that, given he was creating this image of me as this clean-living, whiter than white guy who'd be the darling of blue-chip companies, to align myself with horse racing at such a young age would be contradictory.

I was disappointed with Tony's decision at the time. I was excited by the idea. However, bowing to his superior knowledge, I was happy to go along with pretty much anything that Tony advised. We politely declined Coolmore's offer.

As it transpired, after I'd said no, a year or so later they apparently offered Sir Alex Ferguson the same or a similar deal. Whether they did that because I'd turned it down or whether they were going to use him anyway, I have no idea.

Anyway, Sir Alex was approached, and the horse he got into was a colt called Rock Of Gibraltar. It ran in his colours, under his name; Sir Alex was present at nearly all of the races.

Given that Rock of Gibraltar would go down in history as one of the great milers in recent memory – winning seven Group One races in the process – there was a significant part of me thinking, *that could and should have been me …*

Because of all that ensued – the legal battle between Sir Alex and Coolmore over the horse's future, and very significant stallion fees – with retrospect, I'm very glad that it wasn't me. It could have been a right mess that I could have easily done without! As it turned out, I'd have a Group One winner of my own later down the line.

For many of the intervening years up until I opened my own facility, I'd been writing out cheques for ten grand every month myself for training fees to other trainers. Not being particularly keen on doing that for the rest of my life it was then that I thought, *I need to flip this and train my own horses at a place I own – as well as getting another few owners in to offset some more of the cost.*

Moving forward to 2006, when we were looking for a suitable facility at which to train horses, to begin with, Nicky Vaughan and I first went around looking at farms that might be suitable in my local area. I spoke to the estate agents and said: 'Let me know of anything within a half-hour radius of my house.'

Soon, there were four or five to see. And when I first laid eyes on Manor House Stables, I liked it – but Nicky Vaughan *really* liked it. He definitely saw the potential and scope more than I did at that early stage.

Nowadays when I look at it, I know it was the right decision to buy it. Over time, Manor House Stables has been transformed into something very special.

To get it there, we had to go through a lot. Initially I'd paid £2.2 million for the farm and I knew that, given land values are always stable, I'd always be able to sell it if I had to. From that perspective there wasn't too much risk.

Where there would be significant liability was when I wanted to put in the kind of facilities needed to make the place state of the art: gallops, stables, horse-walkers, trotting rings etc.

To do all of that, I knew I'd be in for around another three quarters of a million pounds of investment on top of the purchase price – none of which I'd get back if the whole venture failed.

After taking six months to get the place up to speed, with only twenty or so horses in the yard, Nicky Vaughan started training horses on my behalf at Manor House Stables.

Initially we had a bit of success. Twenty horses soon became thirty. Then forty, then fifty … and so on. We were doing fine. At this point I had a decision to make. Because I only had barn capacity for twenty horses to start with, as we got more, all I'd do was buy standalone, loose stables that weren't permanent fixtures. With time it became a bit of a cluttered mess.

Did I want a proper place? Or did I want to just turn away business? That was the dilemma. I decided to do the former – which obviously involved another significant amount of investment. I did it all – adding even more new facilities, state of the art barns and staff accommodation.

To fill this new yard I'd built, I needed to expand by finding new owners to bring their horses to be trained at Manor House Stables. At the time it felt like we were a football team racing through the leagues.

Equally, as good as Nicky Vaughan had been at getting us through the lower leagues, I felt as though I needed somebody new to help us make the last, toughest jump to the elite level – the premier league of the racing world.

That new trainer was Tom Dascombe – who himself had experience of training eighty or ninety horses at a time. Better still, when I made the decision to employ Tom, I was also, in effect, buying his business. That meant that all of his existing owners would be coming with him to Manor House Stables. It doubled my string almost overnight.

When I had first approached Tom, he had some conditions of his own.

'I need to speak to my principal backer before I do anything,' he explained.

Fair enough, I thought.

As it turned out, the backer in question was Betfair co-founder Andrew Black. After some discussion, Tom suggested that I sell a stake in Manor House Stables to Andrew in order to build more stables and more facilities like a veterinary centre and a swimming pool for the horses.

And that's exactly what we did. It would have been too much stress for me to do it on my own. Andrew is still in the business on a fifty-fifty arrangement.

Since then, Manor House Stables has gone from strength to strength. In 2018 we went through the domestic one million pound season earnings barrier – which was gratifying. Reaching a total of seventy winners was similarly pleasing.

Of course, who could forget that we'd won a race-in-a-million when Brown Panther – a horse I bred myself and co-owned with Andrew Black – won the 2015 Dubai Gold Cup.

There have been many other highlights too. Being invited to join the Queen's procession at Royal Ascot one year was one of them. It was a real honour and I was very excited to go with Louise.

We had to appear at Windsor Castle in the morning for a

lunch with the Queen. It was really interesting; all the rooms were colour coded. We stood and talked with other guests until a few corgis appeared – signalling that the Queen had arrived.

We all stood to attention and then sat down for lunch. Mindful of my etiquette, I was being careful to hold my fork in the correct hand and so on. I needn't have worried. I looked over at the Queen and she was throwing bits of her starter down to her corgis!

After lunch, we all went in the horse-drawn carriages up Ascot's straight mile. I wouldn't say I felt adrenaline when the national anthem started, but I can't deny that I felt a slight tingle up my spine.

Prior to meeting the Queen, we had all been briefed. We were told that, whenever we addressed her, we were to remove our hats. We pulled in at the finishing post and turned to go under the tunnel into the parade ring whereupon we were told that the Queen would get out, stand for a moment before going in. At that point we were told to wait and follow her in.

As we stood there admiring the parade ring as she was looking at some of the runners for the first race, she turned round and we swept in as we'd been instructed. At the time, I was as close to her as anybody. When she walked into the royal lift, there were perhaps fifteen of us standing outside.

'Come on,' she said, 'we can all squeeze in.'

Being the first one, I obeyed – while also taking my hat off as I thought that was the correct etiquette.

'If you'd put your hat back on,' she then said, with voice raised, 'we might all be able to fit in this lift!'

I sheepishly put my hat back on. I was mortified. And to this day I have absolutely no idea if she was being serious or was joking. Louise, meanwhile, was nudging me from the other side, trying desperately not to laugh because I'd just been bollocked by the Queen.

I'd like to think that this was just the Queen waiving etiquette so that we could all fit in the lift. But equally, I'm not sure. Regardless, Louise maintains to this day that that's why I've never made it to the Queen's honours list. But that's another story altogether …

Looking back on my first years in racing, I now see what the attraction was, and still is for me. As much as I'd been a racing enthusiast since I was a kid, it wasn't until I owned my own facilities and could see what was involved in training elite equine athletes, that I saw the obvious similarities with top-level football.

Because, like I was, these animals are athletes, I was able to apply some of the mind-set I'd applied throughout my football career to my secondary career. The approach was the same: everything had to be perfect, no detail missed, no resting on laurels – all so that these animals could win and keep winning just like I'd tried to do on the football pitch for all those years.

As such, whatever I do for the rest of my life, I'm certain that training racehorses and running the business will be a huge part of it. I've got my dad to thank for all those cream cakes!

REBØOT_20

ASKING FOR HELP

To my surprise, I found myself standing at a figurative cliff edge in 2014. A lifetime of that certain type of mentality, of behaviour, had led me to a point where I had to seek professional help. Yes, that's right, me! Given how resistant I'd been to any kind of psychology throughout my career, even I couldn't escape the irony of where I now found myself.

I suppose, with the benefit of hindsight, this personal wake-up call had quietly crept up on me. Throughout my playing career I'd been, to put it mildly, an extremely focused and driven person. That's not exactly uncommon for people who reach the top of their profession as I did.

I think I took it a little further, though.

Some have even said that they've seen a cold darkness in me – a characteristic that I suppose is at odds with the good-natured, media friendly persona I've always put out there on view. But really, as I've explained, that was always a front created by my agent, long ago.

The truth is, inside, I have raged at times – particularly when I was younger. My mother will confirm that. As a youngster, if I didn't take my frustrations out by punching five or six holes in my bedroom wall if we lost a five-a-side, I'd take them out on her verbally.

At various other times throughout my early career I was unforgivably nasty to her. During the process of writing this book, my dad made more than one reference to the fact that he has never heard me apologise for anything. On match days, nobody dared say a word to me. My wife Louise will tell you all about that.

That my family and Louise tolerated half of what I threw at them and still kept backing me is one of the most profound examples of unconditional love that I can think of. And as much as I try to justify it to myself with that old adage 'you always hurt the ones you love most,' I think even I knew, deep down inside, that it was wrong.

There is no doubt that this maniacal focus on success propelled me through my career. Added to my footballing ability, this dark force is what drove me to the heights I reached. I doubt anyone in my close circles would say that I was ever that easy to live with. But the honest truth is, as far as I was concerned, I was just being Michael Owen – doing what I needed to do to be me.

By the summer of 2014, a year into retirement, it had reached a stage where it was becoming apparent that the bloody-minded way I'd approached my football career, just wasn't compatible with normal, family life.

As they say, something had to give.

The issue that eventually brought everything to a head had been simmering for some time. For years, because of my own inner demons, I was intentionally really hard on Louise about subjects that I knew would push her buttons most – not least her close relationship with our daughter Gemma.

Let me be very clear and say that none of this was in any way a reflection on how I felt about either Gemma or Louise. I love them both with all of me; I now know that it was just my flaws and insecurities at play.

I'd take everything out on Louise, though – I'd accuse her of spending all her time with her eldest and ignoring the other kids. It wasn't even true.

On one hand I'd criticise her lifelong passion for dressage and then turn it against her – even though, on the other, I'd do everything humanly possible to support her in her pursuit of it. It made no sense.

We'd continually get into arguments about petty things and I'd always resort to the same, predictable tactics whereby I turned everything back on her. I was like a broken record: always repeating the same song.

Inside I knew that I adored Louise and would never, ever want to split up. Yet, I could feel everything slipping away.

As time passed, Louise began questioning our future together, as she was absolutely entitled to do. Given that she'd been with me since we were teenagers – through times when we had nothing, to a lifestyle beyond all our wildest dreams – for her to question our viability at all was a reflection of how bad things had become because of me.

The problem became most magnified while we were all on holiday in Dubai that year. I was picking, needling – being nasty. I knew what I was doing, but couldn't stop it. As I stared into an abyss called divorce, panicking, I called Steve McNally, the doctor at Manchester United.

For some reason I've always gravitated towards doctors throughout my career. I saw a lot of them, remember. Steve was no exception. I always really valued his opinions and his view was that we should get some counselling as soon as possible.

I say we – but by this point, as stubborn as I can be – even I knew that it was me who had the problem. As much as there always has to be room for adjustment on both sides of a marriage, I knew beyond doubt that I was the one who had to change in order to become a normal husband and a loving dad.

Our whole future as a family hinged on me being mature enough to look inwardly for once – to face aspects of my character that, while effective during my playing career, were completely destructive outside of it.

Not long after our return from Dubai, Louise and I went to counselling – initially together and thereafter I continued for more sessions on my own. The whole process was a revelation. Soon I started to feel like a new person – like I'd shed an enormous burden. I had just needed someone to talk to and to show me what was in front of me all along: I deeply loved my wife; I wholeheartedly loved my family.

As soon as I reconciled with this quite simple understanding, all the anger and resentment that I'd felt building up over time just slipped away. I started feeling that I could view the rest of my life through new eyes.

When I did, I left all the anger and the focus that had driven me to great success for years, in the dust. These few weeks in 2014 were so pivotal.

The culmination was that I stopped being Michael Owen

the footballer and embarked on the path to a new Michael – a normal person.

I was rebooting my life.

Looking back, maybe I was going through a process that every ex-footballer goes through. You spend your life thinking about the next game, the next goal, or save – or whatever. You focus on training, eating, sleeping and doing everything you can to be the best player you can. You do this for as many years as your body will allow and you do so knowing that it's a short career with no guarantees thereafter.

Then, one day, it all stops.

You get up the next morning and you're no longer a footballer. The problem is, as much as your body no longer has to play the game, your mind continues. It knows nothing else.

I'd been primed to be a footballer since I was six years old. I channelled my mind into being the best I possibly could be for twenty eight years without pause. How was I meant to suddenly stop doing and feeling how I'd done for all these years? The answer was that I couldn't. Without the focus of football, I inevitably diverted some of the more unpleasant aspects of my personality into general life – family, friends and business etc.

As I said, these single-minded, relentlessly ambitious traits were perfectly acceptable as part of a football career. Indeed, they contributed hugely to the length and success of it. Without them, I'd never have scored the goals I scored, when I scored them, or lifted any of the trophies that I did.

But in day-to-day family life, to continue down the same path would have split my close family up. I came to realise that I needed separation from football.

There is another irony here that I'd like to explain.

When I was a seventeen-year-old, having just passed my driving test, I used to drive back and forth from home through the Mersey Tunnel in the morning and again in the late afternoon.

At first, I thought nothing of it. It was merely part of the road that took me to Melwood, my place of work.

As time passed, I started to look at the tunnel differently. After 1998 in France and all of the accompanying hoo-ha, somehow I realised, as immature and inexperienced as I still was, that I needed to establish some kind of separation – a clear delineation between my football life and my family life.

Given how critical my family's support had been in every aspect of my career, it was so important to me that – no matter what I did on the football pitch and regardless of how crazy life got – the close family circle would always be retained no matter what.

As early as 1998, the Mersey Tunnel became the divide.

When I drove to work in the morning, entered the tunnel and emerged on the Liverpool side, I was Michael Owen the footballer. When I came home and reappeared on the side closer to home, I was Michael, Terry and Janette's son and a brother to my siblings.

As years passed, while all the goals, the accolades and the dressing room banter ensued on the work side of the tunnel, I always knew that, at the end of the day, I could be back at home, among the family unit and within an hour of leaving Melwood, be being called a knob by one of my brothers in the pub!

Also, unlike other Liverpool players who lived in the city, I never had to deal with all the frenetic madness – the fans on your doorstep when you came home from training that I know guys like Carra had to. As much as Liverpool was my world, I could escape it whereas they couldn't (or chose not to).

Don't get me wrong. I knew that my life changed when I broke into the Liverpool first team at the age of seventeen. But instead of everything that went along with the fame and the money becoming a new life, I wanted it just to be a *separate* life. There was a clear difference that was important. My family has always meant everything to me.

Inevitably, people have often asked me how I managed to deal with all the fame and its inevitable trappings – particularly when it all came to me at such a tender age.

The answer is a simple one: my feet never, ever left the ground because I always had the family, on the other side of the tunnel, to keep them there. They didn't care how famous I was, or how much I was getting paid. To them, I was always just Mike. And that has never changed since.

The same applies to friends. I have never even considered accumulating celebrity mates. In fact, when I see famous people suddenly becoming mates with all kinds of other similar people, it actually makes me cringe. That would feel so unnatural to me – and so shallow and stereotypical. I still have the same best mate, Michael Jones, that I've had since I was a kid.

Jonesy's father was the manager at Colwyn Bay and, via our parents, we've always been best mates. Even today, we talk every day and see each other every day. People joke about us as if we're the ones that are married! But I never give the friendship any thought. Jonesy's just my best mate because he always has been.

As part of this effort to retain normality, because I was so young when fame and money descended on me, between my parents and my agent Tony Stephens, pretty much everything has been taken care of for me.

From day one, there was a complete support network in place. What I needed to know, they told me. What I didn't – death threats, stalker fan correspondence etc. they protected me from.

From the beginning, my mother looked after my finances fastidiously. There was never even the slightest possibility that I'd blow my earnings. She's like a Rottweiler in that sense – always worrying, stressing and protecting. No matter how much money there was, she always looked after it on my behalf.

Even today, if I won the lottery, she'd still worry about how to divide the money up: who in the family should get what and how to keep everyone happy.

As embarrassing as this admission is, I only recently started using my own bank account, at the age of thirty eight. Up until then, my mother paid all the bills and managed everything. Even though I've lived in a big house since 1998, with all kinds of expenses going out the door every day, that's just how it has always been. It's not a case of me being entitled or lazy, I just never knew any different.

I built my own house after the World Cup in '98, just down the road from where we live now. Louise and I loved designing it and planning everything. We moved in sometime in 1999.

Around the same time, because I could, I bought houses for all of my family on a new development that was being built at St. David's Park near Ewloe. Initially, I bought the first show-home on the development for my mum and dad. Then I started feeling bad that my siblings would feel left out, so I bought one of all the other designs of show-home for each of Terry, Andy, Karen and Lesley.

Really, it was the absolute least that I could do. The family has always lived in each other's pockets in the best possible sense. I had the money so I thought *why not?* They all still live there today – I'm as close to my family as I've ever been. We're in each other's lives almost every day.

Terry, my eldest brother, now works for me having previously worked at British Aerospace for a number of years. He's 49.

When he was younger he played football and was quite talented. For a while he played at a League Of Wales level as a midfielder and would have got paid to play football. If I were to describe his character, I would say that he's always been very content.

Like the horses he looks after as my gardener/groom, he likes his routine. Like my dad, he's quite quiet, a little shy – and has no real desire to go out and earn ten million quid. He's happy earning his money, going to the gym every day and having his weekends when he can go down the pub with his mates and go on the odd holiday. He's just a Steady-Eddie. That's Terry to a tee.

My other brother, Andy, also worked at British Aerospace for many years. Like Terry, he initially built wings for the Airbus planes but, as he got more qualified, he went into the area of product support. Often he'd have to fly around the world to fix grounded planes. He has since left to pursue other ventures.

Andy played football, too, and was a beast of a striker. He was always a great shape for a footballer and had loads of pace. What he lacked, I think, was self-confidence. Seemingly, he got loads of chances because he was so quick. But he wasn't the greatest finisher.

Andy is the polar opposite to Terry. He's definitely one for always wondering if the grass is greener. Consequently, he's always thinking of new ways to make money or new business ideas to set up.

Of all of my siblings, Andy would be the one who struggled most with what I became – not because he was jealous, but more because he hates the thought that he would ever need anything from his younger brother.

As much as he was obviously very grateful when I bought him the house, he has always retained this desire to be independent and to never be seen to rely on me in any way. He's got a lot of pride has Andy and I respect him hugely for it.

Karen, my elder sister, is the really determined one in the family. She works hard and is fiercely loyal. Looking back, I think that growing up as the middle sibling of five perhaps shaped her a little. You could say she's the odd one out. My two elder brothers are a similar age – then there was a decent gap to Karen – then another decent gap to my younger sister and me.

To that end, she probably had quite a challenging upbringing being poked and prodded by the two pairs on either side. But she's a fighter. She started her own workplace-related business and has done really, really well from nothing. Now she employs a dozen people-plus. She'll talk the arse off a donkey too. My mum and her can go anywhere and will be in full-blown conversation with someone within ten seconds! Everyone loves Karen.

Lesley, my younger sister, has always been friendly with my wife Louise. She always came to the games and spent time in the players' lounge and got along with other players' wives. She's my great little sister. She's an interior designer, very driven and enthusiastic. As I said, she and I spent a lot of time together when we were kids.

The Owen family unit – albeit that it has extended into husbands, wives and more kids – is exactly what it always was. I'll be forever grateful for the fact that, because they were there keeping me grounded, I was able to have my cake and eat it perhaps more than most footballers have. I still think about them whenever I drive through the Mersey Tunnel.

Now that my life-changing liaison with the idea of splitting up with Louise and the family in 2014 has passed, I'm pretty sure that everyone who knows me will say that I'm now a completely different person – in the best possible way.

The staff at Manor House Stables used to think I was a right weirdo. I'd go to the races, sit in the box at Chester on my own, reading the paper, not wanting to talk to anyone. That's just how I was.

Nowadays, I'll talk to pretty much anyone. I'll be the first to want to go the pub with my mates and I'll be the last to want to come home at the end of the night. At 3am, they'll all be saying: 'Let's go home, we're almost forty!' But for me, it feels like I'm living life in reverse on some level.

Because my early life was just so utterly bizarre and brilliant at the same time, I never had the opportunity to do lots of things – like going to the pub with a bunch of mates without having to worry about training the next day. Now I can. I'm making up for lost time.

At home I'm a different person, too, around my loved ones. I know for a fact that both Louise and my mother actually get frustrated with me nowadays – 'you're too laid-back!' they'll often tell me.

I don't doubt for a second that the relationship Louise and I have has been so vital in terms of me being the person I am today. In many ways, our relationship has changed so much over the years – I probably wasn't as tuned into these changes as they happened, as much as I should have been.

I have to give Louise an awful lot of credit. With retrospect, she came into a family that wasn't necessarily the easiest to access as an outsider. Because my mother was so involved in my life, I'm sure at times it wasn't easy for Louise.

Was there conflict? I don't know. Was I aware of tension? I don't think I was around enough to *be* aware. It wasn't that I didn't care – it was more that my life has always been very full. Since the age of seventeen, it has felt like I'm forever being pulled in different directions.

At the outset, after we got married in 2004, Louise had no choice to be pulled in these directions with me. Because I was a professional footballer, I called the shots for years. If I said we were moving to Spain with our not quite two-year-old daughter Gemma, Louise went along with it.

Equally, when I decided we were moving to Newcastle, Louise came with me, with Gemma and, later, our son James and our daughter Emily were also born while I was in the North East. All these things I did, and Louise followed – right up until the end of my football career in 2013, before which our third daughter, Jessica, was born while I was still playing at Manchester United.

In the background, while I've been making career moves, Louise has been the absolute bedrock of the family – allowing me to do what I was being paid to do.

Nowadays, certainly post-2014, the dynamics have changed and I'm happy that they have. As much as my life is still very full, I'd like to think I'm much more involved in family life.

I do the school run, go to school meetings, watch dressage, hockey matches and generally do all the things that a loving dad should do. Better still, having levelled with my past and let the dark forces that fuelled me go; I'm so much easier to be around.

Meanwhile, I'm happy to see that Louise has many interests of her own – all of which I'm happy to support. On some level, there has been a reversal of roles. As to the full extent of that reversal, you'd probably have to ask Louise. I think I'm doing ok!

As far as how I interact with and nurture my own kids is concerned, I'm in no doubt that my own life has taught me an awful lot. I'd say – and they'd probably agree – that I'm quite hard as parents go. Hard but also fair, I hope.

Because I've had to work so hard and to keep working hard to maintain the life I created for us, that need for a work ethic in life extends to them. While I obviously don't want life to be a tough struggle for my children, I also don't want them to have everything too easily. There's a balance – and I think, given the way my life has gone – I'm better placed than most to know where that balance is.

I'll help them – and provide them with whatever support and advice that I can – but I also want to see the effort coming from them. This might sound like an old-fashioned mind-set in this day and age, but it's one that I really believe works.

As far as them caring much about what I was once, well, I think I'm in the same boat as most other people with kids. They know I was a pretty decent footballer at one point – but they certainly don't bow at my feet because of it. In fact, I seem to recall a conversation with my son James once – I can't remember how it started.

'So, Dad,' he said, 'were you ever any good? How can you prove it?'

Thinking on my feet, I walked over to the shelf in the sitting room that was home to a few DVDs and video games. I picked out a copy of the Pro Evolution Soccer 2008 video game with me and Cristiano Ronaldo on the front cover.

'There you go,' I said, as I put the game in his hand with the cover face up, 'that was your dad ...'

ACKNOWLEDGEMENTS

During my career, I was only ever focused on the game I was playing and once that was over I was looking forward to the next one. I never stopped for long enough to reflect on what had gone before but having retired six years ago, it felt like the right time to look back.

Writing a book is hard but it was made easier by having Mark Eglinton as my co-writer. I'd like to thank him for his support throughout this process. For getting my thoughts down on paper and making sense of my daily voice notes.

I'm thankful to the team at Reach Sport led on this project by Paul Dove for their editorial help, keen insight, and ongoing support. It is because of their efforts and encouragement that I have been able to get my story out there. Thanks to Rick Cooke, Chris McLoughlin, Simon Monk, Ben Renshaw and Claire Brown.

A very special thanks to my right hand man, Steve Wood. I am eternally grateful to you for being my sounding board, keeping me company on those long trips to Asia and reading those early drafts of the book.

To Sir Alex, Jamie Carragher, my dad, Tony Stephens and Glenn Hoddle – thank you for taking the time to put pen to paper and sharing those memories.

Thank you – you have all contributed to an autobiography I am proud of.

Michael

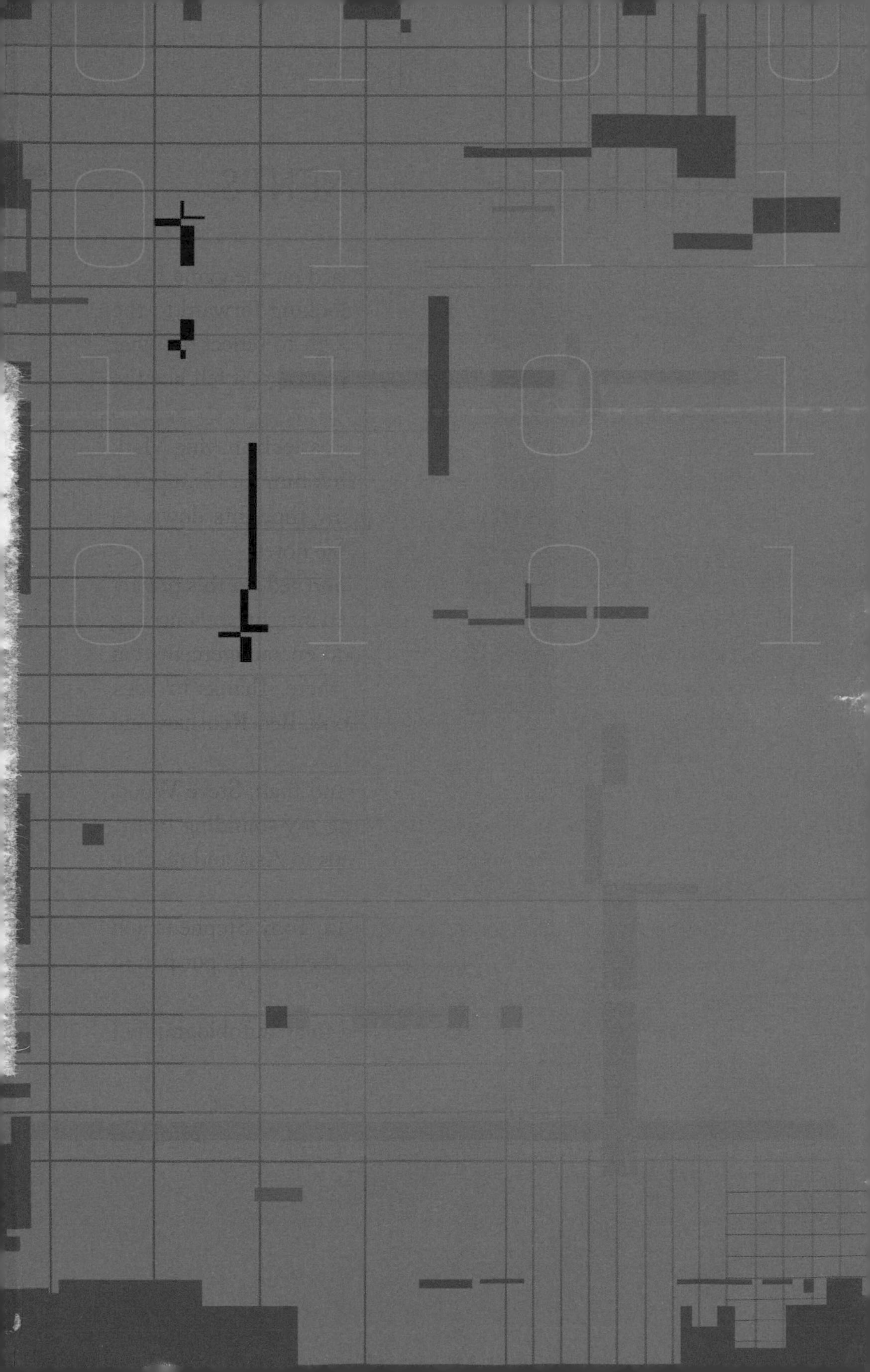

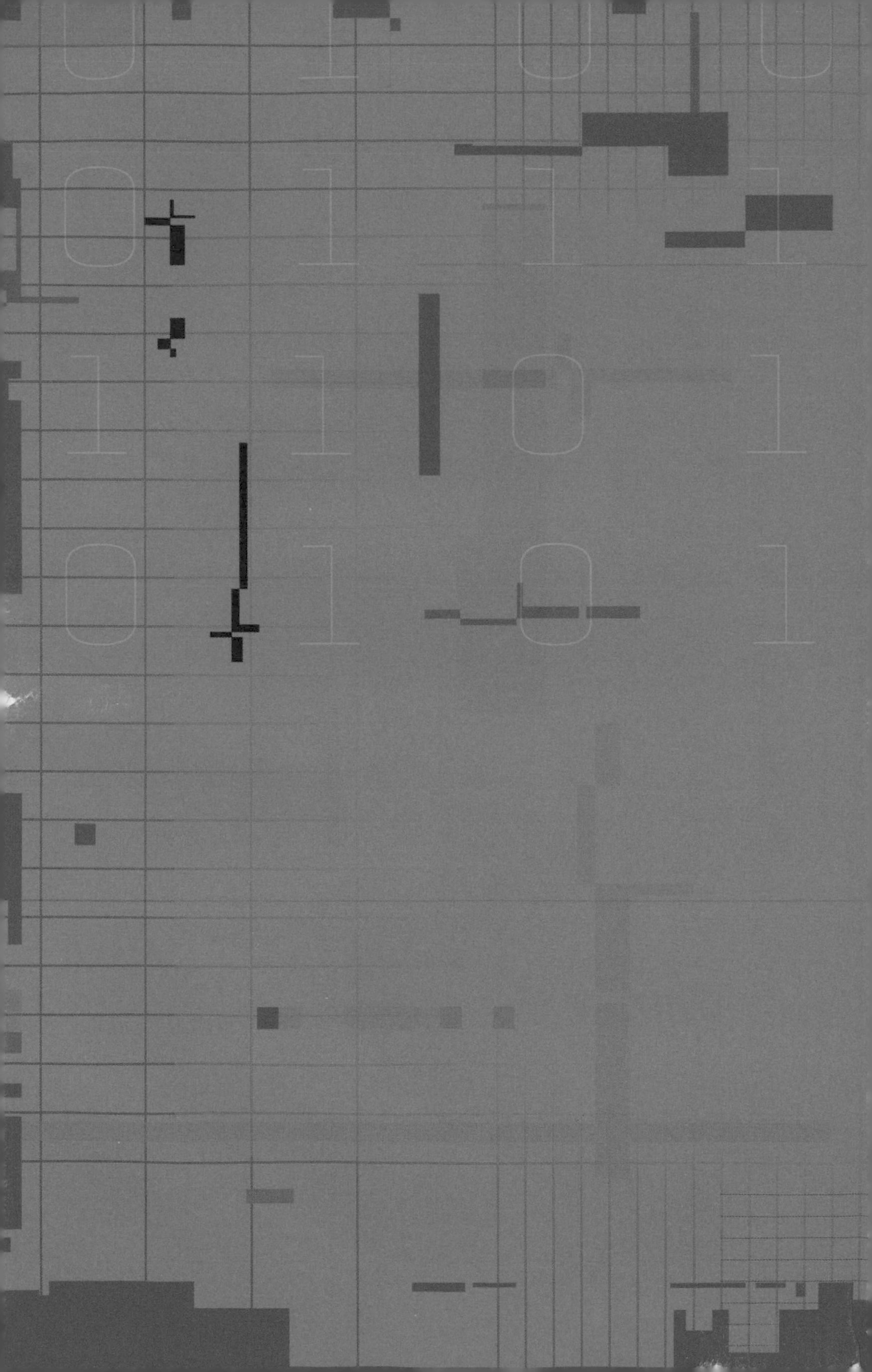